Advancing Entrepreneurship in the United Arab Emirates

Wasif A. Minhas

Advancing Entrepreneurship in the United Arab Emirates

Start-up Challenges and Opportunities

palgrave
macmillan

Wasif A. Minhas
Higher Colleges of Technology
Sharjah, United Arab Emirates

ISBN 978-3-319-76435-1   ISBN 978-3-319-76436-8 (eBook)
https://doi.org/10.1007/978-3-319-76436-8

Library of Congress Control Number: 2018936327

© The Editor(s) (if applicable) and The Author(s) 2018
This work is subject to copyright. All rights are solely and exclusively licensed by the Publisher, whether the whole or part of the material is concerned, specifically the rights of translation, reprinting, reuse of illustrations, recitation, broadcasting, reproduction on microfilms or in any other physical way, and transmission or information storage and retrieval, electronic adaptation, computer software, or by similar or dissimilar methodology now known or hereafter developed.
The use of general descriptive names, registered names, trademarks, service marks, etc. in this publication does not imply, even in the absence of a specific statement, that such names are exempt from the relevant protective laws and regulations and therefore free for general use.
The publisher, the authors and the editors are safe to assume that the advice and information in this book are believed to be true and accurate at the date of publication. Neither the publisher nor the authors or the editors give a warranty, express or implied, with respect to the material contained herein or for any errors or omissions that may have been made. The publisher remains neutral with regard to jurisdictional claims in published maps and institutional affiliations.

Printed on acid-free paper

This Palgrave Macmillan imprint is published by the registered company Springer International Publishing AG part of Springer Nature.
The registered company address is: Gewerbestrasse 11, 6330 Cham, Switzerland

To the United Arab Emirates. Jewel of the Middle East and an example to all young Countries.

Foreword

I am honored and humbled to write this foreword for a book that delves into a topic which is close to my area of research interest—"Entrepreneurship". The topic is of particular relevance to the United Arab Emirates (UAE) because of a paradigm shift in the growth curve of this nation in the past decades. The outlook of the local Emirati population has undergone a remarkable transformation from the families of the pearl divers to oil exporters to an ambitious, well-educated, innovative young generation who are ready to march ahead on their own.

The global crisis of 2008–2009, resulting in widespread unemployment and unprecedented levels of job loss, provided me with an opportunity to explore the entrepreneurship intentions among the youth of UAE. Almost a decade back, I started carrying out primary research among Emirati youth who had undertaken Business Studies in their undergraduate programs. It was amazing to witness the immense interest among university students in starting their own ventures and, most importantly, Emirati females exhibited exactly the same intentions and entrepreneurial propensity as their male counterparts—a result that was an eye-opener in this part of the globe. They cited job creation as their most important contribution as a future entrepreneur and were extremely confident of their capabilities. However, the students highlighted the need for the right environment with a focus on entrepreneurship education as the prerequisite to their success. They pointed out the need to develop a generation of people who are more creative and risk-taking and prepare them for leadership in the new global marketplace.

My first round of studies on entrepreneurial propensity among the Emirati youth gained the support of Wharton Business School to take this project further ahead and study the performance of the existing entrepreneurial ventures, in the form of family business firms in the UAE. The older-generation entrepreneurs and their family-run businesses form the backbone of the UAE—an estimated 75% of the private economy in the Middle East is governed by 5000 families who generate 70% of regional employment. My results indicated that younger and smaller firms in the UAE had higher market valuations (Tobin's Q) and family firms showed strong financial soundness in terms of returns on assets and equity—a result that was quite contrary to opinions and beliefs about the Middle East.

My research studies showed that on one hand, there was a remarkable success story of the family-owned business which highlighted the glory of the older-generation entrepreneurs in building up the primary and secondary sectors in the UAE. On the other hand, there is a strong spirit of entrepreneurship among young Emiratis who need to be exposed to a conducive environment where they can flourish. Today, the UAE Government has openly recognized the need for economic diversification where entrepreneurship, innovation, start-ups, and new enterprises have to play a significant role in building up a knowledge-based economy. However, one needs to fully understand and appreciate that the older model cannot be applied or implemented in the present context. This was the clear lacuna that was identified in my research—a wide gap that has emerged today between entrepreneurial intentions and implementation. As the nation waits for the glorious history of the family-run firms to repeat itself in the UAE, the ongoing changes in regulations, economic environment, competition, peer pressure, globalization, processes, and practices have made it far more difficult for the present generation to implement their intentions. There is, therefore, a pressing need to bridge this gap by exploring the possible reasons for the high intentions and low implementations.

It gives me immense pleasure to introduce this book *Advancing Entrepreneurship in the United Arab Emirates* which took up the research from the point where I had left it—with a clear focus on understanding the barriers, obstacles, and challenges faced by the Emirati youth during their decision-making process. This research explores the journeys of potential Emirati entrepreneurs in the UAE and provides very interesting insights into some of the personal traits that influence the making of a successful entrepreneur—like the drive for success, the need for achievement, an attitude for taking risks, and the capacity to innovate. The book then goes on to delve beyond the basic motivational, inspirational, and personal characteristics to explore practical solutions in terms of cultural issues, educational background, access to finance, and government support, to name a few.

Finally, the researcher proposes a model of entrepreneurship for the UAE where the themes and sub-themes from the qualitative research were interconnected to identify distinct pathways for the future actions of an individual. This exercise also provides a taxonomy of Emirati entrepreneurs which helps distinguish support for Emirati who are at different stages of their entrepreneurial journey. The model helps us understand and realize why and how two individuals with the same entrepreneurial intentions, ambition, and motivation in their youth end up choosing different career paths later in their lives. This model serves a dual purpose; first, it offers valuable insights to potential entrepreneurs to better understand their own intentions, perceptions, and also be aware of the challenges that lie ahead. Second, once the barriers and obstacles are identified, it gives clear directions to the concerned organizations (government, policymakers, financial organizations, incubators, and educational institutions) to provide suitable support mechanisms that help establish an environment more conducive for further developing entrepreneurship in the UAE.

In this book, Minhas carried out extensive and intensive research to identify the issues, barriers, and challenges that are confronting the Emirati youth today. The book provides the much-needed solutions to empower them to act on their intentions. The publication would prove to be extremely insightful not only to future entrepreneurs but also to government organizations, policymakers, financiers, incubators, and educational institutions that would have to be strongly involved in extending the necessary support to potential entrepreneurs in their future pursuits.

I would like to extend my heartiest congratulations to Minhas for his valuable contribution in this field and the commendable research he has undertaken to explore the opportunities and challenges of the young and aspiring Emirati entrepreneurs.

Higher Education Academy, Heslington, UK Sudipa Majumdar
Middlesex University, Dubai, UAE

Preface

In its short history the United Arab Emirates (UAE) is at a cross roads, yet again. The country is going through widespread structural changes as it tries to make a shift from a fossil fuel to a knowledge based economy. Young Emiratis are needed and expected to lead in this endeavor, especially as entrepreneurs who not only create wealth but jobs and opportunities, to help the UAE establish itself as a leading global economic power house. However, when it comes to young Emiratis, studies conducted in the region highlight participation levels in entrepreneurship are disproportionate to the levels of investment in the sector. Thus, this book seeks to understand some of the reasons behind this entrepreneurial gap, the challenges and opportunities, and ultimately how we may be able to advance entrepreneurship in the UAE. But the rationale to select entrepreneurship as a research focus goes beyond this immediate need and stems from a belief that entrepreneurship is needed so much more than ever before.

As with the UAE, it seems our civilization is also at the cusp of a new transformational phase, but then it always is, whether it be the fourth industrial revolution, geo-political events, or indeed the latest economic calamity. The fact is that our modern civilization is in a constant state of flux that seems to be increasing in intensity. Change, more specifically economic change, is a ubiquitous component of human existence. It has surpassed previously coveted social constructs such as Government or

Religion and now firmly holds its place at the pinnacle of all human concerns. There is a general consensus that answers to all our problems are hidden within the economic sphere.

Globally, national concerns such as education, healthcare, transport, even immigration, to name a few, are inextricably linked to a healthy economy. A quick look at the three recent and major elections around the world highlight this notion well. In the United States, United Kingdom (UK), and France, the economy was top of the agenda for all winning parties. For example, in the UK the word economy was mentioned 83 times in an 88-page Conservative Party manifesto. More importantly a healthy economy was identified as the remedy to meet the five main challenges in the manifesto, "A strong economy that works for everyone" being the first of these giant challenges (The Conservative and Unionist Party Manifesto, 2017).

The Conservative Party manifesto seems a million miles away when looking at entrepreneurship in the UAE but this example highlights a global trend where a healthy economy is the main agenda item for society at large. This book argues that the most sustainable route to achieving a healthy economy is through entrepreneurship. In the case of the UAE, and indeed the wider Gulf region, this specifically requires young citizens to pick entrepreneurship as a career choice. This should not be a difficult sell. The 9–5 life is seen by many in the developed world as a trap. Job opportunities do not match up to individuals' expectations nor their aspirations. In this reality, entrepreneurship as a career choice is increasingly becoming a necessity, but nevertheless requires a paradigm shift.

Emerging from the shadows of the last economic crisis, big business has lost its position as the steward of industry, capable of delivering jobs and a strong economy that works for everyone. This fall from grace has led many to question dependable free market economic principles that have brought so many out of poverty. I believe that notions of an unfettered market and non-intervention are obsolete. Market competition alone is no longer a reliable market regulator. Many markets are now best defined as oligopolies and over grown businesses have hijacked innovation, drip feeding it into the market. In this reality individuals who want to carve out their own success still need the government to intervene and provide support through public private partnerships. This notion goes against the grain of free market ideology but does reflect reality for many small entrepreneurs struggling to compete against the giant corporations.

Above all I have written this book because of the promise of entrepreneurship. Not only because of its potential in the field of social science to predict social outcomes and human behavior but also because of its promise of freedom for "he who dares". We live in extraordinary times, defined by individualism and marred in uncertainty. In an age of colossal problems the need for simple solutions has never been greater. I truly believe entrepreneurship has the potential to provide these solutions and by applying innovation, individual entrepreneurs have an opportunity to play a pivotal role.

Sharjah, UAE   Wasif A. Minhas

Acknowledgments

Praise be to the all mighty the most gracious, most compassionate, without whom none of this would have been possible. This acknowledgment recognizes the people who have made it possible for me to complete this long and challenging endeavor. But it also thanks those who have led to this moment, without whom my life may have been very different. Inevitably, I will miss out some people but this does not in any way diminish the value of their involvement in my life.

Firstly, I extend my gratitude to all the research participants, who went out of their way and took time out of their busy schedules to help me complete this research. Their commitment to family, their passion, dedication and pure energy to better themselves and their country is inspiring. Secondly, I would also like to thank to the Higher Colleges of Technology, which provided access to their resources and allowed me the flexibility to complete this study successfully.

There are a few people in everyone's life whose impact is instrumental and everlasting. My thanks to Keith Rutter, Sandy Mercado, Dr. Adam Unwin, Duane Green, and Michael Dowd. Thank you for taking an interest in me. Thank you for your advice and guidance. Thank you for helping me change my life for the better. You may never realize the extent of your influence on my development as a human being.

My deepest gratitude to my parents, Arshad and Sarwat Minhas, whose endless love, hard work, and sacrifices allowed me the opportunities for a better life. Their teachings, guidance, and patience have inspired me and led me to where I am today. I am also grateful for the love, support, and patience of my wife and children, who make me want to better myself every day. And my gratitude goes to God, with whom all things must start and end.

Contents

1	**Introduction**	1
	References	9
2	**Evolution of Entrepreneurship**	13
	Entrepreneurship in the Eighteenth Century	14
	Entrepreneurship in the Nineteenth Century	16
	Entrepreneurship in the Twentieth Century	19
	Schumpeter's Contribution	20
	The American Perspective	22
	Leibenstein's Theory of X-efficiency	24
	The Austrian Perspective	26
	Government Intervention	26
	Price, Monopolies, and Competition	28
	The Austrian Entrepreneur	31
	References	33
3	**Theoretical Framework for Entrepreneurship in the UAE**	39
	Entrepreneurial Action	39
	Entrepreneurial Motivation	41
	Need for Independence	42

Need for Achievement	44
Entrepreneurial Intentions	46
Theory of Planned Behavior	47
Entrepreneurial Event Model	48
Integrated Model of Entrepreneurial Intentions	50
Environmental Factors	53
Conclusions	57
Operational Definitions	61
References	64

4 Methodology 73
Purpose of Research	73
Research Questions	75
Research Design	76
Population, Sampling Strategy	78
Sources of Data	81
Data Collection	82
Data Analysis	86
Data Presentation Strategy	88
Credibility and Utility	90
Role of the Researcher	90
Legal Issues	91
References	93

5 Entrepreneurship in the UAE (I) 99
Demographic Data	101
Themes	106
Theme One: Personal Characteristics	107
Need for Achievement	107
Need for Independence	111
Risk-Taking Propensity	113
Capacity to Innovate	117
Theme Two: Family	120
Family Circumstance	121
Family Approval	124

	Family Support	126
	Commitment to Family	129
	References	131
6	**Entrepreneurship in the UAE (II)**	**135**
	Individual Context	137
	Theme Three: Culture	139
	Collectivist Nationalism	139
	Perceptions of Entrepreneurship	142
	Religion and Tradition	146
	Reputation	149
	Theme Four: Perceived Behavioral Control	150
	Access to Finance	151
	Access to Support	154
	Competition	157
	Education	160
	Market Knowledge	163
	Time	166
	References	169
7	**Role of Government**	**173**
	Government Support Programs	175
	Government Regulation	179
	Political Role Models	181
	Expectations of Government Support Programs	184
	References	188
8	**The Emirati Entrepreneur**	**191**
	References	213
9	**Emirati Model of Entrepreneurship: Critical Success Factors**	**215**
	Emirati Model of Entrepreneurship	222
	The Entrepreneurial Gap	225

Critical Success Factors 229
  Financial Safety Net for Emirati Entrepreneurs 230
  Expansion of Government Support Programs 231
  Effective Promotion of Government Support Programs 232
  Educational Establishments and Public, Private Sector
    Collaboration 233
  Changes in Government Regulation 235
 References 238

Index 243

List of Figures

Fig. 4.1	Triangulating findings	82
Fig. 5.1	Sample age range of entrepreneurs, employees, and incubator managers	103
Fig. 5.2	Average age of entrepreneurs and employees	103
Fig. 5.3	Business age and number of employees	104
Fig. 8.1	Taxonomy of Emirati entrepreneurs	209
Fig. 9.1	Basic model outline	223
Fig. 9.2	Emirati Model of Entrepreneurship	224

List of Tables

Table 4.1　Sample distribution and criteria　　　　　　　　80
Table 5.1　Demographic statistics　　　　　　　　　　　　102

1

Introduction

The foundations of our modern civilization stand on entrepreneurship. Whether we consider the homes we live in, or the many things we fill them with, all aspects of modern life, even love and happiness, are enhanced by entrepreneurship. Growth in the importance of entrepreneurship is largely due to its recognition as an agent of change. It is increasingly positioned as the key ingredient in changing the fortunes of individuals, communities, and the State. For this reason, countries, especially new ones like Singapore, Kazakhstan, and indeed the United Arab Emirates (UAE), are invested in it wholeheartedly. There are extensive government programs stretching across education, commerce, and industry designed to foster entrepreneurship. All in the hope that one day this investment will forge new avenues for economic growth, development, and international competitive advantage. This is even more important for countries like the UAE and Kazakhstan that have experienced high levels of economic growth riding on waves of natural resources.

State investment in entrepreneurship might be an easy sell but returns on this investment are not easily quantifiable nor indeed reliable. Furthermore, investment in entrepreneurship has not always led to equal increases in the number of start-ups. For example, in 2009 the Global

Entrepreneurship Monitor reported that the UAE has increased start-up activity by 38%; however, in 2011 it also reported that only 4% of all new start-ups were purely Emirati owned (Bosma et al. 2011; El-Sokari et al. 2013). This is in sharp contrast to reportedly high levels of entrepreneurial intentions among undergraduates and an institutional environment conducive to entrepreneurship within the UAE (Gupta et al. 2012; Haan 2004; Kargwell and Inguva 2012; Sowmya et al. 2010).

In a bid to create a diverse economy that is not overly dependent on proceeds from natural resources, the UAE government has decreed the advancement of entrepreneurship as one of its key strategic goals (Government of Abu Dhabi 2008). As a result, a number of organizations have sprung up ready to support budding entrepreneurs (Kargwell and Inguva 2012). The Khalifa Fund and Mohammad Bin Rashid Establishment are two examples of government funded non-profit organizations mandated to promote and support entrepreneurship within the UAE. Despite concerted efforts by the government, and abundant opportunities for would-be entrepreneurs, the number of nascent businesses fully owned by Emiratis is still relatively low (Kerros 2012; Horne et al., 2011 Global Entrepreneurship Monitor). Furthermore, at 20.8% (Makahleh et al. 2012), unemployment rates among UAE Nationals are extraordinarily high for a country that achieved 3.6% growth in 2012 (Horne et al., 2011).

In 2017, the UAE population reached 9.4 million. However, Emirati Nationals only represent approximately 13% of the population (World Population Review 2015). Nationally, 15–29 year olds represent the largest strata of the Emirati population. The same is true for the wider Gulf region, which reportedly has one of the youngest populations on the globe (United Nations 2012). Small and Medium Enterprises (SME) and entrepreneurs who start them are the engines of a healthy economy (Minniti 2008). For example, in Dubai these entrepreneurs represent 95% of all businesses and employ 42% of the work force (Dubai SME 2011). A steady stream of new entrepreneurs, especially based in the technology sector, is vital for the UAE economy (Government of Abu Dhabi 2008; Minniti 2008).

In 2012 UAE's GDP jumped to 3.6% from 1.3% in 2011; despite efforts to diversify the economy the UAE still relies heavily on oil and gas for 82% of its revenues (GEM 2011). The UAE is aiming to build an innovative, knowledge-based economy (Government of Abu Dhabi 2008) which requires the formation of new businesses (Dubai SME 2011). In 2011, Emiratis started only 4% of new businesses in the UAE while unemployment stood approximately at a staggering 20.8% in the same year (GEM 2011; Makahleh et al. 2012). As incubation centers and educational establishments try to enhance their offers for budding entrepreneurs (Dubai SME 2011; Kargwell and Inguva 2012), this book highlights whether their efforts are bearing fruit and provides insights on supporting the government's strategic plan. Overall, this book aims to develop a better understanding of the entrepreneurial process, improve practice, and inform policy.

Disproportionate gaps between entrepreneurial intentions among undergraduates and the realization of those intentions among the same strata, after they graduate, have also been identified in other parts of the world (El-Sokari et al. 2013; Horne et al. 2011; Ismail et al. 2009; Krueger et al. 2000; Liñan et al. 2011). Low rates of nascent businesses pose a significant threat to the UAE's prosperity. Exploring possible reasons for this disconnect between high entrepreneurial intentions and low rates of nascent businesses may help fine tune government policy, which is already focused on expanding entrepreneurial activity among the Emirati population (Government of Abu Dhabi 2008). A limited number of studies conducted within the UAE focus on entrepreneurial intentions and rates of entrepreneurial activity; however, research on the clear gap between entrepreneurial intentions and action is lacking (El-Sokari et al. 2013; Bosma et al. 2011; Kargwell and Inguva 2012; Sowmya et al. 2010; Ismail et al. 2009). Developing an understanding of why and how some Emiratis with entrepreneurial intentions are able to start a business, while others with the same intentions opt to seek employment, will highlight the challenges faced by Emirati entrepreneurs.

This book explores entrepreneurship in the UAE with a focus on Emirati entrepreneurs. Exploring the entrepreneurial gap between intentions and actions by highlighting the lived experience of young Emiratis as they make the transition from education into the workforce helps develop a better understanding of the challenges and opportunities faced by Emiratis today. The book also aims to understand the motivational factors that lead to the choice of starting a business and how they can be supported to advance entrepreneurship in the UAE. Differences in levels of entrepreneurial activity between two countries can account for a 30% to 50% difference in productivity (Reynolds et al. 1999; Zacharakis et al. 2000 cited by Sobel et al. 2007). This book highlights the main challenges Emirati entrepreneurs face in the UAE and makes recommendations on how they can be supported to start new businesses and what were the contributing influences in their decision-making process. Constructing this knowledge can be hugely beneficial to prospective entrepreneurs and public, private organizations that are responsible for supporting and fostering entrepreneurship in the UAE.

Understanding which motivational factors enable Emiratis to follow through on their intentions and which factors act as deterrents is important. At the same time, it is also important to understand the perceptions of existing opportunities, resources, and support mechanisms. Thus, this book is framed around the theory of entrepreneurship and key constructs of motivation, intentions, and environmental factors.

Despite gaining significant prominence over the last two decades, the theory of entrepreneurship still lacks consensus (Casson and Casson 2013; Shane et al. 2003; Swedberg 2000). Often a symbiont of other social sciences, such as economics or sociology, the concept of entrepreneurship has struggled to find its own place in the social framework (Swedberg 2000). This may be due to how the notion of entrepreneurship has developed (Shane et al. 2003). Thus, assessing the evolution of entrepreneurship from a historical perspective and with appropriate definitions is important at this early juncture. Although somewhat fragmented by the ideological divide on intervention, the modern understanding of entrepreneurship is inextricably linked to economic theory (Casson and Casson 2013). This book also explores the Austrian perspective, which has played a significant role in developing the theory of entrepreneurship. This helps to define separate lines of enquiry within entrepreneurship, divided by the individual, micro, and macro level (Shane et al. 2003).

An exploration of entrepreneurship within the UAE context, with a particular focus on opportunities and challenges, a historical review of the evolution of entrepreneurship and its impact at individual, micro, and macro level, and discussions on why entrepreneurship is so crucial within the UAE context and beyond, all these make this book useful for an audience concerned with understanding entrepreneurship in the UAE and indeed the wider gulf region. This book is targeted at new and aspiring entrepreneurs in the UAE trying to navigate their way through the complex emotional journey of starting a business and the organizations, including innovation and entrepreneurship centers, government entities, educational and training establishments, trying to support entrepreneurs and advance entrepreneurship in the UAE.

The entrepreneur and the entrepreneurial process are at the core of this book. However, the theory of entrepreneurship has not been consolidated and lacks a universal definition of entrepreneurship or indeed the entrepreneur (Shane and Venkataraman 2000; Swedberg 2000). In fact, defining entrepreneurs has been highlighted as one of the most difficult aspects within the study of entrepreneurship (Casson 2003). The next chapter will assess the evolution of entrepreneurship and how different notions we now use to define entrepreneurship, and indeed the entrepreneur, have developed. One of the aims here is to separate the constructs of entrepreneurship and the entrepreneur which are at times misconstrued, interchanged or used in conjunction. This exercise will also help define these and other relevant terms that are central to this book.

The following chapters outline the research methodology and provide further information about the research context. This book aims to develop an in-depth understanding of entrepreneurship in the UAE through the lived experiences of first time Emirati entrepreneurs. The phenomenon of low levels of entrepreneurial activity among young Emirati nationals is still relatively unexplored, especially when it comes to the male population. Therefore, a qualitative phenomenological approach, using in-depth semi-structured interviews was proposed to explore the essence of entrepreneurs' experience. In trying to understand the experiences and challenges faced by Emirati entrepreneurs, a qualitative methodology helped establish the meaning of this phenomenon through the view of participants (Creswell 2009; Sun 2009).

This book unravels human experience at the individual level and explores multiple realities without the confines of predetermined frames of outcomes or response as required by quantitative research (Loftus and

Higgs 2010). Interviews were the most appropriate method for data collection because the book aims to develop an in-depth understanding of entrepreneurship as a phenomenon in the UAE (Creswell 2009). Furthermore, given the busy schedules of entrepreneurs, a qualitative approach provided the flexibility to interact with participants in their preferred location and on their own terms (Kirk and Miller 1986).

The research design was built upon in-depth semi-structured interviews to collect context-bound experiences from three different sets of research participants. The two groups comprised of Emiratis who had graduated within the last five years: these graduates would have had entrepreneurial intentions as undergraduates but had since gone on to either (a) start a business (b) or found employment. The last set of participants were (c) incubator managers who were able to provide invaluable insights in exploring the entrepreneurial gap within the UAE.

In trying to develop a research question, Creswell (2009) suggested starting from a central question that is broad so that it does not limit the scope of enquiry; however, this should be followed by sub-questions in order to maintain a focus. The sub-questions should be open and may even be used in data collection. The research question should focus on the relationship between a central phenomenon and how participants view that phenomenon (Creswell 2009). For example, in a study of diplomatic leaders, Murtezaj (2011) explored the relationship between emotional intelligence and how diplomatic leaders viewed its utility in negotiation and handling conflict. Similarly, the overarching aim of this research was to explore and understand reasons behind low levels of entrepreneurial activity among Emirati nationals.

This book focuses on the following central and sub-questions:

Q1. Why is there a gap between entrepreneurial intentions and new business start-up rates among Emirati nationals in the UAE?

- Which factors influence Emiratis to become entrepreneurs or seek employment?
- What are the key challenges and barriers faced by aspiring Emirati entrepreneurs?
- What are the key opportunities to advance entrepreneurship in the UAE?
- How do internal (self-efficacy, motivations, intentions) and external (environmental) factors affect the decision-making process?

A deep dive into the experiences of new and aspiring Emirati entrepreneurs would help better understand the challenges for Emirati start-ups and identify opportunities to advance entrepreneurship within the UAE. Exploring these research questions can also benefit other countries in the region and beyond when it comes to understanding the plight of start-ups and support networks needed to sustain them. One of the most important outcomes of this book related to a more comprehensive understanding of the Emirati, and even the Gulf region, entrepreneurs. This book highlights the quintessential facets of the Emirati entrepreneur—facets that have been neither empirically explored previously nor in appropriate depth.

Using a qualitative approach, the book builds upon the basic assumption that there is no single reality. Instead, reality is subjective and must be judged in the context of individual interpretations (Gall et al. 1999). When viewed through the positivist paradigm, this poses a limitation on generalizability (Flick 2014). However, generalization is not the main aim of this study. A qualitative methodology assumes deep meanings that can be drawn out of the rich experiences of research participants, or informants (Filstead 1979). However, this also assumes that other methodologies are unable to provide a deep perspective. Furthermore, there is an assumption that wider perspectives, that can be generalized, are simply not possible (Sechrest and Sidani 1995).

Adopting a qualitative methodology was based on the assumption that the phenomenon being studied is in a continuous state of flux and that the collection of context-bound perspectives could be effectively interpreted to illustrate a useful picture of the world as it is (Creswell and Miller 2000; Filstead 1979). This also raised questions about generalizability and more importantly the credibility of such a qualitative methodology, which posed a significant limitation. Yet an initial review of literature revealed that entrepreneurs' experiences and interaction with the social environment are highly personal and bound in individual context (Baum et al. 2001; Bosma and Levie 2010). Therefore, a qualitative methodology was the most suitable approach to studying this social phenomenon (Creswell 2009).

Employing a qualitative methodology also assumed that contextual social knowledge and meanings should be viewed through the subject's interpretation (Flick 2014). In this case, the context was of Emirati graduates who wanted to start a business, where some had succeeded but most had not. Therefore, conclusions were drawn from contextual interpretations of Emiratis and the way in which they organized experiences specifically within the UAE (Glasersfeld 1992 cited in Flick 2014). More importantly, there was an assumption that social interactions of research participants could be used to explain low levels of new business start-ups among Emiratis (Creswell and Miller 2000). There was also an assumption that Emirati research participants themselves would be able to interpret their experiences to help draw out meanings and develop a clearer picture of seemingly low levels of entrepreneurial activity among Emiratis (Blumer 1969).

The choice of methodology and the decision to focus on one geographical location makes it difficult to generalize findings and adds further limitations to the study. The age range and, to an extent, the sample size also represented limitations. In the same vein, the researcher's experience and ability to draw conclusions from the data were also assumed. These factors placed further limitations on the study in regard to credibility, transparency, and rigor. However, using software to organize and analyze data allows the audience to follow the line of enquiry and enables them to draw and confirm conclusions for themselves (Filstead 1979). Furthermore, direct quotations from the research participants were used to present research data and findings. Both of these strategies enhanced the research transparency and credibility, while demonstrating rigor (Creswell 2009; Richards and Richards 1991 cited in Welsh 2002).

The extensive time frame and large data set associated with qualitative research presented further limitations. Complex and varied data were also difficult to present and assess. These aspects made it difficult to organize data collection and subsequent analysis. Specifically, concerning interviews, presence of the interviewer increased the likelihood of bias, which can draw into question the credibility of findings (Flick 2014). Therefore, to minimize research bias, participants had no prior association with the researcher. Furthermore, interviews were held in locations that were chosen by the research participants. Interviews taking place in familiar surroundings and chosen by the participants also reduce the chances of bias (Johnson and Onwuegbuzie 2004; Kirk and Miller 1986; Saldana 2011). This study used a computer assisted qualitative data analysis (CAQDAS) called NVivo10 which is the latest software designed to analyze non-numeric qualitative data. It must be emphasized that NVivo10 does not take over the researcher's role as the interpreter, analyzer and evaluator. The researcher still has to use critical thinking to interpret and tease out the meanings behind data (Saldana 2011; Smith and Firth 2011). Instead, NVivo10 is essentially a data management tool that enables the researcher to carry out the analytical process more efficiently and with more transparency (Welsh 2002). The researcher in this case adopted a dual approach by first using NVivo10 to organize data, highlight patterns, and create codes, and then manually analyzed the data to confirm themes and draw conclusions (Welsh 2002).

References

Baum, R., Locke, E., & Smith, K. (2001). A multidimensional model of venture growth. *Academy of Management Journal, 44*(2), 292.

Blumer, H. (1969). *Symbolic interactionism: Perspective and method*. New Jersey: Prentice-Hall.

Bosma, N., & Levie, J. (2010). Executive report. Babson College, Universidad de Desarollo, Háskólinn, Reykjavik and London Business School. *Global entrepreneurship monitor*. Babson Park.

Bosma, N., Wennekers, S., & Amorós, J. (2011). Entrepreneurs and entrepreneurial employees across the globe. Global Entrepreneurship Monitor (Extended) Report.

Casson, M. (2003). *The entrepreneur: An economic theory*. Cheltenham: Edward Elgar Publishing. 1843765632.

Casson, M., & Casson, C. (2013). *The entrepreneur in history: From medieval merchant to modern business leader*. Palgrave Pivot. e-EAN/ISBN: 9781137305824.

Creswell, J. (2009). *Research design: Qualitative, quantitative, and mixed methods* (3rd ed.). Newbury Park: Sage Publications.

Creswell, J. W., & Miller, D. L. (2000). Determining validity in qualitative inquiry. *Theory Into Practice, 39*, 124–134.

Dubai SME. (2011). The role of government in supporting entrepreneurship & SME development. *Dubai Department of Economic Development.* Retrieved from http://www.oecd.org/mena/investment/47246782.pdf

El-Sokari, H., Van Horne, C., Huang, Z., & Al Awad, M. (2013). *GEM UAE: Entrepreneurship- An Emirati perspective.* Global Entrepreneurship Monitor. Retrieved from http://www.gemconsortium.org/docs/2892/gem-uae-entrepreneurship

Filstead, W. J. (1979). Qualitative methods. A need perspective in evaluation research. In T. D. Cook & C. S. Reichardt (Eds.), *Qualitative and quantitative methods in evaluation research* (pp. 33–48). Beverly Hills: Sage Publishing.

Flick, U. (2014). *An introduction to qualitative research.* Sage Publishing. ISBN: 1446297713.

Gall, M. D., Gall, J. P., & Borg, W. R. (1999). *Applying educational research: A practical guide* (4th ed.). White Plains: Addison Wesley Longman.

Government of Abu Dhabi. (2008). *The Abu Dhabi Economic Vision 2030.* Retrieved from https://www.ecouncil.ae/PublicationsEn/economic-vision-2030-full-versionEn.pdf

Gupta, V., Yayla, A., Sikdar, A., & Cha, M. (2012). Institutional environment for entrepreneurship: Evidence from the developmental states of South Korea and United Arab Emirates. *Journal of Developmental Entrepreneurship, 17*(3). https://doi.org/10.1142/S1084946712500136.

Haan, H. (2004). Small enterprises: Women entrepreneurs in the UAE. *Centre for Labour Market Research & Information* (CLMRI). Retrieved from http://www.zu.ac.ae/infoasis/modules/mod8/business/documents/smallenterprisereport.pdf

Horne, C., Huang, V., & Al Awad, M. (2011). Entrepreneurship in the United Arab Emirates. *The Global Entrepreneurship Monitor (GEM).* Retrieved from http://www.gemconsortium.org/docs/2626/gem-uae-2011-report

Ismail, M., et al. (2009). Entrepreneurial intention among Malaysian undergraduates. *International Journal of Business and Management, 4*(10).

Johnson, B., & Onwuegbuzie, A. (2004). Mixed methods research: A research paradigm whose time has come. Educational Researcher. *American Educational Research Association, 33*(7), 14–26.

Kargwell, S., & Inguva, S. (2012). Factors influencing the first generation entrepreneurs: An analytical study on the graduates of UAE universities. *International Journal of Business and Social Science, 3*(7), 143–149.

Kerros, T. (2012). The 'Entrepreneurial Triggers' driving graduate entrepreneurship in the UAE. *The Entrepreneurialist,* 3.

Kirk, J., & Miller, M. (1986). *Reliability and validity in qualitative research qualitative research methods.* Sage Publications. ISSN 0888-5397 ISBN 0803924704.

Krueger, N., Reilly, M., & Carsrud, A. (2000). Competing models of entrepreneurial intentions. *Journal of Business Venturing, 15*(5–6), 411–432.

Liñan, et al. (2011). Regional variations in entrepreneurial cognitions: Start-up intentions of university students in Spain. *Entrepreneurship & Regional Development, 23*(3-4), 187–215.

Loftus, S., & Higgs, J. (2010). Researching the individual in workplace research. *Journal of Education and Work, 23*(4), 377–388. https://doi.org/10.1080/13639080.2010.495712.

Makahleh, S., Badih, S., & Sabry, S. (2012, November 29). UAE unemployment issue to be tackled: Private sector – A main partner in solving unemployment issue. *Gulf News,* http://gulfnews.com/news/uae/government/uae-unemployment-issue-to-be-tackled-1.1112132

Minniti, M. (2008). The role of government policy on entrepreneurial activity: Productive, unproductive, or destructive? *Entrepreneurship Theory & Practice, 32*(5), 779–790.

Murtezaj, V. (2011). *Understanding the role of emotional intelligence in negotiating agreements and diplomatic conflict.* PhD dissertation. Retrieved from: http://swissmc.blackboard.com/bbcswebdav

Reynolds, P. D., Hay, M., & Camp, M. (1999). Global entrepreneurship monitor. Executive report. *Babson College & London Business School.* Babson Park/ London/ UK.

Saldana, J. (2011). *Fundamentals of qualitative research, understanding qualitative research.* Oxford University Press, ISBN: 0199838356.

Sechrest, L., & Sidana, S. (1995). Quantitative and qualitative methods: Is there an alternative? *Evaluation and Program Planning, 18,* 77–87.

Shane, S., & Venkataraman, S. (2000). The promise of entrepreneurship as a field of research. *The Academy of Management Review, 25*(1), 217–226.

Shane, S., Lockea, E., & Collins, C. (2003). Entrepreneurial motivation. Human resource management review. *Elsevier Science Inc, 13,* 257–279. https://doi.org/10.1016/S1053.

Smith, J., & Firth, J. (2011). Qualitative data analysis: The framework approach. *Nurse Researcher, 18*(2), 52–62.

Sobel, R., Clark J., & Lee, D. (2007). Freedom, barriers to entry, entrepreneurship, and economic progress. *Austrian Economic Review.* Springer Science + Business Media, 221–236. https://doi.org/10.1007/s11138-007-0023-3.

Sowmya, D., Majumdar, S., & Gallant, M. (2010). Relevance of education for potential entrepreneurs: An international investigation. *Journal of Small Business and Enterprise Development, 17*(4), 626–640.

Sun, T. (2009). Mixed methods research: Strengths of two methods combined. http://swissmc.blackboard.com/bbcswebdav/courses/5502C1971/Mixed%20Methods%

Swedberg, R. (2000). *Entrepreneurship: The social science View*. Oxford University Press. ISBN: 9780198294627.

United Nations, Department of Economics and Social Affairs. (2012). Retrieved from http://esa.un.org/unpd/wpp/unpp/panel_indicators.htm

Welsh, E. (2002). Dealing with data: Using NVivo in the qualitative data analysis process. *Qualitative Social Research, 3*(2), 3–12.

World Population Review. (2015). Retrieved from http://worldpopulationreview.com/countries/united-arab-emirates-population/

2

Evolution of Entrepreneurship

Although not explicitly proclaimed in its evolutionary development, implicitly entrepreneurship is recognized as the core of a market based social system (Casson and Casson 2013; Krueger et al. 2000; Sobel et al. 2007). Its effects resonate through the very fabric of society, from our basic needs of food, shelter and clothing to the more complex needs of knowledge accumulation, security and information (Casson and Casson 2013). Entrepreneurship is the common denominator that has enabled the masses to fulfill these needs. Entrepreneurship has changed the very nature of life for billions of people. Rather than a life that was otherwise "solitary, poor, nasty, brutish, and short" (Hobbes 1651 XIII.9), entrepreneurship has facilitated substantial improvements in the human condition in regard to security, health and, not least, entertainment (Kirzner 1971). However, because of the many variations in our conception of entrepreneurship, despite its long history of development, the theory of entrepreneurship still lacks consolidation (Shane et al. 2003; Swedberg 2000). Emerging from the shadows of political economy and economic science, historically, entrepreneurship has struggled to gain its rightful place as a key construct of modern civilization (Brown and Thornton

2013; Casson and Casson 2013; Swedberg 2000). This chapter provides an overview of the theory of entrepreneurship and its development over the last three centuries.

Entrepreneurship in the Eighteenth Century

In his essay titled *Essai sur la Nature du Commerce en Général*, Richard Cantillon (1755, translated to English by Saucier, 2010) was one of the first to write extensively about the role of entrepreneurship and entrepreneurs. Cantillon's (1755) work did not have real impact until it was rediscovered by William Jevons (1881) in the nineteenth century (Thornton and Saucier 2010). Jevon (1881) dubbed Cantillon's work as the "the cradle of political economy" (Jevons 1881, p. 342), whereas others called him "the father of economics" (Brown and Thornton 2013; Nevin 2013). Cantillon's influence on modern concepts of political economy is undeniable; however, it is his attention to entrepreneurship and the entrepreneur that is of most interest at this juncture.

Key facets in Cantillon's (1755) conception of entrepreneurship are uncertainty and imperfect information. It was the combination of uncertainty about future events and localized knowledge that led to entrepreneurial opportunities (Brown and Thornton 2013). However, opportunity alone was not enough for entrepreneurship to flourish. It was the entrepreneur, to whom Cantillon allocated a specific function; someone willing to undertake risk in return for a profit. Thus, profit provided impetus to the process of entrepreneurship. Cantillon identified three key economic agents that gave form to a market economy—landowners, entrepreneurs and farmers. The entrepreneur played a pivotal role as a conduit between farmers, landowners, and the market, essentially buying from the farmer at a low price and selling to buyers in the city for a higher price (Hebert and Link 2009). The time-lag between transporting goods and transaction completion represented uncertainty, while limited information of supply and demand available to the farmer and city buyer represented imperfect information. The combination of these two factors and the resulting gap signified the opportunity for entrepreneurship, specifically undertaken by the entrepreneur (Cantillon 1755; Hebert and Link 2009).

In the eighteenth century, Cantillon's (1755) notion of entrepreneurship was in its infancy. For example, he did not delve deeply into the notion of uncertainty and risk (Hebert and Link 2009). Cantillon's depiction of the entrepreneur was criticized for being one dimensional and lacking the vital component of innovation (Aspromourgos 2013). Nevertheless, his ideas on uncertainty, the circular flow of income, the function of the entrepreneur, and indeed the market for entrepreneurs, paved the way for future thinkers. Cantillon's insight on the role of trendsetters and their influence on consumption patterns were extraordinarily ahead of its time (Aspromourgos 2013; Hebert and Link 2009).

After Cantillon (1755), developments in the theory of entrepreneurship were rather anemic and arguably adverse at times (Casson 2005). There were small but noteworthy contributions from a range of writers which added to the personal skill sets and attributes of the entrepreneur and furthered our understanding of entrepreneurship. For example, Abbe' Nicolas Baudeau (1730–1792) added to Cantillon's notion of the entrepreneur by introducing the innovator dimension and emphasizing the importance of intelligence to act (Hoselitz 1960). However, within the same time period there were contrasting lines of enquiry. For example, on the continent, in particular the French quarters, there was a clear separation between capitalist and entrepreneur. Cantillon (1755) Baudeau (1730–1792) and later Say (1767–1832) all saw entrepreneurs and capitalists with distinct roles. Entrepreneurs undertook real uncertainty; they generated real wealth and earned a profit in return. However, since a capitalist would only finance an entrepreneurial venture if the entrepreneur could secure interest payments, the interest earned was likened to a wage. These roles could be undertaken by the same person but were, nevertheless, separate economic functions (Praag 2005). Even though writers such as Anne Robert Jacques Turgot (1727–1781) were not able to provide a clear demarcation between the capitalist and the entrepreneur, there was at least a distinction between their economic functions (Hebert and Link 2009).

In England, however, Adam Smith (1776) and his contemporaries largely ignored the uniqueness of the entrepreneur's function. Smith (1776) wrongly separated the frugal and cautious entrepreneur from the adventurous and irrational entrepreneur. The latter was identified as a hazard to the public and involved in immoral business practice (Link and Link 2009). Therefore, Smith's (1776) ideal entrepreneur comes across as rather unenterprising and unimaginative compared to the modern understanding of the entrepreneur (Hebert and Link 2009; Hoselitz 1960; Link and Link 2009). The diverse lines of enquiry, in the eighteenth century, among English and French writers highlight a rather confused period of development for the theory of entrepreneurship. For example, French writers such as Turgot (1727–1781) and English writers such as Smith (1776) and David Ricardo (1772–1823) were unable to distinguish between capitalists and entrepreneurs, which also led to confusion between profit and interest (Link and Link 2009; Praag 2005). For this reason the entrepreneur's role, at least in English literature, did not fully develop well into the twentieth century. Despite the brilliance of Jeremy Bentham (1748–1832) in identifying the entrepreneur as a proactive, intuitive innovator, quite the opposite of Smith's portrayal, he was a lone voice (Casson 2005; Fontaine 1993; Hebert and Link 2009).

Entrepreneurship in the Nineteenth Century

At the turn of the nineteenth century, Jean Baptiste Say (1767–1832) made significant contributions to the theory of entrepreneurship (Praag 2005). Continuing with Cantillon's (1755) tradition, Say (1803, translated to English by Biddle, 1971) places the entrepreneur at the center of economic activity. However, Say (1803) went much further than Cantillon in detailing key concepts of entrepreneurship that are taken for granted in the modern understanding of entrepreneurship. Say provides a framework for entrepreneurship supported by the market economy, self-interest, and the profit-seeking entrepreneur (Praag 2005). Interestingly, for Say, property rights, underwritten by a political authority, were one of the key stimulants of entrepreneurial activity. In doing so, arguably, Say was one of the first to consider entrepreneurship as a social process, supported by institutions. In this regard, Say recognized the role of a political authority and the external environment in shaping a framework for entrepreneurship (North 1990; Praag 2005).

Say's (1803) treatment of the entrepreneur was also revolutionary, in that he outlined key characteristics that differentiated entrepreneurs from others. Say's entrepreneur could be criticized for not being as innovative or as dynamic as Bentham's (1748–1832). However, Say's entrepreneur was a leader, a self-driven manager who was able to apply product and market knowledge, based on careful calculation and sound judgment (Link and Link 2009; Praag 2005). Furthermore, Say also recognized the need for incentives, wealth creation not being the only incentive, to advance entrepreneurship. Say argued against the zero-sum notion of profit and differentiated between capitalists and entrepreneurs; in doing so, legitimizing profit for the entrepreneur. This was a revolutionary notion in the deeply conservative Christian society of the nineteenth century, where profit was still a dirty word for many (Bosch 1997). Not all of Say's insights were new to entrepreneurship literature; however, he was the first to bring together such a wide range of important concepts and provided a comprehensive account of entrepreneurship, which is still useful in the study of entrepreneurship today (Ekelund and Hébert 2013; Hebert and Link 2009; Praag 2005).

The English school of thought struggled to develop the concept of entrepreneurship throughout the nineteenth century, burdened by Smith's (1776) erroneous notions of the capitalist entrepreneur—what Fritz Redlich calls the "Unfortunate legacy" (Redlich 1966, p. 715 as cited in Ekelund and Hébert 2013). There were noteworthy contributions by German writers such as Thunen (1783–1850) and Mangoldt (1855) whose ideas further developed the function of the entrepreneur, risk, uncertainty and innovation. Interestingly, Mangoldt (1855) emphasized time as a key determinant of uncertainty (Hebert and Link 2009). In the latter half of the nineteenth century, the theory of entrepreneurship gained significant momentum, despite the fact that it was under the flagship of newly rebranded economic theory (Brown and Thornton 2013).

The advent of economics and its most avid propagator, the Austrian School of Economics, saw the role of entrepreneurship through an economic prism. This meant that regardless of clear gains in the understanding of entrepreneurship, it had been relegated to the back seat (Brown and Thornton 2013; Casson and Casson 2013). Instead, the focus turned to the market process as the driving force behind economic progress, existing in a theoretical realm of perfect information and perfect markets, governed by the laws of price formation and resources allocation (Baumol 1968; Hebert and Link 2009).

In the Principles of Economics, Menger (1871, translated by Dingwall and Hoselitz 1976), saw the entrepreneur as someone who, through astute observation, calculation, and decision making, aligned available resources to organize and execute the most efficient production process. For Menger the level of uncertainty faced by entrepreneurs depended on their knowledge and ability to organize and execute this process. In regard to risk, however, Menger (1871) disagrees with Mangoldt (1855), who saw risk bearing as the key function of the entrepreneur. For Menger, "risk is only incidental and the chance of loss is counterbalanced by the chance of profit" (Menger 1871, p. 161; Rothbard 2009).

Menger (1871) did not dwell on key entrepreneurial attributes such as leadership or innovation. However, Von Wieser (1927) a student of Menger, points to a broad definition of the entrepreneur. For Von Wieser, an entrepreneur is not only innovative and creative but also organized and sensitive to market demands and human nature. This multitalented entrepreneur must have the ability to predict market demand and also take risk and show leadership in getting product to market (Von Wieser 1927, translated by Hinrichs 1927). At the time, this was the broadest description of the entrepreneur; but interestingly Von Wieser does not seem to differentiate between "reckless speculators" and "foresighted bankers" (Von Wieser 1927, p. 327). Adam Smith (1776) went to great lengths to highlight the shortcomings of reckless speculators, who he deemed public enemies (Hebert and Link 2009). The advent of Austrian economics also heralded another important development. Instead of entrepreneurial activity advancing economic progress, increasingly economic progress itself was seen as the driving force behind the advancement of entrepreneurship (Baumol 1968; Brown and Thornton 2013). However, other economists at the time, such as Leon Walras (1834–1910), did not make this distinction and saw entrepreneurial activity as the all-encompassing force behind economic progress (Hebert and Link 2009; Walras 1874).

Entrepreneurship in the Twentieth Century

At the turn of the last century the leading British economist Alfred Marshall (1842–1924) made significant inroads into correcting some of the misconstructions of the Smith, Ricardo, and Mills tradition inherited by British scholars (Zaratiegui 2002). Heavily influenced by Darwinism, Marshall's (first published 1890, 8th Ed 1920) approach to entrepreneurship and the entrepreneur reflected the Darwinist notion of survival of the fittest, seeing the entrepreneur as a particular type of organism and asserting that "organisms that tend to survive are best fitted to utilize the environment for their own purposes" (Marshall 1920, p. 242). Apart from the notion of risk which amplified with time-lag, innovation, and coordination, Marshall (1920) also introduced another modern idea of alertness to the entrepreneur. Marshall was also one of the first writers to explicitly discuss the role of education in developing entrepreneurial abilities, favoring experience over formal education.

Marshall (1920) reclassified Smith's (1776) prodigal and frugal entrepreneurs into active and passive entrepreneurs. Active entrepreneurs were problem solvers, using innovation and imagination to find new and alternative ways to satisfy demand. However, the passive entrepreneur was more comfortable copying existing solutions (Marshall 1920). The active and passive entrepreneurs may have been the precursors to Schumpeter's (1939) innovator and adaptor entrepreneurs. As with Say (1803) and Mangoldt (1855) before him and Schumpeter (1939) after him, Marshall differentiated profit in relation to the two types of entrepreneurs. The passive entrepreneur's profit resembles a manager's wage, whereas the active entrepreneur's profit derives from the level of risk undertaken (Marshall 1920). Thus, arguably, Marshall's contributions bridged classical, neoclassical, and modern constructs of entrepreneurship (Praag 2005).

The twentieth century saw the greatest leaps in Entrepreneurship theory. Champions of entrepreneurship such as Schumpeter (1934), Knight (2006), Austrian economists like Mises (1949) and Kirzner (1976), and most recently Baumol (1968) and Casson (2003, 2005), among others, have shaped the modern understanding of entrepreneurship. Frank

Knight (1885–1972) was arguably the first of many influential American writers in the twentieth century to progress the theory of entrepreneurship. In his seminal book *Risk, Uncertainty and Profit*, Knight (2006, first printed 1921) provided clarity to previously ambiguous notions of risk and uncertainty tackled by Cantillon (1755) and Say (1803).

Knight (2006) argued that profit cannot simply be derived from calculable risk in a competitive market. Risk that can be measured can also be insured. Instead, entrepreneurial profit is the reward for undertaking non-quantitative, uninsurable risk that derives from imperfect managerial knowledge—what Knight classified as uncertainty (Langlois and Cosgel 1993). By making this distinction, Knight not only helped better explain entrepreneurial profit, but also challenged previous notions of the entrepreneur function. Dealing with measurable risk became a managerial function, for which there was an entrepreneurial wage. Tackling immeasurable uncertainty, argued Knight (2006), was the real entrepreneur function and source of entrepreneurial profit (Langlois and Cosgel 1993; Praag 1999). Both of these functions may be undertaken by the same individual, nevertheless the two separate functions should not be confused. Unfortunately, Knight does not go further to distinguish between uncertainty borne by the capitalist and whether there is entrepreneurial profit for the capitalist (Redlich 1957). Indeed the role of the investor capitalist as a separate entrepreneurial function has not been fully explored to date. One wonders whether Knight's notion of an entrepreneurial wage and profit and Marshall's active and passive entrepreneur can be equated to angle and commodity investors.

Schumpeter's Contribution

Joseph Schumpeter (1883–1950) has arguably made the greatest contributions to the study of entrepreneurship (Baumol 2010; Casson and Casson 2013; Hebert and Link 2009; Link and Link 2009; Praag 1999, 2005). For Schumpeter (1934; 1939) entrepreneurship is at the core of the circular flow of economic life, which ironically can only truly progress if the circular flow is disturbed by innovation and dynamism. Economic progress emerges from creative destruction, which in turn results from entrepreneurs actively applying innovation to find new production combinations, methods of production, source materials, new markets, or industries (Baumol 2010; Schumpeter 1934). Thus innovation is positioned as a central component in advancing entrepreneurship. Schumpeter (1939) designates entrepreneurship as a disequilibrating force rather than an equilibrating one. The entrepreneur essentially disturbs the status quo, or identifies the best way to do so.

Interestingly, Schumpeter (1934) only reserves the category of innovative entrepreneur for a new business; entrepreneurs in established firms are likened to organizers or managers. For Schumpeter (1934), the entrepreneur initiates "spontaneous and discontinuous change in the channel flow, disturbing the equilibrium, which forever alters and displaces the equilibrium state previously existing" (Schumpeter 1934, p. 64). Furthermore, criteria for an entrepreneur were not defined by simply leading a business: "everyone is an entrepreneur only when he actually carries out new combinations, and loses that character as soon as he has built up his business, when he settles down and is running it as other people run their business" (Schumpeter 1934, p. 78). Arguably, in this vein, overlooking whether the entrepreneur is a capitalist, an organizer of resources or simply a business owner, the entrepreneur possesses a distinctive energy, a unique individual leading a specific type of business (Link and Link 2009). However, it can also be argued that categorizing business owners as managers is detrimental and does not recognize the application of entrepreneurial skills needed to deal with competition or run the business on a day-to-day basis. Nevertheless, innovation became a key criterion for distinguishing entrepreneurs from business owners. This was a crucial insight in further developing our understanding of entrepreneurship and arguably a prelude to Baumol's (2010) Theory of Innovation and Entrepreneurship.

Some have criticized Schumpeter (1934) for overlooking the relationship between risk and uncertainty (Kanbur 1980). For example, Kanbur (1980) argues that Schumpeter's (1934) entrepreneur does not bear risk. Kanbur (1980) also criticized Schumpeter (1934) for focusing on a narrow form of financial risk. In defense of Schumpeter (1939), although there is not a great focus on risk, he did recognize the challenge of uncertainty that plagues all entrepreneurial decisions. Arguably, as later with Knight (2006), Schumpeter (1934) differentiates between calculable, thus insurable, risk and uninsurable uncertainty.

The American Perspective

In the wake of the Second World War Schumpeter moved to the United States and joined Harvard University, where he influenced a number of writers who made significant contributions to the theory of entrepreneurship in their own right (Link and Link 2009; Praag 1999). Most notable of these at the time were Edwin F. Gay (1867–1946) and Arthur H. Cole (1889–1974), both of whom advanced Schumpeter's (1939) ideas of innovation and the entrepreneur as a disequilibrating force (Hebert and Link 2009). For example, Cole (1949) used a case study approach to conduct a variety of longitudinal studies of different entrepreneurial functions. Like Walras (1874), Menger (1871), Von Wieser (1927) and others, Cole was able to identify the entrepreneur as an organizer of factors of production. Similarly, like Cantillon (1755), Say (1803), Menger (1871) and Knight (2006), Cole highlighted decision making under uncertainty as a core entrepreneurial function (Cole 1949).

Cole (1949) also drew on another construct which previously, in the context of entrepreneurship, had only been expressed vaguely by Say (1803), Marshall (1920), and in another context by Keynes (Steele 2001). Cole (1949) introduced the notion of environmental factors influencing entrepreneurship. Schumpeter (1934) had previously highlighted the impact of innovative entrepreneurs upon the environment. However, Cole (1949) took this a step further to identify it as a symbiotic relationship, where entrepreneurship and the environment affected each other, arguably bridging the gap between the Austrian notion of economic activity advancing entrepreneurship and the Schumpeterian notion of entrepreneurship being at the core of all economic progress. Other than economic factors which were already well established, Cole (1949) also identified political and social circumstances but did not delve deeper to explore them. Nevertheless, the introduction of environmental factors influencing the entrepreneur's decision, alongside traditionally well recognized factors such as level of uncertainty and access to resources, was a significant step forward for the theory of entrepreneurship.

Toward the middle of the twentieth century George Shackle (1903–1992), an English Economist, also made valuable contributions to the theory of entrepreneurship. Shackle's (1955) main focus was on uncertainty; like Menger (1871) and Knight (2006), he separated the functions of decision making and bearing uncertainty, arguing that even though entrepreneurs may be responsible for undertaking both functions, nevertheless, the roles should be considered separate because those who wish to "can contract out of uncertainty" (Shackle 1955, p. 82).

Like Cantillon (1755), Menger (1871), and Marshall (1920), Shackle (1955, 1966) saw a direct link between time and uncertainty. However, more importantly, Shackle (1966 p. 86) saw uncertainty, not only tied to external circumstance, but an internal limitation of imagination and that it was only this "bounded uncertainty that will permit him (entrepreneur) to act creatively". This seems to be a modern notion, asserting that entrepreneurs are most creative when faced with the greatest adversities (Baumol 2010; Szirmai et al. 2011). Like Schumpeter (1934) Shackle (1966) saw the entrepreneur as a disequilibrating element; however, it was his psychological approach, internalizing the entrepreneurial process that was most radical (Chell 2008; Hebert and Link 2009).

Over in the United States, the Nobel laureate Theodor Schultz (1902–1998) broadened the theory of entrepreneurship by expanding entrepreneurial behavior, thus risk bearing, beyond the realms of business (Chell 2008). In contrast to Shackle (1966) Schultz (1975) saw entrepreneurship as an equilibrating force. Although he accepted the disequilibrating role of the entrepreneur, Schultz (1975) criticized Schumpeter for not expanding the scope of his disequilibrating entrepreneur to consider other economic agents that work in tandem to bring about equilibrium.

One wonders whether Schultz (1975) was looking at the other side of the same coin. While Schumpeter (1934) identified the entrepreneur as a disequilibrating element, he also highlighted established business owners that were more interested in sustaining equilibrium, as disequilibrium would essentially mean their demise. Arguably, mergers and acquisitions used by established corporations to assimilate new businesses exemplify an effective equilibrating strategy. Furthermore, Schumpeter (1934) defined the entrepreneur according to behavior, not limited to business or ownership, but instead the act of pursuing innovation. In this vein, the Schumpeterian (1934) entrepreneur is not bound by function but rather action, which is close to Schultz's (1975) notion of the entrepreneur.

Schultz (1975) also saw education as a key component to enhance entrepreneurial ability and prepare economic agents, not just entrepreneurs, to steer back toward equilibrium. However, Schultz (1975) faced stern criticism on this subject. For example, like Marshall (1920) and Hayek (1945), Machlup (1980) argued for the importance of experience over formal education in the accumulation of relevant knowledge. For Machlup, the essential component in acquiring relevant knowledge was an individual's ability, or more specifically their level of alertness, to available opportunities. This ability could be exercised most freely through experience. Nevertheless, a combination of both viewpoints may be the most effectual course to adopt, as both experience and education are complementary and compatible in the pursuit of knowledge (Hebert and Link 2009).

Leibenstein's Theory of X-efficiency

Harvey Leibenstein (1922–1994) provided an alternative to the prevailing neoclassical economic view of the near redundant entrepreneur operating in theoretically perfect markets and information (Casson 2003; Hayek 1945; Leibenstein 1968). Leibenstein's (1966) Theory of X-efficiency essentially compensated for the human condition and inertia. He maintained that, unlike machines, human actions, and thus their ability to find the most efficient means to ends, were fraught with inherent inconsistencies (Leibenstein 1966). These inconsistencies in human action led to deficiencies and imperfections in the market which ultimately created opportunities for entrepreneurship (Leibenstein 1966, 1968).

Leibenstein (1968) acknowledged previous notions of entrepreneurial opportunities deriving from gaps in the market and the entrepreneur's ability to organize resources; however, he also maintained that, ultimately, opportunities derived from market deficiencies and imperfections. This was in sharp contrast to the neoclassical economic view which considered all economic agents, including firms, as efficient maximizers of utility (Hayek 1945; Hebert and Link 2009). It was this human inaction or inability that led to a perpetual slack in the market.

Leibenstein (1968) identified the entrepreneur as a scarce resource that was at the core of economic activity. Using four characteristics, Leibenstein (1968, p. 75) defined the entrepreneur with the ability to (a) connect markets, (b) fill gaps created by market deficiencies, (c) organize required inputs, and (d) "create or expand time-binding, input-transforming entities (i.e., firms)". Within the realm of entrepreneurship, Leibenstein also wrote clearly about the role of internal and external motivation in adjusting the behavior of economic agents. For Leibenstein, motivation was connected with three key elements of financial reward, punishment, and social acceptance (Potts 2007).

Leibenstein (1968) may be criticized for not going further in expanding the four characteristics of the entrepreneur; however, these four characteristics did implicitly allude to other qualities postulated by writers. For example, regarding the ability to fill gaps, entrepreneurs would need to exercise sound judgment to make decisions, conduct calculations and bear uncertainty (Casson 2005; Say 1803). There was also another puzzling construct in Leibenstein's work (1968) in that, essentially the entrepreneur's success is directly linked to the demise of others (Potts 2007). This construct can also be found in Schumpeter (1934, p. 153): "what the marginal entrepreneur receives is wholly a matter of indifference for the success of others". Arguably, this takes us back to the Plutonian zero-sum game and does not sit comfortably with the modern notion of the innovating entrepreneur, who succeeds in spite of competition (Audretsch 2013).

In recent times entrepreneurship is increasingly recognized as the driving force behind a healthy economy (Baumol 2010; Casson 2005; Minniti 2008). However, as highlighted above, understanding of this particular notion was muddled with the advent of economics and neoclassical writers such as Menger (1871). The crux of the debate was tangled in whether economic progress led entrepreneurial activity, or as Schumpeter (1934) would have it, was it in fact entrepreneurial activity that advanced economic progress (Brown and Thornton 2013; Casson and Casson 2013; Hebert and Link 2009). Exploring key constructs in the development of entrepreneurship demands closer inspection of the Austrian free market principles of economics. In particular, the next section focuses on the role of the market process and contrasting views on intervention to aid entrepreneurship.

The Austrian Perspective

The market is the most suitable arrangement for connecting entrepreneurs and customers to achieve their personal ends (Mises 1949). According to Mises (1949), human action is the engine that turns the market economy. Individual desires are inextricably linked with other individuals. Fulfillment of these desires requires action and cooperation so that those with desire and those with solutions to desires can transact. This interplay of human action ruled by individual ends, prices, resources, goods, and competition governs the market process (Mises 1949).

More than a physical entity, the market is a process matrix, constructed of infinite individual actions and transactions, past, present, and future (Kirzner 1976; Mises 1949). These transactions are facilitated by the profit motive and price mechanism; similar to a telecommunications network, it simultaneously informs buyers and sellers of potential profits and aids decision making (Hayek 1945). If human action is the engine, then prices are the fuel for a market economy. For Hayek (1945) and Mises (1949), prices were the key component in a functioning market economy. They allow entrepreneurs and customers to calculate and compete for goods and resources in achieving their individual ends (Hayek 1945; Mises 1949; Steele 2001).

Government Intervention

Governments can facilitate markets or harm them. Battles have been fought on this front for over a century. In a free market economy, the government's role would simply be limited to protecting individuals and organizations from the threat of violence and harm (Mises 1949). For Austrian economists, this is as far as government should go; anything beyond this point starts to infringe on civil liberties and produces what Isaiah Berlin (1958) would call negative liberty. Worse still, as the government adopts a bigger role it starts to disrupt and corrupt market data, crucial for effective running of markets and for entrepreneurs to make calculated decisions (Hayek 1945). Interference to control market forces, or any interruption to economic transactions reaching their natural ends, poses a direct threat to the market's integrity (Hayak 1968; Mises 1949). Friedman (1976) blamed government interventions for volatile business cycles. Thus, any form of intervention, whether subsidies to support entrepreneurs, or rent controls to protect customers, is harmful to the economy in the long run.

In sharp contrast to the Austrian view, Keynesian or antitrust thought called for government intervention to rein in unruly market forces that could not be left to their own devices (Audretsch 2007; Steel 2001). This notion questioned whether a free market was possible or even desirable. Although the level of government involvement in trying to control elements of the economy has varied throughout the history of capitalism, as Friedman points out, the market economy has never been truly free and the laissez-faire political, economic system needed to advance free markets has never been realized (Friedman 1964).

Our social development under a mutated form of capitalism has meant certain sections of society have accumulated excessive wealth and power, which they may not have accumulated under a truly free market economy (Buchanan 2000; Fukuyama 2013). Entrepreneurs have not been able to apply disruptive innovation as Schumpeter (1934) had predicted; instead, as Kirzner (1976) pointed out, perceived opportunities remain fulfilled. Therefore, interventionists argue that the government has a direct responsibility to correct market imperfections, such as monopolies and deficiencies in supply and demand (Audretsch 2007; Steel 2001). Ironically, these deficiencies may represent the main source of opportunities for entrepreneurs (Leibenstein 1968).

Economists such as Keynes assumed that specific interventions would lead to predictable market outcomes. Although this view could be defended by observing short-term results, the same could not be said for long-term effects (Hayek 1945). Hayek saw the market economy as a complex phenomenon that could not be fully understood to make predictions; any interference meant only harm in the long-run (Read 1958; Steele 2001). Thus, the opposing arguments for a minimal or big government, intervention or non-intervention are roughly based upon this premise.

Whether one subscribes to the Keynesian or Austrian school of thought, politicians and economists alike are still pondering over the question "to intervene or not to intervene?" (Buchanan 2000). In fact, the raging strife between many economists seems to rest on this very tenet (Besley and Burgess 2002; Mises 1949). Government intervention, in the form of monetary or fiscal policy, may achieve favorable economic outcomes, but this is only a short-term fix and ignores the long-term harm to the economy (Hayek 1968). Whether it is an increase in the money supply or a decrease in interest rates, the short-term benefits of increased demand, decreased unemployment and resulting economic growth are dwarfed by long-term harms of inflation and resulting volatility in the business cycle (Ebeling 2006; Friedman 1964; Mises 1949).

Mises (1949) argued that government interventions created artificial price ceilings, wages, and interest rates, which in turn created a false economic reality (Mises 1949), much like Hayek's view of government interventions sending false price signals to economic agents (Hayek 1968). These interventions create a mismatch between supply and demand, eventually confusing entrepreneurs and derailing the economy, pushing it into a downward spiral. In fact Friedman (1976) argued that the United States is trapped in the boom and bust cycle precisely because of government interventions in the past, the best example being the New Deal and President Roosevelt's attempt to control the economy and unruly capitalism (Friedman 1976). Friedman argued that these types of mistakes explain the turmoil in many economies—what Wicksell (1907) calls "an unending cumulative process of rising prices", continuously fluctuating between inflation and unemployment, boom and bust (Friedman 1968; Friedman 1976; Wicksell 1907 cited in Ebeling 2006. p. 13). Although it should also be noted that Wicksell was writing when the economy was mostly heavily affected by raw materials, where the rise and fall in the prices of coal and the like ushered in the boom or bust (A. Widman, personal communication, December 26, 2015).

Price, Monopolies, and Competition

Austrian logic compels us to let the market process run free and trust it to manage itself. However, this does require a belief in the concept of natural inequality (Schenone and Ravier 2007; Skousen 2005). Interventionists such as Fisher (1911) argued for maintaining a consistent price level through the correction periods of the business cycle, which inevitably ensued after unexpected increases in the price levels. Indeed, if the government could neutralize these unexpected increases in prices then the business cycle could be tamed (Fisher 1911 cited in Ebeling 2006). However, as government increases its grip on the economy, the essential role of competition in regulating the market economy withers away (Read 1958). Government policies that aim to create fairer competition within the economy often mean inefficient firms are propped up and protected from efficient firms (Mises 1949; Rothbard 1963). The latter causes the most harm because inefficient firms are allowed to survive where they should have dissolved, but more importantly the process of discovering new and better ways to satisfy consumer needs gets compromised (Hayek 1968). In the Austrian view, it is precisely these types of interventions that create artificial conditions, suffocating entrepreneurs, and the market process.

Austrian economists would do away with all government interference with competition, even to discourage monopolies, the premise being that, in the long-run, a monopoly only survives as long as the next innovation. However, this does not compensate for the short-term damages in lost opportunities nor does it take into account that homo economicus is an acting individual and once a monopoly is created they will do everything in their power to maintain it. Hayek was writing at a time when markets and indeed capitalism were still developing and firms were fighting to reach the summit. Since then, the economic landscape has changed, many large companies have become giant multinationals who have created de facto monopolies and so the role competition once used to play is now insignificant. In this vein, unregulated markets are saturated with overgrown corporations that suffocate entrepreneurs. Even Adam Smith (1776) acknowledged the tendency of totally free markets to develop anti-competitive monopolies (Bootle 2011). Hayek himself seems to point at this and recognizes that, because competition forces firms to improve, they are "disinclined to compete" (Hayek 1968. p. 19).

When one thinks about the survival of the fittest, in the Marshallian sense, images of businesses locked in intense competition against other businesses come to mind. Efficient businesses survive and inefficient ones face the cull. Therefore, competition acts as a natural regulator within the market (Hayek 1968; Mises 1949; Rothbard 1963). However, while this may be true, competition serves an even higher purpose. Most businesses cease to exist not because of competition but because of their own ineffectiveness. Hayek (1968) sees the real purpose of competition as a means of discovery. As firms and consumers try to outdo each other in order to obtain the most desirable goods and services, they are forced to find new and more efficient means of achieving these ends. Competition facilitates the discovery process, enabling economic actors to discover new possibilities of better serving consumer needs (Hayek 1968).

Much like prices, competition is a key component in a free market (Hayek 1968; Mises 1949). It not only preserves the market but also helps it improve and evolve. It "forces" those who depend on the market not just to imitate the latest improvements but also to continuously innovate in a bid to achieve a competitive advantage (Hayek 1968. p. 19). These notions seem very close to Schumpeter's (1934) innovative entrepreneur. However, Hayek's (1968) use of the word "force" is particularly poignant here and helps delve deeper into the nature of homo economicus. It suggests that the willingness to improve is not voluntary and that if competition was not there, firms would continue as they had always done. Without competition, we might still be using beepers and not smart phones, without competition we might never have had the electric car.

One can understand why firms want to minimize competition; ultimately, it adds to the cost while the only benefit it provides firms is the possibility of being better than their competitors. Without competition, firms would neither face this cost nor seek the benefit. Therefore, it is also logical for firms to aim for a monopoly or forge alliances to create cartels at the very least (Rothbard 1963). Mises (1949) paid particular attention to this topic, outlining at least 17 different circumstances where monopolistic behavior may be observed. Mises (1949) emphasized the role monopoly prices play, rather than just the existence of monopolies. Monopoly prices enabled firms to enjoy greater control over supply and prices (Mises 1949). However, Mises (1949) does not go further to highlight other benefits and reasons firms aim for monopolies. For example, along with greater control over supply and prices, firms can also control quality and indeed innovation. The modern entrepreneur's main weapon is innovation; therefore, if existing firms are able to hijack and drip feed innovation, as many large firms do, then entrepreneurs face an impossible challenge. Proponents of non-intervention are quick to point to Google and Facebook as prime examples of new entrants succeeding because they were efficient and innovative. Whilst this is true, another important factor for their success is the fact that they were operating in relatively immature markets. Another new firm enjoying the same level of success is improbable. What'sApp being bought by Facebook in 2014 highlights this fact well.

The Austrian Entrepreneur

The issue of intervening for entrepreneurship falls under a wider ideological divide which may also explain other facets of contrasting views of entrepreneurship (Reinert 1999). Is entrepreneurship an equilibrating or disequilibrating force? Is entrepreneurship driven by individual entrepreneurs or are entrepreneurs merely a product of the market? In other words, do entrepreneurs create markets or does the market create them? (Boettke and Coyne 2003).

The Austrian view of markets constructed upon perfect knowledge, where the entrepreneur is merely an allocative force for other factors of production, helping to bring the market closer to equilibrium, is sterile (Baumol 2010; Casson and Casson 2013). This view contrasts sharply with the interventionist notion of unpredictable markets that are inherently imperfect and plagued by deficiencies which must be corrected though intervention, either through government or a third party involved in the economic transaction (Steel 2001). In this regard, the entrepreneur is a dynamic disequilibrating force that sustains and rejuvenates markets (Schumpeter 1934).

Kirzner (1976) advanced Mises' (1949) construct of human action to further establish the notion of entrepreneurship within economic theory, which in his view had become increasingly elusive. For Kirzner (1976, p. 31), existing analytical dimensions of "economizing, maximizing and efficiency" were not sufficient to explain human behavior in the market process. Kirzner (1976) added an entrepreneurial element, which was best explained as the individual's alertness to opportunities and the evolving nature of allocative decision making, continually allocating the best means to achieve desired ends.

Alertness to market opportunities is a key tenet of our modern understanding of the entrepreneur. Kirzner's (1976) contribution re-established the entrepreneur's role within the market economy. However, the entrepreneur was still limited to an allocative function, unlike Schumpeter's entrepreneur who actively created opportunities; the Austrian perspective was limited to an entrepreneur taking advantage of existing opportunities. This marked a crucial separation between Austrian thought and prevailing views on entrepreneurship.

In summary, adding the classical Austrian view to the historical analysis of entrepreneurship and entrepreneurs advanced the notion of entrepreneurship as a process, thus highlighting the importance of environmental factors and functions that facilitate entrepreneurship. However, despite Kirzner's (1976) revival, in the Austrian view, the entrepreneur's role diminished in a sterile environment of theoretically perfect knowledge. Contrasting the Austrian view of entrepreneurship with Keynesian or antitrust notions helps develop a realistic picture of how entrepreneurship may be advanced in modern markets. Nevertheless, an emphasis on the central role of the entrepreneur remains elusive in both notions. Instead, the government or the market process is expected to take on a commanding role. Arguably, both the Austrian and Keynesian view of entrepreneurship are bound in different contexts. The Austrian view of entrepreneurship is set at the micro level, whereas Keynesian thought is mainly concerned with the macro level. In both instances, unfortunately, the individual level or the entrepreneur is largely ignored (Audretsch 2007). Even writers like Schumpeter (1934) who have focused on the entrepreneur have not gone far enough to explore how and why they adopt this role (Schultz 1975).

In his seminal book, *The Microtheory of Innovative Entrepreneurship*, Baumol (2010) attempted to fuse historically diverse, micro and macro, notions of entrepreneurship with that of the entrepreneur. In doing so, Baumol (2010) not only places entrepreneurial action within an institutional framework but also brings entrepreneurial personality traits to the fore, traits which were increasingly seen as unreliable measures of predicting entrepreneurial behavior (Bird 1989; Gartner 1988; Krueger and Brazeal 1994; Krueger et al. 2000). The following chapter focuses on the individual entrepreneur and draws out key components that enable individuals to undertake entrepreneurial action. The next chapter outlines the theoretical framework that has guided this study.

References

Aspromourgos, T. (2013). Entrepreneurship, risk and income distribution in Cantillon's Essai. In N. Salvadori, C. Gehrke, I. Steedman, & R. Sturn (Eds.), *Classical political economy and modern theory: Essays in honour of Heinz Kurz* (pp. 105–119). London: Routledge.

Audretsch, D. (2007). *The entrepreneurial society*. Oxford Univer0sity Press. ISBN: 978-0-19-518350-4.

Audretsch, D. (2013). *Public policy in the entrepreneurial society*. Edward Elgar Publishing. ISBN: 1783476923.

Baumol, W. (1968). Entrepreneurship in economic theory. *The American Economic Review, 58*(2), 64–71.

Baumol, W. J. (2010). *The microtheory of innovative entrepreneurship. The Kauffman Foundation Series on Innovation and Entrepreneurship*. Princeton University Press. ISBN: 1400835224.

Besley, T., & Burgess, R. (2002). The political economy of government responsiveness: Theory and evidence from India. *The Quarterly Journal of Economics, 117*(4), 1415–1451.

Bird, B. J. (1989). *Entrepreneurial behavior*. Scott, Foresman Little, Brown College Division. ISBN: 0673397912.

Boettke, P., & Coyne, C. (2003). Entrepreneurship and development: Cause or consequence. In Austrian Economics and Entrepreneurial Studies. *Emerald Insight*, pp. 67–87.

Bootle, R. (2011). *The trouble with markets: Saving capitalism from itself*. Nicholas Brealey Pub. ISBN: 1857885589.

Bosch, G. (1997). Eric Williams and the moral rhetoric of dependency theory. *Callaloo, 20*(4), 817–827.

Brown, C., & Thornton, M. (2013). How entrepreneurship theory created economics. *The Quarterly Journal of Austrian Economics, 16*(4), 401–420.

Buchanan, P. (2000). That the Lumpen should rule: Vulgar capitalism in the post-industrial age. *Journal of American and Comparative Cultures, 23*(4), 1–15.

Cantillon, R. (2010). *Essai sur la nature du commerce en général.* (M. Thornton & C. Saucier, Trans.). Auburn: Ludwig von Mises Institute. Original work published in 1755.

Casson, M. (2003). *The entrepreneur: An economic theory.* Cheltenham: Edward Elgar Publishing. ISBN: 1843765632.

Casson, M. (2005). Entrepreneurship and the theory of the firm. *Journal of Economic Behavior & Organization, 58*(2), 327–348.

Casson, M., & Casson, C. (2013). The *entrepreneur in history: From medieval merchant to modern business leader.* Palgrave Pivot. e-EAN/ISBN: 9781137305824.

Chell, E. (2008). *The entrepreneurial personality: A social construction.* Routledge. London. ISBN: 1134335628.

Cole, A. (1949). *The great mirror of folly: An economic-bibliographical study.* Baker Library, Harvard Graduate School of Business Administration.

Ebeling, M. (2006). *"The great Austrian inflation," The Freeman: Ideas on liberty.* Indianapolis: The Ludwig von Mises Institute.

Ekelund, R., & Hébert, F. (2013). *A history of economic theory and method* (6th Ed.). Minden: Waveland Press. ISBN: 1478611065. Illinois, USA.

Fisher, I. (1911). *The purchasing power of money* (2nd ed.). Macmillan: New York.

Fontaine, P. (1993). The capitalist entrepreneur in eighteenth century economic literature. *Journal of the History of Economic Thought.* Cambridge University Press, *15*(01), 72–89.

Friedman, M. (1964, October 11). The Goldwater view of economics. *New York Times Magazine, 35*, pp. 133–137. Retrieved from: http://0055d26.netsolhost.com/friedman/pdfs/nyt/NYT.10.11.1964.pdf

Friedman, M. (1968). The role of monetary policy. *American Economic Review, 58*(1).

Friedman, M. (1976). *Inflation and unemployment. Nobel memorial lecture.* The University of Chicago. Illinois, USA.

Fukuyama, F. (2013). What is governance? *Governance, 26*(3), 347–368. https://doi.org/10.1111/gove.12035.

Gartner, W. (1988). Who is an entrepreneur? Is the wrong question. *American Journal of Small Business, 12*(4), 11–32.

Hayek, F. A. (1945). The use of knowledge in society. *The American Economic Review, 35*(4), 519–530.

Hayek, F. A. (1968). Competition as a discovery procedure. *QJAE, 5*(3).

Hebert, R., & Link, A. (2009). *A history of entrepreneurship.* London: Routledge.

Hoselitz, B. (1960). Entrepreneurship and economic growth. In *Sociological Aspects of Economic Growth* (pp. 139–158). Glencoe: The Free Press.

Jevons, S. (1881). *Richard Cantillon and the nationality of political economy* (pp. 333–360). Oxford: *Contemporary Review*.

Kanbur, R. (1980). A note on risk taking, entrepreneurship, and Schumpeter. *History of Political Economy, 12*(4), 489–498.

Kirzner, I. (1971). Entrepreneurship & the market approach to development. Liberty Fund. *Online Library of Liberty*. Retrieved from: http://swissmc.blackboard.com/

Kirzner, I. (1976). *Equilibrium versus market process: The foundations of modern Austrian economics*. Kansas City: Sheed & Wad.

Knight, F. (2006). *Risk, uncertainty and profit*. New York: Cosimo. ISBN 1602060053.

Krueger, J., & Carsrud, A. (1994). Entrepreneurial intentions: Applying the theory of planned behaviour. *Entrepreneurship & Regional Development, 5*(4), 315–330.

Krueger, N., Reilly, M., & Carsrud, A. (2000). Competing models of entrepreneurial intentions. *Journal of Business Venturing, 15*(5-6), 411–432.

Langlois, R., & Cosgel, M. (1993). Frank Knight on risk uncertainty and the firm: A new interpretation. *Economic Inquiry, 31*, 456–465.

Leibenstein, H. (1966). Allocative efficiency vs X-efficiency. *The American Economic Review, 56*(3), 393–415.

Leibenstein, H. (1968). Entrepreneurship and development. *American Economic Review, 58*(2), 72–84.

Link, A., & Link, J. (2009). *Government as entrepreneur*. Oxford University Press. United States. ISBN: 0199708843.

Machlup, F. (1980). *Knowledge: Its creation, distribution and economic significance, volume I knowledge and knowledge production*. Princeton: Princeton University Press.

Marshall, A. (1920). *Principles of economics* (8th ed.). (First published 1890, London: Macmillan and Co.). Online Library of Liberty.

Menger, C. (1871). *Principles of economics* (James Dingwall & Bert F. Hoselitz, Trans.). New York: New York University Press, (1976).

Minniti, M. (2008). The role of government policy on entrepreneurial activity: Productive, unproductive, or destructive? *Entrepreneurship Theory & Practice, 32*(5), 779–790.

Mises, L. (1949). *Human action: A treatise on economics*. New Haven: Yale University Press.

Nevin, S. (2013). Richard Cantillon: The father of economics. *History Ireland. Wordwell Ltd, 21*(2), 20–23. https://doi.org/10.2307/41827152.
North, D. (1990). *Institutions, institutional change and economic performance.* Cambridge University Press. ISBN: 9780521397346.
Potts, J. (2007). X-efficacy Vs X-efficiency. In F. Frantz (Eds.). *Renaissance in behavioral economics: Essays in honour of Harvey Leibenstein* (92–104). Routledge. ISBN: 1135994161.
Praag, M. (1999). Some classic views on entrepreneurship. De Economist. *ProQuest Central, 147*(3), 311.
Praag, M. (2005). *Successful entrepreneurship: Confronting economic theory with empirical practice.* Edward Elgar Publishing. London. ISBN: 1845426886.
Read, L. (1958). I, Pencil. My Family Tree as told to Leonard. *Library of economics and liberty, Econlib.* Retrieved from: http://swissmc.blackboard.com/
Redlich, F. (1957). Towards a better theory of risk. *Explorations in Entrepreneurial History, 10,* 33–39.
Reinert, E. (1999). The role of the state in economic growth. *Journal of Economic Studies. MCB University Press, 26*(4/5), 268–326.
Rothbard, M. (1963). *Man, economy and state.* Chapter I: Human action. Ludwig von Mises Institute. Retrieved from: http://swissmc.blackboard.com/
Rothbard, M. (2009). *Review of Austrian economics,* Volume V. Ludwig von Mises Institute. ISBN: 1610161645.
Say, Jean-Baptiste. (1803). *A treatise on political economy.* (C. R. Prinsep, Trans.). and Clement C. Biddle., ed. 1855. Library of economics and liberty. Retrieved October 22, 2014 from the world wide web: http://www.econlib.org/library/Say/sayT.html
Schenone, O., & Ravier, A. (2007). Review of "Vienna & Chicago: Friends or foes? A tale of two schools of free-market economics" by Mark Skousen", *History of Economics Review, 46,* Australian National University (ANU), pp. 190–194.
Schultz, T. (1975). The value of the ability to deal with disequilibria. *Journal of Economic Literature, 13*(3), 827–846.
Schumpeter, J. (1934). *The theory of economic development: An inquiry into profits, capital, credit, interest, and the business cycle.* Transaction Publishers. New Brunswick. ISBN: 0878556982.
Schumpeter, J. (1939). *Business cycles: A theoretical, historical and statistical analysis of the capitalist process.* New York/Toronto/London: McGraw-Hill.
Shackle, G. L. S. (1955). *Uncertainty in economics and other reflections.* New York: Cambridge University Press, *10*(5), p. 267.

Shackle, G. L. S. (1966). *The nature of economic thought: Selected papers 1955–1964*. Cambridge University Press. Cambridge. ISBN: 978052106278.

Shane, S., Lockea, E., & Collins, C. (2003). Entrepreneurial motivation. *Human Resource Management Review.* Elsevier Science Inc, *13*, 257–279. https://doi.org/10.1016/S1053-4822(03)00017-2.

Skousen, M. (2005). *Vienna & Chicago: Friends or foes? A tale of two schools of free-market economics* (p. 318). Washington: Regnery Publishing. ISBN 0-8952-6029-8.

Smith, A. (2007). *Wealth of nations* (First Published 1776). Cosimo Classics Series. New York: Cosimo. ISBN 1602069395.

Sobel, R., Clark J., & Lee, D. (2007). Freedom, barriers to entry, entrepreneurship, and economic progress. Austrian Economic Review. *Springer Science + Business Media*, pp. 221–236. doi:https://doi.org/10.1007/s11138-007-0023-3.

Steele, G. R. (2001). *Keynes and Hayek, The money economy*. London: Routledge.

Swedberg, R. (2000). *Entrepreneurship: The social science View*. Oxford University Press. ISBN: 9780198294627.

Szirmai, A., Naudé, W., & Goedhuys, M. (2011). *Entrepreneurship, innovation, and economic development*. Oxford University Press. ISBN: 0199596514.

Von Wieser, F. (1927). (1851–1926). *Social economics* (1st ed.). (A. Ford Hinrichs, Trans. With a pref. by Wesley Clair Mitchell). London: Allen & Unwin. Translation of Theorie der gesellschaftlichen Wirtschaft. Edition (1927). ASIN: B000NWMXXC.

Walras, L. (1874). *Elements of pure economics*. Translated and annotated by William Jaffe (1954). London: Allen and Unwin.

Zaratiegui, J. (2002). What does profit mean for Alfred Marshall. *International Journal of Applied Economics, 10*(3), 381–402.

3

Theoretical Framework for Entrepreneurship in the UAE

The previous chapter illustrates the lack of consensus and at times even the conflicting views on the theory of entrepreneurship and how we define an entrepreneur. This chapter aims to consolidate some of these views and draw out a theoretical framework that is best suited to guide this research in the UAE context. This process will also help produce operational definitions that are most relevant to this book. It will be useful at this point to explore the key tenets that govern the realms of entrepreneurship. For example, what is it that motivates an entrepreneur to act?

Entrepreneurial Action

The theory of entrepreneurship and how entrepreneurship can be advanced is still to achieve consensus (Alvarez 2010; Casson 2005; Shane et al. 2003; Swedberg 2000). The role of incentives (Say 1803), motivation (Marshall 1920; Leibenstein 1968), and environmental factors (Cole 1949) in facilitating entrepreneurship has informed policy and transformed our understanding of entrepreneurship. However, although these

© The Author(s) 2018
W. A. Minhas, *Advancing Entrepreneurship in the United Arab Emirates*,
https://doi.org/10.1007/978-3-319-76436-8_3

factors are widely recognized as key variables in enhancing entrepreneurship, their application is contested among different schools of thought (Baumol 2010; Reinert 1999; Steele 2001). Furthermore, there are rifts and variations within individual schools of thought. For example, although Mises, Schumpeter, and Kirzner may herald from the Austrian school of economics, their views on entrepreneurship and how it should be advanced vary significantly.

The search for a universal definition of an entrepreneur, based on characteristics, has not been successful (Carsrud and Brännback 2011; Casson 2005; Shaver and Scott 1991). It may be prudent at this stage to heed the advice of Francis Edgeworth (1845–1926), and construct multiple definitions of entrepreneurs, because entrepreneurs are best defined by the context and their choice of economic activity (Hebert and Link 2009). Nevertheless, the discussion thus far suggests that an entrepreneur may be defined either by characteristics or by behavior (Gartner 1988). The entrepreneur must face uncertainty in the pursuit of profit, but through innovation, effective leadership, and decision making is able to organize economic resources and efficiently allocate them to produce the best possible market outcomes. Thus, it also follows that entrepreneurs are also a product of their environment. Therefore, in addition to internal facets, the external environmental factors cannot be ignored (Shane and Venkataraman 2000).

Despite multiple variations, it is widely accepted that an active entrepreneur is the core driver of entrepreneurship (Baumol 2010; Carsrud and Brännback 2011; Casson 2003, 2005). The following sections will look at behavior and in particular what drives entrepreneurs to start new ventures. Ajzen's (1991) Theory of Planned Behavior (TPB) suggests entrepreneurial intentions are the best predictors for entrepreneurial action (Carsrud and Brännback 2011; Krueger and Brazeal 1994; Krueger et al. 2000; Liñan et al. 2011). However, intentions do not necessarily lead to action (Bae et al. 2014; Bahrami 2014; Shane et al. 2003). A crucial link between intentions and action is motivation (Carsrud and Brännback 2011). But while entrepreneurial motivation explains the antecedents of entrepreneurial intentions, antecedents of entrepreneurial motivations need further investigation (Fayolle et al. 2014).

Entrepreneurial Motivation

Traditional origins of motivation theories try to find answers for human action, such as, why we choose certain actions over others and what incentivizes these actions (Schacter et al. 2011). The theory of motivation is largely grounded in the two overarching schools of thought, the psychological and economic frameworks (Alschuler 1967; Carsrud and Brännback 2011; Steel and Konig 2006). Like the theory of entrepreneurship, the theory of motivation lacks clear consensus and there have been calls to define a fact-based, common theory of motivation (Carsrud and Brännback 2011; Graham and Weiner 1996; Steel and Konig 2006). Theories of entrepreneurial motivation can be roughly divided into intrinsic and extrinsic sources of motivation (Carsrud and Brännback 2011; Pervin 2003).

Extrinsic theories of motivation emphasize incentives and external factors that pull entrepreneurs into action, whereas intrinsic theories of motivation focus on the internal drivers that push us into action (Hakim 1989; Kirkwood 2009). Using the intrinsic theoretical framework, a number of entrepreneurial traits can be drawn out to better understand entrepreneurs and their actions (Shane et al. 2003). However, this trait-based approach to entrepreneurial research has been criticized, too, for limited application and generalizability (Aldrich and Zimmer 1986; Bird 1989; Carsrud and Brännback 2011).

Arguably, both the internal and external assessments of entrepreneurial motivation focus on the situation as it exists and fail to account for antecedent influences that should not be ignored when considering the origins of entrepreneurial motivation (Krueger and Carsrud 1994). Furthermore, antecedent influences also affect entrepreneurs' perception of value, and therefore the type of venture they are likely to adopt (Estay et al. 2013). Combining these factors provides a promising framework for explaining entrepreneurial motivation and why they vary among entrepreneurs (Carsrud and Brännback 2011; Fayolle et al. 2014). However, this specific area still lacks extensive empirical research, especially within the UAE (Sikdar and Vel 2011).

In one of the earliest studies of motivation, Murray (1938) used a Thematic Apperception Test and found motivation to be highly individual and context specific. The results of the study demonstrated that individuals were heavily influenced by their experiences, environment, and their conscious and sub-conscious state (Graham and Weiner 1996). More importantly, research participants tended to project their personal and emotional situation onto their aspiration (Murray 1938). Atkinson (1957) and McClelland (1961) later advanced Murray's (1938) work to develop a comprehensive Theory of Achievement, which mainly focuses on internal drivers and the need for achievement. Murray (1938) was arguably one of the first to recognize that motivation, like so many other facets of the human condition, is bound to context.

Need for Independence

In a quantitative study of French entrepreneurs, Estay et al. (2013) went beyond traditional lines of enquiry, concerned with the effect of intentions and motivations on behavior, to investigate the antecedents of entrepreneurial motivation. Independence and development were highlighted as the main antecedents of entrepreneurial motivation. The need for independence motivated entrepreneurs to pursue actions expected to return financial independence and enhance self-determination (Wagner and Ziltener 2008), while development motivated them because of the perception that their action directly led to improvement (Estay et al. 2013). The study sample comprised 235 respondents with a 100% response rate; however, the questionnaire was administered by the local chamber of commerce when new entrepreneurs came to register their business. This, coupled with the fact that the sample was limited to one region of France, questions the validity and reliability, thus the generalizability of the study (Creswell and Miller 2000). Nevertheless, this is a noteworthy study because it highlighted what leads to entrepreneurial motivation and in a way identified the motivation behind ambition.

Differentiating between the situation-specific motivation to start a business and the motivation to continue to run a business is important (Baum et al. 2001). Estay et al. (2013) investigated the later. The motivation to start a business, the need for achievement, independence and development are, arguably, best explained through Bandura's (1977a) social cognition theory where environmental factors and social cognition shape an individual's motivations. In a meta-analysis of twelve studies, Urban (2010) found direct links between culture and an individual's self-concept, personality and cognition in South Africa. Although culture did not directly relate to entrepreneurship, its impact on motivation and aspirations highlighted an indirect link with entrepreneurship. This was similar to earlier studies that found that culture affected entrepreneurship indirectly by affecting attitudes and perceived success in certain actions. However, the same studies found no direct link between entrepreneurship and culture (Krueger and Brazeal 1994; Krueger et al. 2000).

The results of Estay et al. (2013) study resonate with Scheinberg and MacMillan (1988), who also highlighted the need for independence and development as the main motivators for entrepreneurial action. A recent quantitative study of Kuwaiti females conducted by Mutairi and Fayez (2015) also highlighted the need for independence, specifically financial independence as the main motivator to start a business. The same study revealed that female entrepreneurs identified lack of family and institutional support as the main barriers to entrepreneurship (Mutairi and Fayez 2015). The need for independence, especially financial independence, is echoed in empirical data from Saudi Arabia, Bahrain (Sadi and Al-Ghazali 2012), Oman (Mathew 2010), and indeed the UAE (Erogul and McCrohan 2008; Haan 2004; Hossan et al. 2013; Itani et al. 2011). Interestingly, these regional studies also revealed that family and cultural factors were largely perceived as barriers by female entrepreneurs (Mathew 2010; Mutairi and Fayez 2015; Sadi and Al-Ghazali 2012). However, in the UAE, while culture played an important role, family was perceived positively, as a motivational or support mechanism for female entrepreneurs (Haan 2004; Hossan et al. 2013; Itani et al. 2011). In a qualitative study, Erogul and McCrohan (2008) conducted in-depth interviews with 17 female Emirati entrepreneurs to explore the motivation for starting their business.

The study results highlighted the need for independence as a major motivator for female Emiratis to start business ventures. However, unlike European studies, Erogul and McCrohan (2008) found cultural factors played a major role in venture creation among female Emirati entrepreneurs. Although using different approaches, Estay et al. (2013) and Erogul and McCrohan (2008) highlighted the antecedents of motivations for established entrepreneurs. However, these studies adopted a narrow scope and did not go further to explain why independence and development were a source of entrepreneurial motivation. Almost all the regional studies focused on entrepreneurs, as opposed to potential entrepreneurs. Furthermore, these regional studies were largely based on female samples. This only provides a partial view of entrepreneurial motivation in the UAE and its neighboring regions.

Need for Achievement

The achievement motive remains one of the most influential contributions to the theory of motivation (McClelland et al. 1953). Developing the theory further, in his seminal work *The Achieving Society*, McClelland (1961) identified the achievement motive or need for achievement (nAch) as the main predictor of entrepreneurial intentions (Alschuler 1967; Carsrud and Brännback 2011; Estay et al. 2013; Shane et al. 2003). This is unlike power motivation or affiliation motivation, where an individual is solely driven to act in accordance with developing networks or gaining influence to exert his will (Alschuler 1967). The achievement motive drives actions that lead to excellence (McClelland 1961). In pursuing excellence, individuals are more likely to undertake tasks that require higher levels of skill, individual responsibility, recognition, and impact of outcomes. Taking on the role of an entrepreneur meets all of these criteria (Shane et al. 2003). Thus, a career in entrepreneurship is the most likely outcome for individuals who possess a high need for achievement (McClelland 1961).

In a study of 305 mixed nationality young adults in the UAE, Ryan et al. (2011) investigated the relationship between nAch and entrepreneurial potential. The study revealed a strong correlation between nAch and entrepreneurial potential; however, they found low levels of nAch among UAE nationals. Furthermore, the study revealed inconsistent levels of nAch between male and female participants, as female participants displayed higher levels of nAch than their male counterparts (Ryan et al. 2011).

Some studies in the region support motivational disparity between male and female young adults (Bahrami 2014; Haan 2004; Sowmya et al. 2010). The lure of public sector jobs may explain lower levels of nAch in relation to entrepreneurial behavior in some studies (Kargwell and Inguva 2012; Sowmya et al. 2010). However, the bulk of empirical evidence on entrepreneurial motivation among UAE nationals overwhelmingly points to high levels of nAch (El-Sokari et al. 2013; Itani et al. 2011; Sikdar and Vel 2011).

In a study of locus of control (an individual's self-belief in how much they control their own destiny) among first time community entrepreneurs, Diaz and Rodriguez (2003), found significant variations in the motivation of participants. They concluded that nAch can be used to distinguish between owner managers and the innovative Schumpeterian entrepreneur (Diaz and Rodriguez 2003). However, it is not clear whether investigating nascent entrepreneurs, instead of founders of established firms, would have yielded different results. Furthermore, investigations on entrepreneurs' propensity for risk, from a motivational perspective, do not tend to differentiate between insurable risk and real uncertainty (Shane et al. 2003). Entrepreneurs are able to succeed where others would not venture because they see opportunities where others see risk. Thus, it is questionable whether the entrepreneurs and managers interpret risk in the same way (Shane et al. 2003). In later research, McClelland (1985) found the nAch to significantly increase entrepreneurial performance and encouraged entrepreneurial behavior of risk taking and business expansion.

However, nAch also presents an interesting dichotomy. For both Atkinson (1957) and McClelland (1961), the individual with high need for achievement was almost risk averse, opting for medium risk propositions. While nAch has been found to effectively predict entrepreneurial action and distinguish levels of success among entrepreneurs, McClelland (1961, 1985) and many after him found almost no difference between firm founders and managers in regard to risk propensity (Collins et al.

2000; Fineman 1977; Johnson 1990; Low and Macmillan 1988 cited in Shane et al. 2003).

Furthermore, some have argued, that the achievement motive is a better predictor of human behavior within group settings, rather than solitary settings, which raises doubts about using the achievement motive as predictor of entrepreneurial action (Chell 2008; Collins et al. 2000). Nevertheless, a number of studies have also found significant correlations between nAch and propensity for entrepreneurial action (Ahmed 1985; Ryan et al. 2011). Indeed, in a later study, Collins et al. (2004) used meta-analysis to identify the effects of achievement motivation on entrepreneurial behavior. The study revealed that achievement motivation was significantly correlated with entrepreneurial behavior (Collins et al. 2004).

Entrepreneurial Intentions

Entrepreneurial intentions are one of the best predictors for entrepreneurial behavior (Bae et al. 2014; Carsrud and Brännback 2011; Krueger et al. 2000; Liñan et al. 2011). Mechanisms that enable these intentions to reach fruition, through cognition and motivation, have increasingly taken on a central role within entrepreneurship research (Carsrud and Brännback 2011; Shane et al. 2003). From a socio-cognitive point of view, intentions are self-predictors or deciding factors of engagement in actual behavior (Ajzen 1991; Bandura 1977a, b). While the strength of these intentions is often specific to an individual's context, cognition and levels of motivation, intentions nevertheless serve as the best signal for entrepreneurial action (Fayolle et al. 2014; Krueger et al. 2000; Sowmya et al. 2010).

A number of models have been used to explore and expose entrepreneurial intentions; for example, the Model of Implementing Entrepreneurial Ideas (Bird 1988) and the Maximization of the Expected Utility Model (Fayolle et al. 2014). However, the most influential examples can be found in Ajzen's (1991) Theory of Planned Behaviour and Shapero and Sokol's (1982) Entrepreneurial Event Model (SEE) (Carsrud and Brännback 2011; Estay et al. 2013; Fayolle et al. 2014; Liñan et al. 2011).

Theory of Planned Behavior

As an extension of Ajzen and Fishbein's (1980) Theory of Reason and like Bandura's (1977a) Social Learning Theory, Ajzen's (1991) Theory of Planned Behaviour is bound in cognition and perception of reality (Kautonen et al. 2013; Krueger and Carsrud 1994). TPB has been updated in recent years to the Reasoned Action Approach by Fishbein and Ajzen's (2010). However, the older TPB was preferred to the Reasoned Action Approach for two reasons. First, the TPB has been cited in thousands of scholarly papers from a diverse range of disciplines which enables the researcher to compare and contrast research findings with extensive empirical data that has been rigorously testes over a prolonged period of time (Morgan and Bachrach 2011). The second reason related to integration of the TPB with other models that explore entrepreneurial intentions and behaviors (Krueger and Carsrud 1994). For example, Linan et al. (2011) integrated the TPB with Bandura's (1997) Social Learning Theory. This also enables the researcher to home in on existing empirical data that relate precisely to the aims of this study.

TPB uses independent determinants of attitude toward behavior, subjective norms and perceived behavioral control (PBC) as the key constructs of an individual's intentions (Ajzen 1991; Bae et al. 2014; Bahrami 2014; Liñan et al. 2011). Ajzen (1991) postulated that intentions built upon these three constructs were the best predictors of behavior. Attitudes relate to an individual's evaluation of a behavior; subjective norms refer to the individual's social acceptance of a behavior and PBC relates to the perception about the degree of difficulty or success associated with a behavior (Ajzen 1991).

PBC has also been equated to Bandura's (1997) self-efficacy, which relates to an individual's confidence and perceived capabilities of undertaking certain tasks (Ajzen 1991; Shane et al. 2003). These two constructs are important in developing an understanding of the entrepreneurial process and are widely used in entrepreneurship research to predict entrepreneurial intentions (Krueger et al. 2000). Crucially, when compared with the other two constructs of attitude and social norms, variations in PBC seem to be the best predictors of entrepreneurial intentions (Liñan et al. 2011). For example, in a study of entrepreneurial intentions among Saudi students, Almobaireek and Manolova (2011) found a strong relationship between PBC and entrepreneurial intentions, indicating that entrepreneurial intentions are strongly affected by perceptions of success in a certain task. Interestingly this relationship was stronger among female participants as compared to male participants.

As TPB is based on three independent constructs, Ajzen (1991) did not clarify the origin of an individual's PBC, which may be determined by knowledge, innate confidence or environmental factors (Krueger and Brazeal 1994). PBC and self-efficacy seem similar to locus of control. However, Ajzen (1991) differentiated PBC from Rotter's (1966) construct of perceived locus of control. PBC, Ajzen (1991) suggested, evaluates each behavior on its own merit, unlike perceived locus of control which relates to a person's general outlook and approach to a behavior (Ahmed 1985; Diaz and Rodriguez 2003; Kautonen et al. 2013; Krueger et al. 2000; Liñan et al. 2011). This is an important insight as it emphasizes an individual's ability to make calculated decisions to choose one task over another, instead of blindly accepting every opportunity.

Unlike Rotter's (1966) generalized locus of control, assessing a situation on its own merit through PBC also accounts for the achievement motive (Ajzen 1991; Warehime 1972). Furthermore, PBC also suggests that the decision is not based upon the opportunity alone. Instead, an opportunity's attractiveness is weighed against the perception of opportunity, resources, and the individual's perception about their own ability to take advantage (Carsrud and Brännback 2011; Shane et al. 2003). This suggests an improvement in skills and abilities may lead to stronger entrepreneurial intentions. Almobaireek and Manolova (2011) also found education and training to have a significant effect on entrepreneurial intentions.

Entrepreneurial Event Model

SEE uses social dimensions of entrepreneurship, their effect on the perception of desirability, feasibility and their impact on an entrepreneur's propensity to act (Krueger et al. 2000; Shapero and Sokol 1982). In this way, the SEE relates directly to the entrepreneur's behavior. Unlike the TPB, where intentions are the key predictors of behavior, SEE addresses the change in circumstances or displacement events that significantly disturb an entrepreneur's life pattern, leading to behavior change (Shapero and Sokol 1982). Whether it is incentives pulling entrepreneurs or internal drivers pushing them into action, the change in circumstances alludes to how changes in situational factors affect behavior (Hakim 1989; Kirkwood 2009; Naffziger et al. 1994). In this way, the SEE resonates closely with Leibenstein's Theory of X-efficiency. However, Shapero and Sokol (1982) proposed that situational factors were merely objective measures, such as changes in demographics. Instead, an entrepreneur's evaluation of opportunity was driven by perception. This in itself accounts for motivation, creating a knock on effect on intentions and resulting action or behavior (Baum et al. 2001; Krueger and Brazeal 1994).

In the SEE, a change in an individual's modus operandi leads to a change in behavior. However, the choice of behavior depends on the perceived desirability and feasibility associated with different behavior options (Krueger et al. 2000). Perceived desirability relates to the attractiveness of a venture, whereas, perceived feasibility relates to a person's self-belief or capabilities in successfully performing the task (Shapero and Sokol 1982). The TPB, the SEE, and Social Cognition Theory overlap in a number of ways. The notion of perceived desirability in the SEE deals with the here and now; for example, an individual's preference for performing one task over another. This is akin to the construct of attitudes in the TPB. Likewise, perceived feasibility in SEE is similar to the notion of PBC in the TPB, or the concept of self-efficacy in Social Cognition Theory. Essentially, these constructs suggest individuals measure the probability of success relative to their perceived ability to complete the task. Therefore, high levels of perceived ability associated with undertaking an opportunity indicates increased probability of entrepreneurial action (Ajzen 1991; Bandura 1997, 2002; Shapero and Sokol 1982).

The notion that perceptions can be developed and are directly influenced by increased mastery and expectancy, presents an opportunity for those responsible for promoting entrepreneurship and supporting entrepreneurs (Eccles and Wigfield 2002; Ronstadt 1985; Schultz 1975), especially within the UAE and wider region (El-Sokari et al. 2013;

Hossan et al. 2013; Sadi and Al-Ghazali 2012; Sowmya et al. 2010). TPB (Ajzen 1991), SEE (Shapero and Sokol 1982) and Bandura's (1977a) Social Cognition Theory all complement each other and many researchers have combined them to develop integrated models for measuring entrepreneurial intentions (Almobaireek and Manolova 2011; Bae et al. 2014; Bandura 2002; Krueger and Brazeal 1994; Krueger et al. 2000; Liñan et al. 2011).

Integrated Model of Entrepreneurial Intentions

Contemporary authors built upon the above overarching theories for empirical research. Integrating TPB, SEE and self-efficacy, Krueger and Brazeal (1994) developed a Model of Entrepreneurial Potential, which proposed "potential" as the defining link between perception and intentions (Ajzen 1991; Bandura 1977a; Shapero and Sokol 1982). Krueger and Brazeal (1994) suggested that, in addition to tangible resources, entrepreneurs should have access to credible information, as well as emotional and psychological support. This creates the most conducive environment for entrepreneurship where it can be cultivated (Krueger and Brazeal 1994). Like many others (Aldrich and Zimmer 1986; Bird 1989; Naffziger et al. 1994), Krueger and Brazeal (1994) abandoned using demographics or the personal traits approach to understand entrepreneurs, disputing the relevance of static criteria in a fluid and ever-changing environment (Gartner 1988; Krueger and Brazeal 1994) and preferring, instead, to explore perceptions for predicting behavior (Kautonen et al. 2013). This was a positive development in entrepreneurial research, since, with appropriate inputs, perceptions can be changed to influence actual behavior (Eccles and Wigfield 2002; Fayolle et al. 2014; Krueger and Brazeal 1994).

In a later study of 97 senior university students in the United States, Krueger et al. (2000) used SEE with Ajzen's (1991) TPB to assess entrepreneurial intentions. Krueger et al. (2000) applied a correlational analysis to the SEE and TPB models separately, then integrated both models and applied the same approach. The study found that while separately both models were reasonably apt at predicting entrepreneurial intentions, integrating both models produced a more precise measure of entrepreneurial intentions. This finding corroborates research conducted in the UAE.

Bahrami (2014) applied the SEE model to a sample of 232 participants from diverse backgrounds and found no significant correlations between social behavior moderators and entrepreneurial intentions. Bahrami (2014) explains this by noting that the diverse sample may have diluted the data. However, this example also highlights the benefit of incorporating multiple models to produce hybrid research instruments. Similarly, Krueger et al. (2000), applying TPB, found social norms to have no significant effect on intentions; they proposed a further investigation to clarify this inconsistency (Krueger et al. 2000). Other studies, using a similar model, also found social norms to have no direct effect; however, social norms did seem to have an impact on attitudes and PBC (Liñan et al. 2011). Thus, social norms affected entrepreneurial behavior indirectly.

In a quantitative cross-sectional study of regional variations in entrepreneurial cognition and intentions, in Spain, Liñan et al. (2011) synthesized the seminal theories of Ajzen (1991) and Bandura (1977a) to develop the Entrepreneurial Intention Questionnaire (EIQ). The results of the questionnaire helped produce a comprehensive model of entrepreneurial intentions. This entrepreneurial intention model was based on two independent variables of motivational and environmental factors, with entrepreneurial intentions as the dependent variable. Liñan et al. (2011) found that motivational factors directly influenced entrepreneurial intentions while environmental factors indirectly influenced entrepreneurial intentions through their effect on motivational factors.

A valuable contribution of Liñan's et al. (2011) work was the integration of Bandura's (1977a) Social Learning Theory into the entrepreneurial intentions model to explain the origin of perceptions, something that Ajzen (1991) and Shapero and Sokol's (1982) models were lacking. Liñan et al. (2011) filled this void by examining the role of socio-cultural (external) factors on an entrepreneur's perceptions of desirability and feasibility. However, key external factors such as entrepreneurial education, mentorship and other support mechanisms were not included in the

EIQ. Other studies conducted in the UAE and elsewhere identify a range of environmental factors that influence an individual's perception of the social environment, such as education, culture and gender (El-Sokari et al. 2013; Majumdar and Varadarajan 2013; Saeed et al. 2013; Sowmya et al. 2010).

Interestingly, Majumdar and Varadarajan (2013) found no significant differences in the entrepreneurial intentions of male and female university students. However, this does not necessarily contradict other regional studies, mentioned above, that highlight significant gender differences in the aspirations of entrepreneurs. Majumdar and Varadarajan's (2013) study focused on undergraduates and entrepreneurial intentions whereas others (El-Sokari et al. 2013; Saeed et al. 2013; Sowmya et al. 2010) focused on entrepreneurs and were social factors that affected their behavior.

Given the uncertainty and risk involved in entrepreneurial ventures, individuals who perceive these factors as barriers that are difficult to overcome, rather than opportunities, would be less willing to start new businesses (McMullen and Shepherd 2006; Shane et al. 2003). In a meta-analysis study about entrepreneurial intentions, Bae et al. (2014) concluded that self-efficacy and the individuals' beliefs in their ability to successfully perform entrepreneurial tasks are mediators between entrepreneurial education and entrepreneurial intentions (Bandura 1977a, 2002).

Similarly, in a study of female entrepreneurs in the UAE, Sowmya et al. (2010) found that despite the existence of entrepreneurial intention and perceived opportunities, entrepreneurial intentions were hampered by insecurity. This may have been caused by entrepreneurs' perceived lack of experience or negative perceptions about the environment. These findings were echoed across many studies in the region which identified entrepreneurial intentions among Emiratis but also recognized the mismatch between intentions and their realization (Almobaireek and Manolova 2011; Bahrami 2014; Haan 2004; Hossan et al. 2013; Itani et al. 2011; Sadi and Al-Ghazali 2012; Sikdar and Vel 2011; Sowmya et al. 2010; Zeffane 2014). Empirical research in the UAE and wider region has called on governments and other key stakeholders to bridge the gap between high entrepreneurial intentions and the actual creation of enterprises among Emiratis (Haan 2004; Itani et al. 2011; Sowmya et al. 2010; Zeffane 2014). The identification of environmental and motivational factors influencing entrepreneurial intentions is critical to formulate solutions.

Environmental Factors

Entrepreneurship requires entrepreneurs and entrepreneurs are a product of their environment: thus, an environment conducive to entrepreneurship is crucial for its success (Krueger and Brazeal 1994; Shapero 1981; Valliere 2008). Along with self-efficacy, an individual's evaluation of entrepreneurial success in relation to a given opportunity is strongly linked with their perceptions of the environment and its capacity to support entrepreneurial action (Bandura 1977a, b, 1997, 2002). The entrepreneurial environment is constructed with institutions and in this regard the influence of environmental factors may be explained by institutional economic theory (Nee and Young 1991; North 1990). Weber's protestant work ethic was undoubtedly adopted because of social, cultural, and religious stimuli and would certainly support this notion (Kim 2012). Specific to entrepreneurship, perceptions of the environment can influence entrepreneurs' judgment about expected outcomes (Minniti 2008; Naffziger et al. 1994; Valliere 2008). Thus, when exploring the gap between entrepreneurial intentions and action, perceived suitability of the environment may provide valuable insights.

Environmental factors can be further divided into formal and informal factors (North 1990). Informal factors include perceptions of social and cultural support and acceptance of entrepreneurial action. These also include perceptions of the environmental capability and key constructs such as education, propensity to innovate, and capacity to facilitate entrepreneurial opportunities. Formal environmental factors mainly focus on government policy, regulation, infrastructure, and finance (Alvarez 2010). Although Ajzen (1991) and Shapero and Sokol (1982) considered the role of informal social and cultural environmental factors, their models did not explicitly explore the influence of formal factors. Despite efforts of later researchers (Almobaireek and Manolova 2011; Krueger and Brazeal 1994; Liñan et al. 2011) who integrated Bandura's (1977a) social cognition theory to better understand environmental influences on behavior, empirical evidence on entrepreneurs' perceptions of formal environmental factors, especially in the UAE, remains scarce.

Investigating the influence of environmental factors on behavior is complex. Formal and informal institutions that define the environment are bound in context, fluid in nature and interchangeable according to geographical regions, cultures, and the country's stage of development (Bosma and Levie 2010; Naffziger et al. 1994; North 1990). For example, cultural perceptions can derive from family and friends or wider national superstructure, while at the same time culture is interchangeable, depending on historic and religious factors (Alvarez 2010; Liñan et al. 2011). Religion itself is an interesting factor because in the UAE it is a formal institution, whereas in other parts of the world it does not feature as an institution at all.

In most Western countries, finance is part of the formal environment structure (Alvarez 2010). However, in the UAE and indeed the wider Middle East region, finance falls under a wider spectrum ranging from formal to informal. For example, empirical evidence on SME finance in the UAE highlights family and friends as the main sources of finance. Furthermore, the terms and conditions of finance vary significantly when comparing different lenders and regions with the UAE (Rocha 2010). Therefore, studying the effect of environmental factors on behavior posed a number of challenges. Nevertheless, despite the inherent complexities, influence of environmental factors on UAE entrepreneurs demanded further investigation.

The models discussed above suggest that attitudes and beliefs influence perceptions and often tend to have a greater influence on behavior than objective facts (Krueger and Brazeal 1994; Shapero and Sokol 1982). Thus, instead of categorizing formal and informal environmental factors, this current study aimed to investigate if, and which, environmental factors influence entrepreneurs' perceptions in the UAE.

Applying the structural equation model on a sample of 380 experts, Casero et al. (2013) tested the effects of education and training, research and development transfer, and cultural and social norms on entrepreneurial capacity. The results indicated social and cultural norms to have the greatest effect on entrepreneurial capacity. The findings also highlighted an indirect, rather than the expected direct link between education and training with entrepreneurial capacity Casero et al. (2013).

The results suggested that education and training was not a defining factor for starting a business. However, its strong influence on cultural and social norms highlighted the indirect effect on entrepreneurial capacity. Arguably, here too there may be issues with design and method (Shane et al. 2003). Education and training are broad constructs with significantly different means and ends. The education and training section of the questionnaire used in the survey focuses on education rather than training. Therefore, this particular construct may need further investigation.

In a study of environmental conditions and their effect on entrepreneurial activity in Spain, Alvarez (2010) also concurred with Casero et al. (2013) findings, in that cultural and social factors greatly influenced entrepreneurial activity. These studies are in sharp contrast to the majority of empirical evidence collected from the UAE. For example, in a quantitative study of 232 participants, Bahrami (2014) found no significant relationships between demographic and cultural factors with entrepreneurial intentions in the UAE. Similarly, in a qualitative study of 16 female entrepreneurs, Itani et al. (2011) found that culture mattered but played an insignificant role in predicting entrepreneurial action.

Empirical data on culture and its insignificant effects on entrepreneurship seem to be contradictory to a society deeply embedded in culture and tradition. Shane et al. (2003) notion of limitation in method may be relevant here as Itani et al. (2011) focused on a female-only sample. Furthermore, Bahrami's (2014) sample consisted of mixed nationalities; arguably, the sample did not prescribe to specific culture values, making it difficult for the research instrument to pick up significant cultural references specific to the UAE. Other studies highlight the perceived importance placed on education and training. For example, using a case study approach with 30 participants, Sikdar and Vel (2011) investigated the entrepreneurial process in the UAE by evaluating how entrepreneurs interacted with different elements of the environments. In doing so, they highlighted the most important environmental factors to UAE's nascent entrepreneurs. The study highlighted education and training as one of the most significant variables in entrepreneurial action. Interestingly, the same study also revealed that nascent UAE entrepreneurs valued institutional support mechanisms (Sikdar and Vel 2011).

Similarly, as mentioned earlier, Sowmya et al. (2010) found Emiratis valued the role of education in fostering entrepreneurship; however, they felt that current opportunities did little to prepare young graduates for entrepreneurship. These findings were echoed by Itani et al. (2011), who specifically highlighted the area of financial and management training, where UAE entrepreneurs perceived they had the lowest capabilities. Some research findings in Europe may help explain why Sowmya et al. (2010) found negative perceptions about entrepreneurial educational programs. For example, Oosterbeek et al. (2010) found that a leading entrepreneurship education program in Europe had insignificant effects on increasing entrepreneurial skills. In fact, the program had negative effects on entrepreneurial intentions and was deemed detrimental to building entrepreneurial capacity. This may be explained by limitations in the education programs; however, we also need to consider the fact that some individuals simply choose to shy away from starting a business after understanding the challenges involved.

Investigations on environmental factors and their effect on entrepreneurial intentions have produced diverse and at times conflicting findings. While some inconsistencies may be explained by inappropriate methods (Shane et al. 2003), changes in context also play a part. For example, while some study results indicate insignificant relationships between social and cultural norms and entrepreneurial intentions (Krueger and Brazeal 1994; Liñan et al. 2011), others highlighted these as the most significant antecedents of entrepreneurial intentions Casero et al. (2013).

Similarly, other studies indicate a stronger correlation between culture and entrepreneurial intentions in the Middle East, when compared with the United States (Erogul and McCrohan 2008; Itani et al. 2011; Krueger et al. 2000). As mentioned earlier, research conducted within the UAE and wider region has also produced conflicting results. For example, elsewhere in the Middle East, the informal institution of family seems to have a negative influence on entrepreneurs, especially female entrepreneurs. However, in the UAE family represents a positive influence (Itani et al. 2011; Matthew 2010; Sadi and Al-Ghazali 2012).

The UAE government has launched a wide range of education initiatives and specialist programs, such as the Khalifa Fund and campus based business incubators, to promote entrepreneurship (Kerros 2012). These efforts have also been well documented in the media, which would support Sikdar and Vel's (2011) findings of high levels of perceived value associated with education and training and institutional support. However, perceptions about the level of education and training and institutional support available were largely negative (Sikdar and Vel 2011), perceptions that were corroborated by Sowmya et al. (2010). This indicates a gap between government efforts and their perceived value for UAE entrepreneurs. This area certainly demands further investigation.

Conclusions

The evolutionary progress of entrepreneurship and our understanding of the entrepreneur can be marked by specific moments in history. Some constructs have echoed consistently throughout the relatively short and sporadic history of the theory of entrepreneurship. The entrepreneur as a decision maker and leader has almost unanimous acceptance as a key construct in what defines an entrepreneur (Baumol 2010; Cantillon 2010; Casson and Casson 2013; Marhsall 1920; Menger 1871; Mises 1949; Say 1803; Schumpeter 1934; Shackle 1966). Similarly, the entrepreneur as an organizer, allocator and an employer (user) of other economic factors has also been widely recognized as an important entrepreneurial function (Baumol 1968; Casson 2005; Kirzner 1971, 1976; Mises 1949; Say 1803; Schumpeter 1934; Walras 1874; Wieser 1914 cited in Rothbard 2009).

Cantillon's (2010) notions of risk and uncertainty have reverberated over the last three centuries through the works of Thunen (1850), Mangoldt (1855), Menger (1871), Cole (1949) and Casson (2005). The fact that these concepts were later granted further clarity by Knight (2006), in what became known as the "Knightian Uncertainty", is a testament to their importance in how we perceive entrepreneurship and the role of the entrepreneur (McMullen and Shepherd 2006). Following in the footsteps of Say (1803) and Menger (1871), Marshall's (1920) distinction between the entrepreneur and the manager was particularly useful and arguably aided Schumpeter (1934) in developing the concept of the innovating entrepreneurs.

Innovativeness is perhaps the most enduring quality by which we recognize entrepreneurs today. Although the inception of this concept can be traced back to Bentham (1748–1832) and Thunen (1850), Schumpeter's (1934) treatment of the entrepreneur, defined by innovation and their role in society, added another dimension to the theory of entrepreneurship. Research within the UAE has also highlighted the diverse range of entrepreneur characteristics and the difficulty in defining the entrepreneur within the UAE context (Bahrami 2014; Itani et al. 2011). However, it would be interesting to explore whether common characteristics exist within the narrower context of Emirati entrepreneurs.

Developments in the theory of entrepreneurship have led to a better understanding of key concepts, for example, distinctions between risk and uncertainty or separation between the functions of an entrepreneur and manager. It has also led to the rejection of certain constructs. For example, the notion that only capitalists can be entrepreneurs or that entrepreneurs must also be owners has almost disappeared from the theory of entrepreneurship (Schumpeter 1934; Smith 2007; Ricardo (1772–1823); Von Wieser 1927). The same can be said for an entrepreneur simply being an arbitrageur (Cantillon 2010; Kirzner 1976; Walras 1874), a contractor (Bentham 1748–1832), or pursuing solely economic benefit (Carsrud and Brännback 2011; Marshall 1920; Say 1803). Arguably, these constructs have been amalgamated into our conceptual understanding of the entrepreneur. For, although entrepreneurs may not be solely defined by any one of these notions, they may adopt one or more of these functions. In this respect, the individual entrepreneur is at the center of entrepreneurship.

The evolution of entrepreneurship itself is also tied to historical milestones. Certain elements within the process of entrepreneurship have widespread historical acceptance. For example, apart from the entrepreneur, there is a clear historical tradition that recognizes the role of knowledge relative to time. Similarly, opportunities and resources are crucial to the process of entrepreneurship (Cantillon 2010; Cole 1949; Hayek 1945; Kirzner 1976; Leibenstein 1968; Menger 1871; Mises 1949; Say 1803; Schumpeter 1934; Shackle 1966). Incentives and education are recognized as key components within the process of entrepreneurship (Hayek 1945; Machlup 1980; Marshall 1920; Menger 1871; Say 1803; Schultz 1975). Risk and uncertainty are also omnipresent, as they not only help create opportunities but also separate entrepreneurs from rent seekers or managers (Bamoul 2010; Cantillon 2010; Knight 2006; Leibenstein 1968).

Early calls for market regulation or an institutional framework to facilitate entrepreneurship can be traced back to Cantillon (2010) and Say (1803). However, these were later given further clarity by Cole (1949), whose notion of environmental factors encompassed everything within entrepreneurship that was external to the entrepreneur. Despite Austrian calls for purely free market principles to advance entrepreneurship (Hayek 1945; Mises 1949), the case for non-intervention is obsolete. Most recently, the need for effective intervention and institutional frameworks to support entrepreneurship has gained further recognition (Baumol 2010; Boettke and Coyne 2003; Nee and Young 1991; North 1990). However, it is also clear that intervention must go beyond the traditional paradigm of capital, for example, subsidies or tax breaks or indeed a purely government led intervention (Holtz-Eakin 2000; Li 2002). Arguably, these tend to be rigid, at times irrelevant, and thus useless to entrepreneurs.

Purely capital based interventions do not discriminate against inefficient firms. They create the free rider scenario and distort economic and competitive conditions within the entrepreneurial ecosystem (Bhat and Khan 2014; Buera et al. 2012). Instead, empirical research suggests the need for responsive policies that are suitable for the diverse needs of entrepreneurs and indeed entrepreneurship (Groenewegen and Steen 2007; Holtz-Eakin 2000). In addition to capital, interventions need to focus on key factors such as knowledge and information, emotional support and developing a culture of entrepreneurship (Grossman 2008; Krueger and Brazeal 1994; Naude 2013). In this regard, intervention cannot solely be the responsibility of government or respective agencies. Instead, existing social institutions, such as education, media, and private support networks, need to play an active role in supporting entrepreneurship (Casson 2003; Groenewegen and Steen 2007; Henrekson and Sanandaji 2010).

Within the UAE context, effective intervention to foster an entrepreneurial culture, and providing access to relevant information and emotional support have been highlighted by a number of studies (Erogul and McCrohan 2008; Itani et al. 2011; Matthew 2010; Sadi and Al-Ghazali 2012). Indeed, a number of government led programs are working toward achieving these very objectives (Kerros 2012; Saeed et al. 2013; Sikdar and Vel 2011). However, the effectiveness of these programs has also been questioned (Erogul and McCrohan 2008; Itani et al. 2011; Sowmya et al. 2010). Therefore, it would be interesting to explore the perceived value that entrepreneurs associate with government programs and indeed other informal institutions of family and culture.

Throughout the literature review, motivation emerges as a crucial component within the entrepreneurial process and the main link between entrepreneurial intentions and action (Ajzen 1991; Carsrud and Brannback 2011). This is because motivation seems to be behind every step an entrepreneur takes. It is a dynamic, multidimensional facet affecting different stages of the entrepreneurial process, with individual context being the only constant (Baum et al. 2001; Eccles and Wigfield 2002; Johnson 1990; Murray 1938; Nuttin 1984). The need for achievement and independence appear to influence entrepreneurial behavior most significantly (Collins et al. 2004). As with entrepreneurship (Fayolle et al. 2014; Hebert and Link 2009; Krueger and Carsrud 1994), it may also be useful to consider motivation within a contextual framework, building upon separate notions of instrumental and final motivation (Nuttin 1984).

Similar to locus of control, need for achievement may represent a general disposition, which may explain inconsistent empirical data on the relationship between achievement motivation, and entrepreneurial behavior (Chell 2008; Collins et al. 2000; Collins et al. 2004; Diaz and Rodriguez 2003). Instead, when studying entrepreneurial behavior, it may be useful to consider situation-specific motivation (Ahmed 1985; Baum et al. 2001). Similar to PBC (Ajzen 1991), situation-specific motivation considers individual motivation according to context: this is particularly useful in the study of entrepreneurial behavior because it is inherently bound in context (Baum et al. 2001). In this regard, rather than just exploring the final and instrumental motivation, which are multidimensional (Johnson 1990; Nuttin 1984), it would be beneficial to explore how the nature of entrepreneurial motivation changes from one situation to another (Baum et al. 2001).

Entrepreneurial intentions are the best signals for entrepreneurial action (Fayolle et al. 2014; Krueger et al. 2000). The TPB (Ajzen 1991) and the SEE (Shapero and Sokol 1982) emerge as two of the most salient models to explore entrepreneurial intentions. However, integrated models, especially those that incorporate environmental factors, such as Bandura's (1977a) Social Cognition Theory, seem to provide a better understanding of entrepreneurial intentions. Within these models, the attractiveness of certain propositions and perceived ability to succeed in the pursuit of those propositions were highlighted as the main factors influencing entrepreneurial intentions. An individual's perceived capability of succeeding in a task has the strongest bearing on whether that task will be undertaken. The fact that an individual's perception of his/her capabilities can be changed represents a significant opportunity to advance entrepreneurship.

Although data are limited, empirical research in Europe and in the Middle East reveals that environmental factors do not seem to have a direct influence on entrepreneurial intentions. However, recent studies in Europe and the Middle East have developed sophisticated models to compensate for deficiencies of TPB and SEE in recognizing environmental factors. Interestingly, these models revealed stronger and more direct relationships between environmental factors and entrepreneurial intentions. Nevertheless, environmental factors do not appear often enough in research focusing on entrepreneurial intentions.

Operational Definitions

The entrepreneur and the entrepreneurial process are at the core of this book. However, the theory of entrepreneurship has not been consolidated and lacks a universal definition of entrepreneurship or indeed the entrepreneur (Shane and Venkataraman 2000; Swedberg 2000). In fact, defining the entrepreneurs has been highlighted as one of the most difficult aspects within the study of entrepreneurship (Casson 2003). Similarly, a universal definition of the entrepreneur, based on characteristics is also lacking (Carsrud and Brännback 2011; Casson 2003, 2005; Shaver and Scott 1991). This section defines entrepreneurship and the entrepreneur, among other terms relevant to this book. For example, despite multiple definitions, the entrepreneur, as we see her, is defined through specific behaviors and characteristics.

An entrepreneur undertakes risk and uncertainty, is an innovator, a decision maker and a leader (Baumol 2010; Cantillon 2010; Casson and Casson 2013; Marhsall 1920; Menger 1871; Schumpeter 1934; Shackle 1966), an organizer, allocator, and an employer (user) of other economic factors (Baumol 1968; Casson 2005; Kirzner 1971, 1976; Mises 1949; Say 1803; Schumpeter 1934; Walras 1874 translated by Jaffe (1954); Von Wieser, (1851-1926)). In this vein,

> an entrepreneur is someone who faces uncertainty and accepts risk in the pursuit of profit, but, through innovation, effective leadership and decision making is able to organize economic resources and efficiently allocate them to produce the best possible market outcomes.

Thus, it also follows that entrepreneurs are a product of their environment. The search for a single definition of the entrepreneur, most relevant to this book, revealed the following:

> everyone is an entrepreneur only when he actually carries out new combinations, and loses that character as soon as he has built up his business, when he settles down and is running it as other people run their business. (Schumpeter 1934, p.78)

The concept of entrepreneurship is also fragmented. Despite multiple variations, the entrepreneur and entrepreneurship are inseparable and the entrepreneur is widely accepted as the core driver of entrepreneurship (Baumol 2010; Carsrud and Brännback 2011; Casson 2003, 2005). Nevertheless the concept of entrepreneurship is at times confused with that of entrepreneur by authors who fail to distinguish between two distinct functions (Shane et al. 2003). For example, in a recent book titled *Organizing Entrepreneurial Judgment*, Foss and Klein (2012) define entrepreneurship by seven functions, namely small-business management, imagination and creativity, innovation, alertness to opportunities, ability to adjust, leadership, and judgment. However, arguably, all seven concepts highlighted are more applicable to the entrepreneur rather than entrepreneurship.

Others describe entrepreneurship as entrepreneurial opportunities (Alvarez and Busenitz 2001) or entrepreneurial behavior (Miller 1983). Arguably, these descriptions are not entirely helpful to the central concept of entrepreneurship (Eckhardt and Shane 2003) relative to this book. The concept of entrepreneurship most relevant to this book describes it as a function or a process that facilitates the entrepreneur or entrepreneurial activity (Shane and Venkataraman 2000). The following definition best describes entrepreneurship in relation to this study.

Entrepreneurship can be defined as "a process by which individuals – either on their own or within organizations – pursue opportunities" (Stevenson and Jarillo 1990, p. 23)

Other key concepts in the study were less difficult to define and are as follows.

Entrepreneurial action can be defined as a "contextually embedded process while retaining the entrepreneur as a reflexive and strategically thinking subject" (Berglund 2005, p. 2). Entrepreneurial action can be driven by personality traits (Delmar and Davidson 2000), entrepreneurial intentions (Krueger et al. 2000), contextual pressures (Reynolds 1991), and the direct and indirect effects of the external factors (Berglund 2005, p. 3).

Environmental factors can be defined as "status of the economy, the availability of venture capital, the actions of competitors, and government regulations" (Shane et al. 2003, p. 258). These also include social and cultural influence (Bandura 1986) and formal and informal support networks (Liñan and Fernandez-Serrano 2014)

Intentions can be defined as those which "capture the motivational factors that influence a behavior; they are indications of how hard people are willing to try, or how much of an effort they are planning to exert, in order to perform the behavior" (Ajzen 1991, p. 181)

Self-efficacy can be defined as "people's beliefs about their capabilities to produce designated levels of performance that exercise influence over events and affect their lives. Self-efficacy beliefs determine how people feel, think, motivate themselves, and behave" (Bandura 1994 para 1–2).

Motivation can be defined as the purpose or psychological cause of an action (Schacter et al. 2011), "what activates a person, what makes individuals choose one behavior over another" (Carsrud and Brännback 2011, p. 11). Motivations influence "who pursues entrepreneurial opportunities, who assembles resources, and how people undertake the entrepreneurial process" (Shane et al. 2003, p. 258).

References

Ahmed, S. (1985). nAch, risk-taking propensity, locus of control and entrepreneurship. *Personality and Individual Differences, 6*(6), 781–782.

Ajzen, I. (1991). The theory of planned behaviour. *Organizational Behaviour and Human Decision Processes, 50*(2), 179–211.

Ajzen, I., & Fishbein, M. (1980). *Understanding attitudes and predicting social behavior*. Englewood Cliffs: Prentice-Hall.

Aldrich, H., & Zimmer, C. (1986). Entrepreneurship through social networks. In D. Sexton & R. Smilor (Eds.), *The art and science of entrepreneurship* (pp. 3–23). Cambridge, MA: Ballinger.

Almobaireek, W., & Manolova, T. (2011). Who wants to be an entrepreneur? Entrepreneurial intentions among Saudi university students. *African Journal of Business Management, 6*(11), 4029–4040. https://doi.org/10.5897/AJBM11.1521.

Alschuler, A. (1967). *The achievement motivation and the development project: A summary and review*. Center for Research and Development on Educational Differences. Harvard University Press.

Alvarez, S. (2010). Theories of entrepreneurship: Alternative assumptions and the study of entrepreneurial action. *Foundations and Trends in Entrepreneurship, 1*(3), 105–148.

Alvarez, S., & Busenitz, L. (2001). The entrepreneurship of resource-based theory. *Journal of Management, 27*, 755–775.

Atkinson, J. W. (1957). Motivational determinants of risk-taking behavior. *Psychological Review, 64*, 359–372.

Bae, T., Qian, S., Miao, C., & Fiet, J. (2014). The relationship between entrepreneurship education and entrepreneurial intentions: A meta-analytic review. *Entrepreneurship Theory & Practice, 4*, 217–254.

Bahrami, S. (2014). Entrepreneurship intentions and perceptions in the UAE: A study of moderating effects of gender, culture and family. *International Journal of Small Business and Entrepreneurship Research, 2*(4), 37–50.

Bandura, A. (1977a). *Social learning theory*. New York: General Learning Press.

Bandura, A. (1977b). Self-efficacy: Toward a unifying theory of behavioral change. *Psychological Review, 84*(2), 191–215.

Bandura, A. (1986). The explanatory and predictive scope of self-efficacy theory. *Journal of Clinical and Social Psychology, 4*, 359–373.

Bandura, A. (1994). Self-efficacy. In V. S. Ramachaudran (Ed.), *Encyclopedia of human behavior* (Vol. 4, pp. 71–81). Cambridge: Academic Press.

Bandura, A. (1997). *Self-efficacy: The exercise of control*. New York: Freeman.

Bandura, A. (2002). Social cognitive theory in cultural context. *Applied Psychology, 51*(2), 269–290.

Baum, J. R., Locke, E. A., & Smith, K. G. (2001). A multidimensional model of venture growth. *Academy of Management Journal, 44*, 292–303.

Baumol, W. (1968). Entrepreneurship in economic theory. *The American Economic Review, 58*(2), 64–71.

Baumol, W. J. (2010). *The Microtheory of innovative entrepreneurship*. The Kauffman Foundation Series on Innovation and Entrepreneurship. Princeton University Press. ISBN: 1400835224.

Berglund, H. (2005). *Toward a theory of entrepreneurial action: Exploring risk, opportunity and self in technology entrepreneurship*. Chalmers Publication Library. ISBN: 91-7291-697-4.

Bhat, S., & Khan, R. (2014). *Government policy ecosystem for entrepreneurship development in MSEs sector*. MPRA.

Bird, B. J. (1989). *Entrepreneurial behavior*. Glenview: Scott, Foresman/Little, Brown College Division. 0673397912.

Boettke, P., & Coyne, C. (2003). Entrepreneurship and development: Cause or consequence. In *Austrian Economics and Entrepreneurial Studies. Emerald insight* (pp. 67–87). Bingley: Emerald Publishing Group.

Bosma, N., & Levie, J. (2010). Executive report. Babson College, Universidad del Desarollo, Ha´sko´linn, Reykjavik and London Business School. *Global entrepreneurship monitor*. Babson Park.

Buera, F., Benjamin, M., & Yongseok, S. (2012). Well-intended policies. *Review of Economic Dynamics, 16*, 216–230.

Cantillon, R. (2010). *Essai sur la nature du commerce en général.* (M. Thornton, & C. Saucier, Trans.) United States: Ludwig von Mises Institute. (Original work published in 1755).

Carsrud, A., & Brännback, M. (2011). Entrepreneurial motivations: What do we still need to know? *Journal of Small Business Management, 49*(1), 9–26.

Casero, C., Mogollón, R., & Roldán, J. (2013). A structural model of the antecedents to entrepreneurial capacity. *International Small Business Journal, 30*(8), 850–872.

Casson, M. (2003). *The Entrepreneur: An economic theory.* London: Edward Elgar Publishing. ISBN 1843765632.

Casson, M. (2005). Entrepreneurship and the theory of the firm. *Journal of Economic Behavior & Organization, 58*(2), 327–348.

Casson, M., & Casson, C. (2013). *The entrepreneur in history: From medieval merchant to modern business leader.* Palgrave Pivot. e-EAN/ISBN: 9781137305824.

Chell, E. (2008). *The entrepreneurial personality: A social construction.* London: Routledge. ISBN 1134335628.

Cole, A. (1949). *The great mirror of folly: An economic-bibliographical study.* Baker Library, Harvard Graduate School of Business Administration.

Collins, C., Locke, E., & Hanges, P. (2000). *The relationship of need for achievement to entrepreneurial behavior: A meta-analysis.* Working paper, University of Maryland, College Park.

Collins, C. J., Hanges, P. J., & Locke, E. A. (2004). The relationship of achievement motivation to entrepreneurial behavior: A meta-analysis. *Human Performance, Taylor & Francis, 17*(1), 95–117.

Creswell, J. W., & Miller, D. L. (2000). Determining validity in qualitative inquiry. *Theory Into Practice, 39*, 124–134.

Delmar, F., & Davidson, P. (2000). Where do they come from? Prevalence and characteristics of nascent entrepreneurs. *Entrepreneurship & Regional Development, 12*, 1–23.

Diaz, F., & Rodriguez, A. (2003). Locus of control, nAch and values of community entrepreneurs. Social behavior and personality. *ProQuest Central, 31*(8), 739.

Eccles, J., & Wigfield, A. (2002). Motivational beliefs, values, and goals. *Annual Review of Psychology. ProQuest Central, 53*, 109–132.

Eckhardt, J. T., & Shane, S. A. (2003). Opportunities and entrepreneurship. *Journal of Management, 29*(3), 333–349.

El-Sokari, H., Van Horne, C., Huang, Z., & Al Awad, M. (2013). *GEM UAE: Entrepreneurship-An Emirati perspective.* Global Entrepreneurship

Monitor. Retrieved from: http://www.gemconsortium.org/docs/2892/gem-uae-entrepreneurship

Erogul, M., & McCrohan, D. (2008). Preliminary investigation of Emirati women entrepreneurs in the UAE. *African Journal of Business Management, 2*(10), 177–185.

Estay, C., Durrieu, F., & Akhter, M. (2013). Entrepreneurship: From motivation to start-up. *Springer Science+Business Media New, 11*, 243–267.

Fayolle, A., Liñán, F., & Moriano, A. (2014). Beyond entrepreneurial intentions: Values and motivations in entrepreneurship. *International Entrepreneurship and Management Journal, 10*(4), 679–689.

Fineman, S. (1977). The achievement motive construct and its measurement: Where are we now? *British Journal of Psychology, 68*, 1–22. https://doi.org/10.1111/j.2044-8295.

Fishbein, M., & Ajzen, I. (2010). *Predicting and changing behavior: The reasoned action approach.* New York: Taylor & Francis.

Foss, N., & Klein, P. (2012). *Organizing entrepreneurial judgment.* Cambridge: Cambridge University Press. ISBN: 9780521697262.

Gartner, W. (1988). Who is an entrepreneur? Is the wrong question. *American journal of small business, 12*(4), 11–32.

Graham, S., & Weiner, B. (1996). *Theories and principles of motivation.* London: Prentice Hall.

Groenewegen, J., & Steen, M. (2007). The evolutionary policy maker. *Journal of Economic Issues. ProQuest Central, 41*(2), 351.

Grossman, S. (2008). The case of business improvement districts: Special district public-private cooperation in community revitalization. *Public Performance & Management Review, 32*(2), 290–308.

Haan, H. (2004). *Small enterprises: Women entrepreneurs in the UAE.* Centre for Labour Market Research & Information (CLMRI). Retrieved from http://www.zu.ac.ae/infoasis/modules/mod8/business/documents/smallenterprisereport.pdf

Hakim, C. (1989). New recruits to self-employment in the 1980s. *Employment Gazette, 97*, 286–297.

Hayek, F. A. (1945). The use of knowledge in society. *The American Economic Review, 35*(4), 519–530.

Hebert, R., & Link, A. (2009). *A history of entrepreneurship.* London: Routledge.

Henrekson, M., & Sanandaji, T. (2010). The interaction of entrepreneurship and institutions. *Journal of Institutional Economics, 7*(1), 47–75.

Holtz-Eakin, D. (2000). Public policy toward entrepreneurship. *Small Business Economics, 15*(4), 283–291.

Hossan, C., Parakandi, M., & Saber, H. (2013). Entrepreneurial knowledge, preferences and barriers of female business students in the Middle East. *Journal of Business and Policy Research, 8*(2), 83–99.

Itani, H., Sidani, S., & Baalbaki, I. (2011). United Arab Emirates female entrepreneurs: Motivations and frustrations. *Equality, Diversity and Inclusion: An International Journal, 30*(5), 409–424.

Johnson, R. (1990). Toward a multidimensional model of entrepreneurship: The case of achievement motivation and the entrepreneur. *Entrepreneurship Theory & Practice, 14*(3), 39–54.

Kargwell, S., & Inguva, S. (2012). Factors influencing the first generation entrepreneurs: An analytical study on the graduates of UAE universities. *International Journal of Business and Social Science, 3*(7), 143–149.

Kautonen, T., Gelderen, G., & Tornikoski, E. (2013). Predicting entrepreneurial behaviour: A test of the theory of planned behaviour. *Applied Economics, 45*(6), 697–707. https://doi.org/10.1080/00036846.2011.610750.

Kerros, T. (2012). The 'Entrepreneurial Triggers' driving graduate entrepreneurship in the UAE. *The Entrepreneurialist, 3*.

Kim, S. H. (2012). *Max Weber. The Stanford encyclopedia of philosophy*. Retrieved from http://plato.stanford.edu/archives/fall2012/entries/weber.

Kirkwood, J. (2009). Motivational factors in a push-pull theory of entrepreneurship. *Gender in Management an International Journal, 24*(5), 346–364.

Kirzner, I. (1971). Entrepreneurship & the market approach to development. Liberty Fund. *Online Library of Liberty*. Retrieved from http://swissmc.blackboard.com/

Kirzner, I. (1976). *Equilibrium versus market process: The foundations of modern Austrian economics*. Kansas City: Sheed & Wad.

Knight, F. (2006). *Risk, uncertainty and profit*. Cosimo, Inc. ISBN: 1602060053

Krueger, J., & Carsrud, A. (1994). Entrepreneurial intentions: Applying the theory of planned behaviour. *Entrepreneurship & Regional Development, 5*(4), 315–330.

Krueger, N., & Brazeal, D. (1994). Entrepreneurial potential and potential entrepreneurs. *Entrepreneurship Theory and Practice, 18*, 91–104.

Krueger, N., Reilly, M., & Carsrud, A. (2000). Competing models of entrepreneurial intentions. *Journal of Business Venturing, 15*(5–6), 411–432.

Leibenstein, H. (1968). Entrepreneurship and development. *American Economic Review, 58*(2), 72–84.

Li, W. (2002). Entrepreneurship and government subsidies: A general equilibrium analysis. *Journal of Economic Dynamics and Control, 26*(11), 1815–1844.

Liñan, et al. (2011). Regional variations in entrepreneurial cognitions: Start-up intentions of university students in Spain. *Entrepreneurship & Regional Development, 23*(3–4), 187–215.

Liñan, F., & Fernandez-Serrano, J. (2014). National culture, entrepreneurship and economic development: different patterns across the European Union. *Small Business Economics, 42*(4), 685–701.

Machlup, F. (1980). *Knowledge: Its creation, distribution and economic significance, Volume I knowledge and knowledge production.* Princeton: Princeton University Press.

Majumdar, S., & Varadarajan, D. (2013). Students' attitude towards entrepreneurship: Does gender matter in the UAE? *Foresight, 15*(4), 278–293.

Mathew, V. (2010). Women entrepreneurship in Middle East: Understanding barriers and use of ICT for entrepreneurship development. *Journal of International Entrepreneurship & Management 6*, 163–181. Springer Science+Business Media.

Marshall, A. (1920). *Principles of economics* (8th ed.). (First published 1890, London: Macmillan and Co.). Online Library of Liberty.

McClelland, D. (1961). *The Achieving Society.* Free Press Paperback. New York: Van Nostrand.

McClelland, D. (1985). How motives, skills, and values determine what people do. *American Psychological Association., 40*(7), 812–825.

McClelland, C., Atkinson, W., Clark, A., & Lowell, L. (1953). *The achievement motive.* New York: Appleton-Century-Croft.

McMullen, J., & Shepherd, D. (2006). Entrepreneurial action and the role of uncertainty in the theory of the entrepreneur. *Academy of Management Review, 31*(1), 132–152. https://doi.org/10.5465/AMR.2006.19379628.

Menger, C. (1871). *Principles of economics,* (James Dingwall, & Bert F. Hoselitz Trans.). New York: New York University Press. (1976).

Miller, D. (1983). The correlates of entrepreneurship in three types of firms. *Management Science, 29,* 770–791.

Minniti, M. (2008). The role of government policy on entrepreneurial activity: Productive, unproductive, or destructive? *Entrepreneurship Theory & Practice, 32*(5), 779–790.

Mises, L. (1949). *Human action: A treatise on economics.* New Haven: Yale University Press.

Morgan, P., & Bachrach, C. (2011). Is the Theory of planned behaviour an appropriate model for human fertility? *Vienna Yearbook of Population Research, 9,* 11–18.

Murray, H. A. (1938). *Explorations in personality*. New York: Oxford University Press.

Mutairi, A., & Fayez, F. (2015). Factors motivating female entrepreneurs in Kuwait. *Journal of Applied Management and Entrepreneurship, 20*(1), 50.

Naffziger, W., Hornsby, J., & Kuratko, F. (1994). A proposed research model of entrepreneurial motivation. *Entrepreneurship Theory & Practice, 18*, 29–42.

Naude, W. (2013). *Entrepreneurship and economic development: Theory, evidence and policy*. (Discussion Paper No. 7507). Maastricht: University of Maastricht, Institute for the Study of Labor.

Nee, V., & Young, F. (1991). Peasant entrepreneurs in China's second economy: An institutional analysis. *Economic Development and Cultural Change, 39*(2), 293–310.

North, D. (1990). *Institutions, institutional change and economic performance*. Cambridge University Press. ISBN: 9780521397346

Nuttin, J. (1984). *Motivation, planning, and action: A relational theory of behavior dynamics*. Hillsdale: Erlbaum.

Oosterbeek, H., Praag, M., & Ijsselstein, A. (2010). The impact of entrepreneurship education on entrepreneurship skills and motivation. *European Economic Review, 54*, 442–454.

Pervin, L. (2003). *The science of personality*. Oxford University Press. ISBN: 9780195151022.

Reinert, E. (1999). The role of the state in economic growth. *Journal of Economic Studies. MCB University Press, 26*(4/5), 268–326.

Reynolds, P. (1991). Sociology and entrepreneurship: Concepts and contributions. *Entrepreneurship Theory and Practice, 16*(2), 47–70.

Rocha, R., Farazi, S., Khuori, R., & Pearce, D. (2010). *The status of bank lending to SMEs in the Middle East and North Africa Region: The results of a joint survey of the Union of Arab Banks and the World Bank*. Washington, DC/Bruit: The World Bank & The Union of Arab Banks.

Ronstadt, C. (1985). The educated entrepreneurs: A new era of entrepreneurial education is beginning. *American Journal of Small Business., 70*(1), 7–23.

Rothbard, M. (2009). *Review of Austrian Economics*, Volume 5 of Volume 1–10. Ludwig von Mises Institute. ISBN 1610161645. https://mises.org/library/review-austrianeconomics-volumes-1-10.

Rotter, J. B. (1966). Generalized expectancies for internal versus external control of reinforcement. *Psychological Monographs, General and Applied, 80*, 1. American Psychological Association.

Ryan, J., Tipu, S., & Zeffane, R. (2011). Need for achievement and entrepreneurial potential: a study of young adults in the UAE. *Education, Business and Society: Contemporary Middle Eastern Issues, 4*(3), 153–166.

Sadi, M., & Al-Ghazali, B. (2012). The dynamics of entrepreneurial motivation among women: A comparative study of business women in Saudi Arabia and Bahrain. *Asian Academy of Management Journal, 17*(1), 97–113.

Saeed, S., Yousafzai, S. Y., Yani-De-Soriano, M., & Muffatto, M. (2013). The role of perceived university support in the formation of students' entrepreneurial intention. *Journal of Small Business Management.* https://doi.org/10.1111/jsbm.12090.

Say, Jean-Baptiste. (1803). *A treatise on political economy.* C. R. Prinsep, trans. and Clement C. Biddle., ed. 1855. Library of Economics and Liberty. Retrieved October 22, 2014 from the World Wide Web: http://www.econlib.org/library/Say/sayT.html

Schacter, D., Gilbert, D., Wegner, D., & Hood, B. (2011). *Psychology: European edition.* Palgrave Macmillan. ISBN: 0230343678.

Scheinberg, S., & MacMillan, I. C. (1988). An 11 country study of motivations to start a business. In B. A. Kirchoff, W. A. Long, W. E. McMullan, K. H. Vesper, & W. E. Wetzel (Eds.), *Frontiers of entrepreneurship research* (pp. 669–687). Wellesley: Babson College.

Schultz, T. (1975). The value of the ability to deal with disequilibria. *Journal of Economic Literature, 13*(3), 827–846.

Schumpeter, J. (1934). *The theory of economic development: An inquiry into profits, capital, credit, interest, and the business cycle.* Transaction Publishers. United States. ISBN: 0878556982.

Shackle, G. L. S. (1966). *The nature of economic thought: Selected papers 1955–1964.* Cambridge University Press. London. ISBN: 978052106278.

Shane, S., & Venkataraman, S. (2000). The promise of entrepreneurship as a field of research. *The Academy of Management Review, 25*(1), 217–226.

Shane, S., Lockea, E., & Collins, C. (2003). Entrepreneurial motivation. *Human Resource Management Review. Elsevier Science Inc, 13,* 257–279. https://doi.org/10.1016/S1053-4822(03)00017-2.

Shapero, A. (1981). Self-renewing economies. *Economic Development Commentary, 5*(4), 19–22.

Shapero, A., & Sokol, L. (1982). The social dimensions of entrepreneurship. In C. Kent, D. Sexton, & K. H. Vesper (Eds.), *Encyclopedia of entrepreneurship* (pp. 72–90). Englewood Cliffs: Prentice-Hall.

Shaver, K., & Scott, L. (1991). Person, process, choice: The psychology of new venture creation. *Entrepreneurship Theory & Practice, 16*(2), 23–45.

Sikdar, A., & Vel, P. (2011). Factors influencing entrepreneurial value creation in the UAE-An exploratory study. *International Journal of Business and Social Science, 2*(6), 77.

Smith, A. (2007). *Wealth of nations*. First Published 1776. Cosimo Classics Series. New York: Cosimo. ISBN 1602069395.

Sowmya, D., Majumdar, S., & Gallant, M. (2010). Relevance of education for potential entrepreneurs: An international investigation. *Journal of Small Business and Enterprise Development, 17*(4), 626–640.

Steel, P., & Konig, C. (2006). Integrated theories of motivation. *Academy of Management Review, 31*(4), 889–913.

Steele, G. R. (2001). *Keynes and Hayek, The money economy*. Abingdon: Routledge.

Stevenson, H., & Jarillo, C. (1990). A paradigm of entrepreneurship: Entrepreneurial management. *Strategic Management Journal, 11*, 17–27.

Swedberg, R. (2000). *Entrepreneurship: The social science View*. Oxford University Press. ISBN: 9780198294627

Urban, B. (2010). Antecedents of entrepreneurship, with a focus on culture in an emerging country context. *Problems and Perspectives in Management, 8*(1), 114–126.

Valliere, D. (2008). Re-conceptualizing entrepreneurial framework conditions. *Journal of International Entrepreneurship & Management, 6*, 97–112. https://doi.org/10.1007/s11365-008-0077-0. Springer Science + Business Media.

Von Wieser, F. (1927). (1851–1926). *Social economics* (1st ed.). (A. Ford Hinrichs, Trans. With a pref. by Wesley Clair Mitchell). London: Allen & Unwin. Translation of Theorie der gesellschaftlichen Wirtschaft. Edition (1927). ASIN: B000NWMXXC.

Wagner, K., & Ziltener, A. (2008). *The nascent entrepreneur at the crossroads: Entrepreneurial motives as determinants for different type of entrepreneurs*. Discussion Papers on Entrepreneurship and Innovation.

Walras, L. (1874). *Elements of pure economics*. Translated and annotated by William Jaffe (1954). Allen and Unwin. London.

Warehime, R. G. (1972). Generalized expectancy for locus of control and academic performance. *Psychological Reports, 30*, 314.

Zeffane, R. (2014). Does collectivism necessarily negate the spirit of entrepreneurship? *International Journal of Entrepreneurial Behaviour & Research, 20*(3), 278–296.

4

Methodology

This short chapter outlines the research methodology and design adopted for this study. The types of methodology, whether qualitative, quantitative, or mixed, should be determined by the nature of the phenomenon being studied (Creswell 2009). In trying to unravel context-bound experiences of young Emirati nationals, the following chapter justifies a qualitative approach using open-ended in-depth interviews. After an outline of the research aim, objectives, and questions, the population and sampling strategies are discussed. The last two sections of the chapter highlight data collection procedures and the software used to conduct analysis.

Purpose of Research

A number of studies in the UAE identified entrepreneurial intentions among young Emiratis (Bahrami 2014; Haan 2004; Hossan et al. 2013; Itani et al. 2011; Sikdar and Vel 2011; Sowmya et al. 2010; Zeffane 2014). However, high levels of entrepreneurial intentions do not translate into entrepreneurial action (Itani et al. 2011; Haan 2004; Sowmya et al. 2010).

This study proposed to explore the gap between entrepreneurial intentions and action by highlighting key factors within the entrepreneurial process and how they ultimately influence young Emiratis.

The study aimed to understand which factors motivate and support young Emirati entrepreneurs to start their businesses and which factors act as deterrents. This drew out key constructs of motivation, intentions, and environmental factors, such as culture, education, and government support that explain the entrepreneurial gap within the UAE. A qualitative approach was suitable for an exploratory study of this nature because it aims to develop an in-depth understanding of entrepreneurship through the lived experiences of first time entrepreneurs (Flick 2014; Creswell 2009; Sun 2009).

Despite extensive government efforts, the number of start-ups fully owned by Emirati nationals is still relatively low (Haan 2004; Kerros 2012). A study by the Global Entrepreneurship Monitor (GEM) (2011) highlighted that entrepreneurial activity within the UAE as a whole experienced a downward trend after its peak in 2008. Only 4% of new entrepreneurs were Emirati and almost no new business ventures (2.3%) operated in the medium to high technology sectors (Bosma and Levie 2010; El-Sokari et al. 2013). Furthermore, at 20.8% (Makahleh et al. 2012), unemployment rates among Emirati nationals are extraordinarily high for a country that achieved 3.6% growth in 2012.

Small Business Enterprises and entrepreneurs who start these businesses are the engines of a healthy economy (Minniti 2008). For example, in Dubai they represent 95% of all businesses and employ 42% of the work force (Dubai SME 2011). A steady stream of new entrepreneurs, especially based in the technology sector, is vital for the UAE economy (Government of Abu Dhabi 2008). In a bid to create a diverse economy that is not overly dependent on proceeds from natural resources, the UAE government decreed entrepreneurship as one of its strategic goals (Government of Abu Dhabi 2008). As a result, a number of organizations have sprung up, ready to support budding entrepreneurs, for example, the Khalifa Fund and Mohammad Bin Rashid Establishment (Hossan et al. 2013; Itani et al. 2011; Kargwell and Inguva 2012).

The relatively low level of entrepreneurial activity among UAE nationals represents a significant problem. A qualitative, phenomenological approach, using open-ended in-depth interviews was planned to gain a better understanding of why entrepreneurial activity is so low among UAE Nationals. Findings from this study should aid educational institutions in developing entrepreneurial education. The findings will also help government institutions like the Khalifa Fund to assess whether their efforts to help foster a diverse knowledge-based economy are on course (Government of Abu Dhabi 2008).

Research Questions

In developing research questions, Creswell (2009) suggested starting from a central question that is broad so it does not limit the scope of enquiry; however, this should be followed by sub-questions in order to maintain a focus. Sub-questions should be open-ended and may even be used in data collection. Research question should focus on the relationship between a central phenomenon and how participants view the phenomenon (Creswell 2009). For example, in a study of diplomatic leaders, Murtezaj (2011) explored the relationship between Emotional Intelligence and how diplomatic leaders viewed its utility in negotiation and handling conflict. In a study of female UAE entrepreneurs, Erogul and McCrohan (2008) explored the motivation and support network of female Emirati entrepreneurs. Similarly, the overarching aim of this research was to explore and understand reasons behind low levels of entrepreneurial activity among Emirati nationals.

With these factors in mind, the research focused on the central and sub-questions highlighted below:

Q1. Why is there a gap between entrepreneurial intentions and new business start-up rates among Emirati nationals in the UAE?
- Which factors influence Emiratis to become entrepreneurs or seek employment?
- What are the key challenges and barriers faced by aspiring Emirati entrepreneurs?
- How do internal factors (self-efficacy, motivations, intentions) and external factors (environmental factors such as education, family, government) affect the decision-making process?

Research Design

Reality is grounded in recognizing the individuality of experience and its inductive nature (ontological position). If this is considered as the foundation of how reality is constructed (epistemological position), then one would employ a discursive approach, subscribe to constructivism and apply a qualitative methodology (Creswell 2009; Flick 2014; Slevitch 2011; Sun 2009). Qualitative research is rooted in constructivist philosophy and tends to focus on individual experience and our interpretation of that experience to explain a certain reality (Creswell 2009; Sun 2009).

The type of methodology, whether qualitative, quantitative or mixed, should be determined by the nature of the phenomenon being studied (Creswell 2009; Onwuegbuzie et al. 2009). There are certain situations where a qualitative, quantitative, or mixed methodology is best suited to meet the research needs (Campbell and Fisk 1959). For example, if the topic of study is relatively new or previously unexplored, then a qualitative approach is useful in gaining an initial understanding. However, if the area of interest is well established with theoretical foundations or hypotheses, then quantitative research is better suited, as it enables the researcher to test and accept or reject the null hypothesis.

The scientific, deductive nature of quantitative research enables it to claim validity and reliability (Creswell and Miller 2000; Flick 2014). This is particularly useful when the researchers want to make generalizations and apply findings from the sample to the wider population. On the other hand, if the aim of the researcher is to get an in-depth understanding of an issue, or the research needs demand credibility and utility, then a qualitative approach would be suitable. This is certainly true if the research is trying to understand human experience and how that experience is interpreted by participants and the researcher.

There are aspects of human life and social phenomena that cannot be studied under laboratory or controlled conditions: "human beings have agency and intentionality" (Loftus and Higgs 2010. p.386) and this is where qualitative research can best serve researchers. The study titled "Understanding the Role of Emotional Intelligence in Negotiating Agreements and Diplomatic Conflict" (Murtezaj 2011) demonstrated how the credibility and utility offered by qualitative research is quintessential in certain circumstances. Murtezaj (2011) highlighted the lack of research in this area, especially on the role of diplomats and how they handle conflict.

This lack of research and the newness of the topic highlighted a need for a qualitative approach (Creswell 2009). Furthermore, if we consider the research questions that needed to be explored, for example, "What is the leader diplomat's strategy in handling conflicts?", then this also called for a qualitative approach (Murtezaj 2011. p.23). The researcher did not have the benefit of an existing database of possible strategies that diplomatic leaders used in handling conflict. Data on whether diplomatic leaders recognized the role of emotional intelligence in handling conflict also did not exist (Murtezaj 2011. p.19). Therefore, it can be argued that a qualitative approach was the only credible strategy, which could have been used for this particular study.

Using a phenomenological approach and in-depth interviews enabled the researcher to explore and interpret highly personal experiences of diplomatic leaders (Murtezaj 2011; Sun 2009). It can be argued that the richness and depth of meanings identified by this approach would not have been possible through a quantitative approach. Human experience is "context bound" (Smith and Heshusius 1986, as cited in Slevitch 2011. p.77) and qualitative research enables the researcher to unravel this context and uncover deep meanings to understand and interpret human experience at an intimate level that quantitative research cannot reach.

This exploratory study aimed to develop an in-depth understanding of entrepreneurship through the lived experiences of first time entrepreneurs and graduates with entrepreneurial intentions (Sun 2009). First time entrepreneurs had gone through the experience of starting a business for the first time in the UAE. Unraveling these context-bound experiences uncovered deep meanings that are hugely beneficial to potential entrepreneurs and ensured the study had credibility and utility (Slevitch 2011).

In trying to understand the experiences and challenges faced by graduates aspiring to become entrepreneurs, qualitative research provided a number of advantages and challenges. In order to provide a narrower focus, the study homes in on Emirati graduates who had graduated within the last five years and had opened a small to medium sized business for the first time, or had chosen the employment route, within the UAE. In order to gain data from multiple sources and to triangulate, the study also collected the perspective of incubation center managers (Denzin 2006; Filstead 1979).

The literature review revealed many factors within the entrepreneurial process to be multidimensional and bound in individual context (Baum et al. 2001; Eccles and Wigfield 2002; Johnson 1990). Thus, adopting a qualitative phenomenological approach was particularly useful. It enabled the researcher to identify the essence of entrepreneurs' experience. The researcher was able to explore human experience on an individual basis and explore multiple realities without the confines of predetermined frames of outcomes or response as required by quantitative research (Loftus and Higgs 2010).

Interviews were the most appropriate method for data collection. Given the busy schedules of entrepreneurs, a qualitative approach provided the flexibility to interact with participants in their preferred location and on their own terms (Kirk and Miller 1986). For example, data collection and timetables were built around the participants' schedules, and they chose to focus on the experiences and challenges that they felt were most relevant. Interviews and other qualitative methods tend to take much longer than a quick survey. Despite the fact that interviews were planned around participants' schedules, finding participants who were willing to sacrifice an hour or so of their time was probably the biggest practical challenge to the study. This issue has also been highlighted by other researchers (Flick 2014; Onwuegbuzie et al. 2009). Nevertheless, a qualitative approach provided an in-depth understanding of seemingly low levels of entrepreneurial activity among young Emirati nationals.

Population, Sampling Strategy

Creswell (2009) suggested that a sample size of 3–10 participants was sufficient in qualitative inquiries; however, to enhance "credibility and trustworthiness" a sample size between 10 and 20 may be needed (Saldana 2011, p. 34). This study employed purposeful and criterion based sampling techniques to ensure that a wide spectrum of relevant perspectives was included to enhance credibility and utility (Filstead 1979). A sample of ten participants was proposed for this study.

As mentioned earlier, in trying to understand the experiences and challenges faced by graduates aspiring to become entrepreneurs, qualitative research provided a number of advantages and challenges. In order to provide a narrower focus, the study homes in on Emirati graduates who had graduated within the last five years and had opened a small- to medium-sized business for the first time, or had chosen the employment route, within the UAE. In order to gain data from multiple sources and to triangulate, the study also collected the perspectives of incubation center managers.

Purposeful sampling was used to identify participants who had direct experiences relevant to the study (Creswell 2009). For example: (a) four individuals who had started a business within three to five years of graduation, (b) four individuals who had not started a business within three to five years of graduation, but had instead opted for employment. These individuals were able to provide a unique perspective of experiences that had led them to make very different choices. Furthermore, including the perspectives of (c) two incubation managers was also beneficial to the study, as these individuals had worked with a large number of people who had successfully started a business and those whose business ventures had failed (Table 4.1).

The main sample of four entrepreneurs and four employed Emirati nationals had an equal number of male and female participants. Furthermore, the sample of two incubator managers was also made up of one male and one female participant. It was important to have a mixed gender sample because most of the research in the region tended to be gender specific. Criterion sampling helped qualify participants and ensured the most suitable participants were invited to participate, which also added to the credibility of the research (Creswell 2009; Flick 2014). Each segment of the sample had experienced the phenomenon but from uniquely different perspectives. Therefore, criterion based sampling was justified; however, the qualifying criteria were specific to each segment.

For example, the qualifying criteria for (a) entrepreneurs included: (i) UAE nationals, (ii) education level of Bachelor's or above, (iii) started a

Table 4.1 Sample distribution and criteria

Sample segments	Entrepreneurs (a)	Employed (b)	Incubator managers (c)
Sample size (10) Distribution	4	4	2
Sample labels	Ent01 to Ent04	Emp01 to Emp04	Inc01 to Inc02
Gender balance	50/50	50/50	50/50
Minimum relevant experience	Non-applicable	Non-applicable	3–5 years
Nationality	UAE nationals	UAE nationals	Non-applicable
Education level	Minimum bachelors graduation	Minimum bachelors graduation	Non-applicable
Graduated within	3–5 years	3–5 years	Non-applicable
Key criterion (a)	Must own and manage a running business in the UAE	Must be employed in the UAE	Must be employed in a business incubator in the UAE
Key criterion (b)	Had intentions of starting a business before/after graduation	Had intentions of starting a business before/after graduation	Non-applicable

business within three to five years of graduation. Qualifying criteria for (b) non-entrepreneurs included: (i) UAE Nationals, (ii) education level of Bachelor's or above, having graduated within the last three to five years, (iii) had entrepreneurial intentions as undergraduates or even after graduating, (iv) now employed. Both sample segments "a" and "b" must have had entrepreneurial intentions as undergraduates. Qualifying criteria for (c) incubator managers included: (i) works in an incubation center or similar agency with a mandate to support and promote entrepreneurship, (ii) at least three years' experience in a front line role within the UAE. This approach ensured that a credible sample whose experiences were highly relevant was employed and these individuals were most suitable to answer the research questions(Creswell 2009; Flick 2014).

Sources of Data

A significant proportion of the proposed sample was made up of graduates from one of the largest Higher Education institutions in the UAE. The institution has a student body of approximately 20,000 students, all of whom are UAE Nationals. It has large campuses in five out of the seven Emirates within the UAE and its graduates are well sought after by employers, often ending up in jobs of high responsibility.

The study had planned to identify segments "a" and "b" of the sample through the Higher Colleges of Technology alumni database contact list. Similarly segment "c" was identified through the College's contacts list. Individuals (segment c) and organizations who have been trying to support new entrepreneurs provided a unique perspective that was used to confirm, or investigate further, the perspectives of segments "a" and "b". The researcher was already in contact with a number of these organizations who were eager to participate in research that attempted to develop a better understanding of entrepreneurial activity within the UAE.

In order to gain access to different sample segments, relevant permissions were required from separate bodies, including the research committee at the author's institution, and of course the participants. Using multiple data sources enabled the researcher to triangulate findings, which further enhanced credibility and utility (Creswell 2009; Sun 2009). The researcher is currently employed at a Higher Education Institution focused on entrepreneurship, which also provided easier access to the participants. However, it should be clarified that all efforts were made to ensure participants and the researcher did not have prior acquaintance. Saldana (2011) warns against the researcher finding participants among existing friends as it increases the chances of bias (Fig. 4.1).

Among the four types of triangulation highlighted by Denzin (2006), this study used the triangulation of data. Interview responses from three different sources (Sample a, b, c) with different perspectives were crosschecked and contrasted with each other to validate data and draw conclusions. The aim of data triangulation was not solely to validate findings (Denzin 2006). Additionally, data triangulation enabled the researcher to

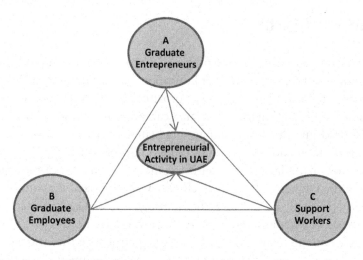

Fig. 4.1 Triangulating findings

gain a deeper understanding of critical issues affecting Emirati graduates (Flick et al. 2004). In this way, the researcher was able to bring together findings and justify conclusions (Denzin and Lincoln 1994; Hastings 2010). This process also enhanced the credibility and utility of the study (Creswell 2003).

Data Collection

A qualitative, phenomenological approach, using open-ended in-depth interviews, was used to gain a deeper understanding of why entrepreneurial activity is so low among Emirati graduates and which factors influence them in making the decision to become entrepreneurs or find paid employment. The interviews were semi-structured; for example, interviews with different sample segments followed a similar line of questioning. However, the open-ended nature of questioning ensured participants were able to choose the direction of experiences they wanted to explore.

Open-ended in-depth interviews allowed the researcher flexibility to control the line of enquiry and focus questioning to draw out important aspects of the informants' experiences. In doing so, the researcher was able to draw out answers to what, how, and why research participants held certain beliefs (Creswell 2009). The researcher's ability to sense the meanings behind responses and redirect the line of questioning was crucial to this process. However, clarifying responses and making meanings can potentially lead to bias. As the researcher clarified responses, the language and words that were used could have potentially deviated from the intended meaning. This highlights a limitation of qualitative research (Kvale and Brinkmann 2009).

Furthermore, there was a danger the researcher might lead informants in a different direction (Kvale and Brinkmann 2009). The semi-structured nature of the interviews and use of a similar line of questioning minimized this risk. The researcher also avoided rephrasing words and instead focused on the what, how, and why. Using consistent types of questions, for example, introductory, follow-up, probing, specific and direct questions, also helped develop a level of consistency, minimized the threat of bias, and improved credibility (Creswell 2003; Kvale and Brinkmann 2009).

Participants who volunteer to participate sacrifice their time, which should be considered by the researcher (Creswell 2009). Therefore, interviews were conducted within 45 minutes and a digital audio recording device was used to record them. The interviews were held at the participant's own place of work; however, a suitable area for the interviews, such as a "quiet room", was negotiated prior to the interview (Kirk and Miller 1986; Saldana 2011, p. 38). The researcher chose not to adopt the repertory grid suggested by Hair et al. (2009); however, some important constructs were identified prior to the interviews. For example, it was made clear to participants that entrepreneurial intentions and other factors such as employment status were to be discussed. The researcher also used pen and paper to record key junctures in the interview and personal memos to improve accuracy, identify relevant words for coding, and to inform interpretation and analysis.

The interviews were conducted in English; however, the UAE represents a unique proposition for researchers. The national language is only the third most spoken language in the country, Hindi and English being most widely spoken. The study mainly aimed to focus on UAE National graduates who had studied an English curriculum, and so language did not represent a large risk. However, language does not exist in isolation;

it is intertwined with culture, thus, additional challenges had been overcome (Risager 2006).

For example, the challenge of conducting this research was not just limited to superficial linguistic barriers, for example, explaining the meaning of words and so on. Potentially, participants can find it difficult to understand the meaning of references which can only be deciphered by understanding the culture (Hair et al. 2009; Risager 2006). These issues further deepen with the use of industry specific vocabulary. In planning for data collection, at least three layers of national, organizational, and group culture were negotiated (Karahanna et al. 1998, cited in Raitoharju et al. 2009). In such cases, meanings can get lost in translation, which represent a threat to credibility and utility.

The researcher ensured the language used in interviews was simple and as far as possible, minimized cultural references in order to minimize misunderstandings. The researcher also paid particular attention to conversational technology and credulous listening (Hair et al. 2009). For example, this involved receptive listening and using participants' own words and language to confirm or clarify the meaning of their statements (Hair et al. 2009; Moustakas 1994; Murtezaj 2011). This ensured that participants were relaxed and more likely to share the deeper meanings behind their experiences.

Once the sample of ten participants had been identified, they were given an opportunity to ensure they gained relevant permissions from their employers, if necessary, and confirm interview dates. A time frame of three weeks was needed to gain relevant approvals. Therefore, relevant approvals were sought six weeks prior to conducting research. Once the research participants confirmed their participation, emails, followed up by telephone calls, were sent to potential participants. The emails included important information, for example, the nature and aims of the research, the fact that participants' privacy would not be compromised and a consent form (see appendix A for standard email and B for consent form). All respondents were identified by pseudonyms and so their identity and privacy were not compromised.

The actual data collection through interviews spanned over four weeks. Once participants had agreed to participate, they were sent emails with schedules and locations. A courtesy email was sent a week in advance as a reminder, followed up by a phone call the day before the interview. The researcher had planned to interview segment "a" in the first week, followed by segment "b" in the second week, and segment "c" in the third week. The fourth week had been allocated to cover any missed appointments.

The sample of male entrepreneurs was particularly difficult to obtain. The planned process of sample identification did not produce a relevant sample of male entrepreneurs who had graduated within the last four to five years. This particular sample segment was sought through female participants, instead of the University contacts list or incubator managers. In contrast, the high number of potential female participants was identified relatively quickly. The researcher also had to find two additional participants because interviews with two participants in segment "a" and "b" were not deemed suitable.

Through the interview process it was found that one of the participants from segment "b" did not meet the criteria, mainly because they had never had entrepreneurial intentions. This was despite the fact that they had indicated entrepreneurial intentions during the initial contact process. An interview from one of the participants from segment "a" was deemed unsuitable because the interview process showed that the participant had not started a formal business entity, in that he did not have a business license. In both instances, replacements were successfully identified and interviewed; thus, the overall impact on the study was minimal.

The five open-ended questions below utilized the elicitation approach as suggested by Hair et al. (2009) and Saldana (2011) and were used to open the interview with sample segment "a", the entrepreneurs:

1. When did you have intentions of starting a business? Were there any personal risks you had to overcome?
2. How did you come up with your business idea? And how did you make it happen?
3. What role did friends and family or organizations play in supporting you to start the business?
4. How would you describe the conditions for entrepreneurship within the UAE? How easy was it to finance your business?

5. After having established the business, how has the nature of challenges changed and what advice would you give aspiring entrepreneurs?

Data Analysis

The choice of data analysis is dependent upon the research question, methodology, type of data and the analytical models available to articulate findings (Onwuegbuzie et al. 2009; Saldana 2011). Unlike quantitative research, where the data analysis begins in earnest once the researcher has collected relevant data, in qualitative research the heavy task of data analysis begins alongside data collection (Brause 2012; Sun 2009). This facet of interpreting findings, patterns, and themes to construct meaning as data emerges, makes data analysis one of the most difficult aspects of qualitative research (Saldana 2011).

Interview data tends to be extensive and contains unique perspectives of human experience, which make the analysis time consuming (Smith and Firth 2011). Furthermore, in a study such as this, where data was coming from multiple sources, it became harder to manage data and effectively identify themes (Filstead 1979). Some scholars argue that using CAQDAS in analyzing qualitative data can improve rigor (Richards and Richards 1991 cited in Welsh 2002).

This study used a CAQDAS called NVivo10 which is the latest software designed to analyze non-numeric qualitative data. It must be emphasized that NVivo10 does not take over the researcher's role as the interpreter, analyzer and evaluator. The researcher still has to use critical thinking to interpret and tease out the meanings behind data (Saldana 2011; Smith and Firth 2011). Instead, NVivo10 is essentially a data management tool that enables the researcher to carry out the analytical process more efficiently and with more transparency (Welsh 2002). The researcher in this case adopted a dual approach by first using NVivo10 to organize data, highlight patterns, and create codes, and then manually analyzed the data to confirm themes and draw conclusions (Welsh 2002).

NVivo10 enabled the researcher to keep all of the data in one place to add codes, known as "nodes" in NVivo10, and navigate across the data to identify themes and patterns more efficiently and effectively (Kikooma 2010; QRS 2013; Welsh 2002). The researcher also added memos and their interpretations as the themes emerged. Different functions in the application were then used to identify interconnectivities between themes. In the traditional sense, nodes can potentially double up as a research journal enabling the research to keep track of different levels of understanding and how it changed as new knowledge was constructed (QRS 2013). For example, NVivo10 was able to separate memos as independent nodes or include them as part of the main body of data.

The researcher avoided using a transcription service built into the NVivo10 software and interviews were transcribed manually within two days to ensure a deeper understanding of the data and to start the interpretive and analytical process (Mclellan et al. 2003). Entries on NVivo served as a research journal and provided an audit trail. Furthermore, the participants were offered an opportunity to see the transcribed interviews to ensure that they represented a true picture of the discussions. Only two of them chose to do so, but this nevertheless served as a check on the accuracy of the transcriptions. This process of member checking also ensured accuracy and improved credibility (Harper and Cole 2012).

In practice, the researcher found NVivo10's coding strips function most useful in analyzing transcribed interviews, as this function highlighted themes and where these themes overlapped. Recalling the data according to nodes was also a useful function in comparing themes in different interviews. This function also helped organize data more efficiently and justify findings according to direct quotes from the participants. This process was integral in triangulating data as it assisted the researcher in comparing responses of different samples according to relevant themes and validating them by contrasting with responses from incubator managers (Denzin 2006). Furthermore, the researcher was able to gain a deeper understanding of the emerging data, which also helped justify conclusions (Denzin and Lincoln 1994).

The ability to change codes and categories at any stage of the research process was also an advantage. Most importantly, the analytical process was brought to the forefront and it became more accessible, making it more transparent (Cambra and Wilson 2011; Saldana 2011). Transparency also has an added benefit for readers as they can use the data and researcher's interpretations to construct their own meanings. In delivering transparency, NVivo10 helped the researcher overcome some of the biggest criticisms of qualitative research, such as lack of rigor and trustworthiness and in doing so enhance credibility and utility (Kikooma 2010; Smith and Firth 2011).

Data Presentation Strategy

The choice of data presentation strategy in qualitative research depends on a number of factors, such as the type of methodology, audience, and overall purpose of the research (Saldana 2011). For example, a researcher conducting research for an art exhibition will choose a different presentation strategy compared to a researcher conducting research to inform social policy. Ultimately, all research aims to persuade and convince target audiences of research findings (Brause 2012; Saldana 2011). The style in which data is presented, and interpretations are justified, determines the degree to which readers are likely to be persuaded by the research findings.

This study's purpose of researching entrepreneurship within the UAE aimed to add to the existing body of knowledge and inform policy. Therefore, an analytical and formal style was most appropriate; what Saldana (2011, p. 148) would call "writing analytically and formally". Direct quotations from participants were used to outline key data and links with emerging themes in the results section, but with caution. Excessively long quotes can defeat the objective; therefore, attention was paid to quote the most relevant information and cut out unnecessary passages (Saldana 2011). It is important to note that careful attention has been taken not to manipulate quotations from participants. This along with the fact that English was not the first language for any of the participants means that, at times, quotations do not adhere to grammar rules. Qualitative interview-based studies on entrepreneurship have used this approach to good effect. For example, Erogul and McCrohan (2008) used direct quotations from interviewees to present interview data. This practice connects the audience with the research and makes the analytical process transparent, enabling them to better understand the line of enquiry and findings. Ultimately, this helps persuade the audience and adds to the research credibility and utility.

It can be argued that, despite ensuring credibility and utility, a study can fail to persuade its readers if the art of data presentation is inappropriate. This study complies with the American Psychological Association (APA) writing format (APA 2017). Correctly following a predetermined writing format can highlight to readers the researcher's ability to be consistent and meticulous. This can go on to help persuade readers of the research findings (Saldana 2011).

Using a CAQDAS such as NVivo10 enabled the researcher to present data in multiple ways. Although this study did not use the graphics function from NVivo10, its graphics function has the capacity to show linkages between quotations, matrices to highlight how categories developed and diagrams to illustrate how themes emerged or how the whole research process developed (Smith and Firth 2011). Using graphs, tables and figures to highlight and analyze evidence was also in line with the formal and analytical style. This type of data presentation strategy provides visual summaries and also helps the audience grasp the essence of the findings (Saldana 2011). This not only adds to the research credibility and utility, but also provides readers better accessibility to the analytical and overall research process, which also adds to its persuasiveness.

The discussion section used participant views and theoretical literature to derive interpretations and justify conclusions, which also strengthened the study's persuasive powers. This section used key words such as "For example…Mr C felt…", "Therefore… arguably…", "This is in line with what Mr so and so (2001) found in…", "This means…". Using all three in conjunction made the findings more persuasive. In order to improve accessibility, headings and subheadings were used to highlight the flow of the report and help the reader signpost different sections of the study (Saldana 2011). Saldana (2011) suggested using text rich features such as *italics* or **boldface** to emphasize important statements, codes, themes, and so on. For example, using the boldface feature to highlight key junctures or wording in participant quotations should enable readers to focus on the most important information within the quotation. However, the latest APA guidelines discourage the use of this beneficial approach. Similarly, using diagrams to illustrate interconnectivity among participants' views, literature, categories, and emerging themes also enhanced data presentation.

Credibility and Utility

Employing strategies such as a rigorous methodology, approved by the supervisor, and personal reflexivity to recognize how the researcher's bias and involvement may affect the research enhances credibility and utility (Creswell 2009; Kikooma 2010; Sun 2009). One-to-one, in-depth interviews, using open-ended questions also enabled the researcher to understand deep meanings behind the experiences of participants (Saldana 2009). Furthermore, the semi-structured nature of interviews provided flexibility to explore experiences of greater relevance or clarify meanings of ideas discussed. This quality of exploring, interpreting experiences of individuals, highly relevant to the phenomenon and finding deep meanings to the central question gives qualitative research credibility.

Credibility ensures findings can be applied to other situations that are similar in context, which gives qualitative research utility. However, the process of understanding and interpreting participants' experience must be transparent (Smith and Firth 2011). Using the CAQDAS, NVivo10, helped the researcher provide better access to different stages of the analytical process and how conclusions were reached, which improved credibility and transparency. The software also created an audit trail which served as a secondary transparency mechanism, enabling the reader to gain an insight into the process and journey the researcher took to construct knowledge, further enhancing credibility and utility (Kikooma 2010).

Role of the Researcher

The researcher's inability to recognize, declare or plan against his or her bias can threaten the credibility of qualitative research (Creswell 2003). This researcher is currently employed as a lecturer in entrepreneurship and it could be argued, much like segment "c" a support worker, might be trying to support and promote entrepreneurship. Although the researcher had only been working in the UAE for four years at the time of conduction research, current and historical involvement in entrepreneurship as a lecturer, entrepreneur and close contact with participants during the interview all create a potential for bias (Sun 2009). The research findings are certainly of interest to the researcher. Therefore, the issue of recognizing and minimizing bias to ensure credibility has been dealt with head on.

The researcher paid particular attention to conversational technology and credulous listening (Hair et al. 2009) and applied a realist reporting approach wherever possible (Saldana 2011). For example, this involved receptive listening and using participants' own words and language to confirm or clarify the meaning of their statements (Hair et al. 2009; Moustakas 1994, cited in Murtezaj 2011). CAQDAS was helpful again as the participants' perspective was transcribed and evidenced on NVivo10. Lastly, the researcher's interpretations were based on evidence provided by participants, which were then cross-referenced with existing literature to draw conclusions (Park 2006).

In this way, the researcher was able to maintain objectivity and findings were justified through specific evidence highlighted by the study. The use of a CAQDAS in particular granted audience access to the research process and brought the meaning-making process to forefront. This also ensured that results were not affected by bias, and thus improved accessibility, transparency while increasing credibility and utility (Brause 2012; Creswell 2009; Saldana 2009).

Legal Issues

A paper on ethical practice published by the British Sociological Association (BSA) emphasized the importance of minimizing ambiguity. In gaining approvals for research, the rationale should be clear to understand for stakeholders (BSA 2002). The research proposal needed to be communicated to the researcher's employer, the Ministry of Education, and research participants. Therefore, appropriate efforts were made in adapting language or simplifying complicated facets of the research process to meet the needs of different stakeholders.

Gaining consent from research participants is a major concern for all researchers carrying out social research. Although most institutions have ethical guidelines based on the Belmont report (1979), many have developed adapted guidelines appropriate for the local setting (Smith 2003).

The British Educational Research Association (BERA 2011) emphasized the voluntary nature of informed consent and that it must be gained before the research begins (BERA 2011). Informed consent is not simply limited to gaining permission from research subjects to participate. It was the researcher's responsibility to ensure potential participants were fully aware of what was involved, for example, the nature of the research and its connotations.

It can be argued that the process of informed consent, based on high ethical standards, is complicated in the UAE. One has to overcome the initial barrier posed by language only to find oneself in a cultural minefield. For example, even if a female potential research participant is an adult, it is still a requirement to gain consent from her legal guardian. The nature of the proposed research ensures confidentiality as the names and personal details were not shared with the public. However, the fact that some details may have to be shared with reviewers indicates the limitations of confidentiality, which was also shared with participants (Smith 2003).

A consent form was designed in line with high ethical standards, using guidelines outlined by the APA, Newcastle University (UK) and Zayed University (UAE) to ensure adherence to international standards and local cultural sensitivity. Appropriate measures were taken to ensure potential participants and others involved in the decision-making process were able to understand the purpose of the research, how it may be used and its consequences (BSA 2002). The consent form itself highlighted the voluntary nature of participants' involvement and their right to withdraw at any stage of the research. It also assured them that their individual privacy and data would be protected at all times. (See appendix A for standard email and appendix B for consent form).

The security of data provided by participants and the privacy of each participant had to be strictly observed. Recorded interview data, analysis and all other related files were stored on the researcher's personal computer and each file was password protected. Participants have been referred to as numbers and corresponding sample group, for example, entrepreneur interviewees were referred to as Ent01M, Ent02F and so on. The researcher had planned to share findings and conclusions directly related to each participant in order to confirm and gain final consent;

however, none of the participants showed a preference for this option. In fact, only two participants agreed to read the transcribed interviews to confirm they represented a true picture of what the participant wanted to convey.

In summary this chapter highlights the qualitative phenomenological methodology used to collect data from a sample of ten research participants. This chapter justifies the use of this methodology to explore possible explanations for the central research question of low levels of entrepreneurial activity among Emirati graduates. The chapter also details the research strategy and how this study tries to enhance credibility and utility. The next chapters from here on in focus on the key factors that affect entrepreneurs, and the challenges and opportunities these factors represent for advancing entrepreneurship in the UAE.

References

APA. (2017). *American Psychological Association*, APA Style. Retrieved from; http://www.apastyle.org/?_ga=2.46604207.969075372.1509190046-783947205.1509190046

Bahrami, S. (2014). Entrepreneurship intentions and perceptions in the UAE: A study of moderating effects of gender, culture and family. *International Journal of Small Business and Entrepreneurship Research, 2*(4), 37–50.

Baum, R., Locke, E., & Smith, K. (2001). A multidimensional model of venture growth. *Academy of Management Journal, 44*(2), 292.

Bosma, N., & Levie, J. (2010). Executive report. Babson College, Universidad del Desarollo, Ha'sko'linn, Reykjavik and London Business School. *Global entrepreneurship monitor*. Babson Park.

Brause, R. (2012). *Writing your doctoral dissertation: Invisible rules for success*. London/New York: Taylor and Francis.

British Sociological Association. (2002). *Statement of ethical practice for the British sociological association (BSA)*. Retrieved from: http://www.britsoc.co.uk/media/27107/StatementofEthicalPractice.pdf

Cambra, J., & Wilson, A. (2011). Qualitative data analysis software: Will it ever become mainstream? *International Journal of Market Research, 53*(1), 17–24.

Campbell, D. T., & Fiske, D. W. (1959). Convergent and discriminant validation by the multitrait-multimethod matrix. *Psychological Bulletin, 56*, 81–105.

Creswell, J. W. (2003). *Qualitative inquiry & research design: Choosing among five approaches.* Thousand Oaks: Sage Publications, Inc.
Creswell, J. (2009). *Research design: Qualitative, quantitative, and mixed methods* (3rd ed.). Newbury Park: Sage Publications.
Creswell, J. W., & Miller, D. L. (2000). Determining validity in qualitative inquiry. *Theory Into Practice, 39,* 124–134.
Denzin, N. (2006). *The research act: A theoretical introduction to sociological methods.* McGraw-Hill. ISBN: 0070163618.
Denzin, N., & Lincoln, Y. (1994). *Handbook of qualitative research.* London: Sage Publications. ISBN: 0803946791.
Dubai SME. (2011). The role of government in supporting entrepreneurship & SME development. *Dubai Department of Economic Development.* Retrieved from http://www.oecd.org/mena/investment/47246782.pdf
Eccles, J., & Wigfield, A. (2002). Motivational beliefs, values, and goals. *Annual Review of Psychology. ProQuest Central, 53,* 109–132.
El-Sokari, H., Van Horne, C., Huang, Z., & Al Awad, M. (2013). GEM UAE: Entrepreneurship- An Emirati perspective. *Global Entrepreneurship Monitor.* Retrieved from http://www.gemconsortium.org/docs/2892/gem-uae-entrepreneurship-an-emirati-perspective
Erogul, M., & McCrohan, D. (2008). Preliminary investigation of Emirati women entrepreneurs in the UAE. *African Journal of Business Management, 2*(10), 177–185.
Filstead, W. J. (1979). Qualitative methods. A need perspective in evaluation research. In T. D. Cook & C. S. Reichardt (Eds.), *Qualitative and quantitative methods in evaluation research* (pp. 33–48). Beverly Hills: Sage Publications.
Flick, U. (2014). *An introduction to qualitative research.* Sage Publishing. ISBN: 1446297713.
Flick, U., Kardoff, E., & Steinke, I. (2004). *A companion to qualitative research.* Sage Publications, London. ISBN: 1848605234.
Government of Abu Dhabi. (2008). *The Abu Dhabi Economic Vision 2030.* Retrieved from: https://www.ecouncil.ae/PublicationsEn/economic-vision-2030-full-versionEn.pdf
Haan, H. (2004). *Small enterprises: Women entrepreneurs in the UAE.* Centre for Labour Market Research & Information (CLMRI). Retrieved from http://www.zu.ac.ae/infoasis/modules/mod8/business/documents/smallenterpriserepor

Hair, N., Rose, S., & Clark, M. (2009). Using qualitative repertory grid techniques to explore perceptions of business-to-business online customer experience. *Journal of Customer Behaviour, 8*(1), 51–65. https://doi.org/10.1362/1 47539209X414380.

Harper, M., & Cole, P. (2012). Member checking: Can benefits be gained similar to group therapy? *The Qualitative Report, 17*(2), 510–517. Retrieved from http://nsuworks.nova.edu/tqr/vol17/iss2/1.

Hastings, S. (2010). Triangulation. Salkind, N. (2010). *Encyclopedia of research design*. Sage Publications, Inc. Thousand Oaks. ISBN: 9781412961288.

Hossan, C., Parakandi, M., & Saber, H. (2013). Entrepreneurial knowledge, preferences and barriers of female business students in the Middle East. *Journal of Business and Policy Research, 8*(2), 83–99.

Itani, H., Sidani, S., & Baalbaki, I. (2011). United Arab Emirates female entrepreneurs: Motivations and frustrations. *Equality, Diversity and Inclusion: An International Journal, 30*(5), 409–424.

Johnson, R. (1990). Toward a multidimensional model of entrepreneurship: The case of achievement motivation and the entrepreneur. *Entrepreneurship Theory & Practice*, 39–54.

Kargwell, S., & Inguva, S. (2012). Factors influencing the first generation entrepreneurs: An analytical study on the graduates of UAE universities. *International Journal of Business and Social Science, 3*(7), 143–149.

Kerros, T. (2012).The 'Entrepreneurial Triggers' driving graduate entrepreneurship in the UAE. *The Entrepreneurialist, 3*.

Kikooma, J. F. (2010). Using qualitative data analysis software in a social constructionist study of entrepreneurship. *Qualitative Research Journal, 10*(1), 40–51. https://doi.org/10.3316/QRJ1001040.

Kirk, J., & Miller, M. (1986). *Reliability and validity in qualitative research qualitative research methods*. Sage Publications. ISSN 0888–5397 ISBN 0803924704.

Kvale, S., & Brinkmann, S. (2009). *Interviews: Learning the craft of qualitative research Interviewing*. Sage Publications. ISBN 0761925422.

Loftus, S., & Higgs, J. (2010). Researching the individual in workplace research. *Journal of Education and Work, ResearchGate*. https://doi.org/10.1080/13639 080.2010.495712.

Makahleh, S., Badih, S., & Sabry, S. (2012, November 29). UAE unemployment issue to be tackled: Private sector: A main partner in solving unemployment issue. *Gulf News*, Retrieved from http://gulfnews.com/news/uae/government/uae-unemployment-issue-to-be-tackled

Mclellan, E., Macqueen, K., & Neidig, J. (2003). Beyond the qualitative interview: Data preparation and transcription. *Field Methods*. Sage Publications. 15(1), pp. 63–84. https://doi.org/10.1177/1525822X02239573.

Minniti, M. (2008). The role of government policy on entrepreneurial activity: Productive, unproductive, or destructive? *Entrepreneurship Theory & Practice*, 779–790.

Moustakas, C. (1994). *Phenomenological research methods*. Sage Publications. ISBN: 145220747X.

Murtezaj, V. (2011). *Understanding the role of emotional intelligence in negotiating agreements and diplomatic conflict*. PhD Dissertation. Retrieved from: http://swissmc.blackboard.com/bbcswebdav

Onwuegbuzie, A., Johnson, R., & Collins, K. (2009). Call for mixed analysis: A philosophical framework for combining qualitative and quantitative approaches. *International Journal of Multiple Research Approaches*, 3(2), 114–139.

Park, P. (2006). Knowledge and participatory research. In P. Reason & H. Bradbury (Eds.), *Handbook of action research: Participative inquiry and practice (Concise)* (pp. 83–93). London: Sage Publications.

QRS. (2013). What is NVivo. *QSR International Pty Ltd*, Retrieved from: http://www.qsrinternational.com/nvivo/what-is-nvivo

Raitoharju, R., Heiro, E., Kini, R., & D'Cruz, M. (2009). Challenges of multicultural data collection and analysis: Experiences from the health information system research. *The Electronic Journal of Business Research Methods*, 7(1), 75–82.

Risager, K. (2006). Language and culture in a global perspective. In K. Risager (Ed.), *Language and culture: Global flows and local complexity* (pp. 1–18). Clevedon: Multilingual Matters.

Saldana, J. (2009). *The coding manual for qualitative researchers*. London: Sage Publishing.

Saldana, J. (2011). *Fundamentals of qualitative research, understanding qualitative research*. Oxford University Press. ISBN: 0199838356.

Sikdar, A., & Vel, P. (2011). Factors influencing entrepreneurial value creation in the UAE—an exploratory study. *International Journal of Business and Social Science*, 2(6), 77.

Slevitch, L. (2011). Qualitative and quantitative methodologies compared: Ontological and epistemological perspectives. *Journal of Quality Assurance in Hospitality & Tourism*, 12(1), 73–81. https://doi.org/10.1080/1528008X.2011.541810.

Smith, D. (2003). Five principles for research ethics: Cover your bases with these ethical strategies. *American Psychological Association, 34*(1), 56.

Smith, J., & Firth, J. (2011). Qualitative data analysis: The framework approach. *Nurse Researcher, 18*(2), 52–62.

Sowmya, D., Majumdar, S., & Gallant, M. (2010). Relevance of education for potential entrepreneurs: An international investigation. *Journal of Small Business and Enterprise Development, 17*(4), 626–640.

Sun, T. (2009). *Mixed methods research: Strengths of two methods combined.* http://swissmc.blackboard.com/bbcswebdav/courses/5502C1971/Mixed%20Methods%

The Belmont Report: Ethical Principles and Guidelines for the Protection of Human Subjects of Research. (1979). *United States, National Commission for the protection of human subjects of biomedical and behavioral research.* Retrieved from http://ohsr.od.nih.gov/guidelines/belmont.html

The British Educational Research Association (BERA). (2011). *Ethical guidelines for educational research.* Retrieved from: http://content.yudu.com/Library/A2xnp5/Bera/resources/index.htm?referrerUrl=http://free.yudu.com/item/details/2023387/Bera

Welsh, E. (2002). Dealing with data: Using NVivo in the qualitative data analysis process. *Qualitative Social Research, 3*(2), 1–7.

Zeffane, R. (2014). Does collectivism necessarily negate the spirit of entrepreneurship? *International Journal of Entrepreneurial Behaviour & Research, 20*(3), 278–296.

5

Entrepreneurship in the UAE (I)

This book explores the entrepreneurial gap in the UAE and highlights key factors that affect the process of entrepreneurship for Emiratis. A qualitative, phenomenological approach, using open-ended semi-structured interviews, was employed to gain a better understanding of the phenomenon. Specifically, it examined the lived experiences of young Emiratis who graduated within the last three to five years and have either succeeded or failed in realizing their entrepreneurial intentions. An additional sample of incubator managers was also employed to triangulate findings.

This chapter reports on the research results, outlining main themes that emerged from interviews, their relevance to explaining the entrepreneurial gap and related challenges and opportunities within the UAE. This chapter is divided into five sections. The first section provides an overview of demographic statistics of research participants, highlighting key factors relevant to each sample segment. The following four sections report on and analyze the four major themes and eighteen sub-themes that have emerged from interviews. The role of government has far reaching consequences for Emiratis and emerges as a corner stone of Emirati society. Therefore, this fifth theme, along with four related sub-themes,

© The Author(s) 2018
W. A. Minhas, *Advancing Entrepreneurship in the United Arab Emirates*,
https://doi.org/10.1007/978-3-319-76436-8_5

has been outlined separately in Chap. 7: "Role of Government". The chapter concludes with a short summary.

The five major themes that emerged from interviews are personal characteristics, family, culture, perceived behavior control, and role of government. Although there were some commonalities in family and culture, a decision was made to keep these themes independent because the aim of this study focused on gaining a deeper understanding rather than the ability to generalize. The first theme, personal characteristics, included the sub-themes of need for achievement (nAch), need for independence, risk-taking propensity, and capacity to innovate.

The second theme of family included the sub-themes of family circumstance, family approval, family support, and commitment to family. The third theme of culture included the sub-themes of collectivist nationalism, perceptions of entrepreneurship, religion and tradition and lastly, reputation. The fourth theme of perceived behavior control included the sub-themes of access to finance, access to support, competition, education, market knowledge and time. Finally the fifth theme, role of government, included the sub-themes of political role models, government support programs (GSPs), government regulations, and expectations of GSPs. All of the themes were supported by direct quotations from the participants themselves.

Later sections further analyze and summarize these themes and draw out their relevance to the main research objectives. These sections confirm some of the complexities in exploring the phenomenon of entrepreneurship bound in individual experiences and context. This also highlights the interconnected nature of themes that have emerged, their roles at different stages of the entrepreneurial process, and how individuals interacted with them as they endeavored to realize their entrepreneurial intentions.

The chapter also discusses the findings, further exploring the interconnected nature of major themes and their implications for entrepreneurship in the UAE. Research on entrepreneurship often focuses on motivations as the staple of entrepreneurial intention; however, these studies seldom explore the origins of these motivations and the individuals they affect (Stephan et al. 2015). The section highlights different stages of the entrepreneurial process identified in the analyses and makes connections between different factors to propose an Emirati Model of Entrepreneurship (EME).

Demographic Data

The following section provides demographic statistics. The real names of participants have been omitted. The sample of four graduates that managed to start a business is represented as, for example, "**Ent01M**". The "Ent" indicates they are entrepreneurs, the number indicates the sample count and M or F indicates whether they were male or female. Similarly, "**Emp01F**" is used to represent the sample of graduates who failed to start a business but found employment. In the same way, "**Inc01F**" represents the smaller sample of two incubator managers (Table 5.1).

As the table above indicates, an equal number of male and female participants were used in interviews. Excluding the incubator manager sample, participants' age ranged from 24 to 36 years, with an average of 28.75 years. With the exception of two participants, each graduate was from a different subject area. Subject areas have been omitted but they ranged from Accounting to Mechanical Engineering. With the exception of one participant who graduated five years ago, the sample had graduated within the last two years. All of the participants were Emiratis, UAQ nationals working in Sharjah or Dubai. However, their permanent residence was located in a range of different Emirates. For the incubator managers sample, the "(Bus)" highlighted in Table 5.1 under "number of employees", indicates the number of businesses currently under incubation.

Interestingly, when comparing the average age of each sample group separately, there was a noticeable difference. For example, the average age of entrepreneurs was 30.75 years whereas the employees' average was 26.75 years. The four-year difference may indicate that these entrepreneurs did not jump into starting a business straight away and waited after graduation. This notion is supported by the fact that nearly all entrepreneurs interviewed were previously employed for a short while and some continued to post-graduate education (Fig. 5.1).

Further attention to the entrepreneur sample also highlighted that all of the businesses were in their nascent stage. The number of employees ranged from 7 to 4 and the average age of these businesses was 2.25 years. This had positive implications for the study as the participants were able to provide the latest insights into the experience of opening a business from an Emirati perspective (Figs. 5.2 and 5.3).

Table 5.1 Demographic statistics

Sample Code	Age	Location	Gender	Length of Time	Education Level	Year of Graduation	Number of Employees	Turnover	Previously Employed
Ent01M	34	Dubai	M	2	MBA	2013	7	Not broken even	Yes
Ent04M	36	Dubai	M	1.5	MBA	2010	6	Not broken even	Yes
Ent03F	27	Ajman	F	3.5	BA	2013	4	133,000 AED	No
Ent02F	26	Dubai	F	2	MA	2015	6	In profit undisclosed	Yes
Emp01F	24	Sharjah	F	1.5	BA	2013	n/a	n/a	n/a
Emp02M	29	Al Ain	M	10	BA	2015	n/a	n/a	n/a
Emp03F	24	Sharjah	F	2	BA	2013	n/a	n/a	n/a
Emp04M	30	UAQ	M	9	BA	2014	n/a	n/a	n/a
Inc01F	29	Dubai	F	3	MA	2010	8 (Bus)	n/a	n/a
Inc02M	47	Dubai	M	12	MBA	2009	9–12 (Bus)	n/a	n/a

Entrepreneurship in the UAE (I)

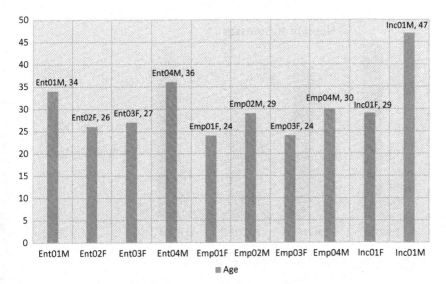

Fig. 5.1 Sample age range of entrepreneurs, employees, and incubator managers

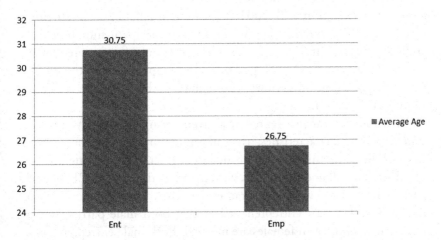

Fig. 5.2 Average age of entrepreneurs and employees

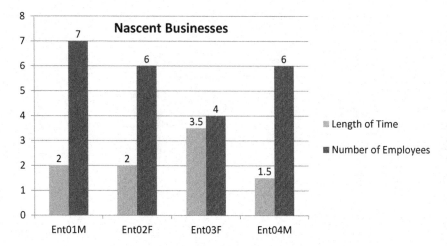

Fig. 5.3 Business age and number of employees

In addition to the statistical data, it was also beneficial to highlight the individual context of each participant. The literature review emphasized the importance of individual context in qualitative phenomenological studies (Baum et al. 2001; Eccles and Wigfield 2002). Providing insights into the individual context of each participant should help the audience better understand the phenomenon of entrepreneurship in the UAE context. This practice also helps support the themes that emerge from interviews and enhance the research credibility (Smith et al. 2009).

The eight participants represent a diverse sample, but they also share some common characteristics. They all wanted to start a business at some stage of their life; this was one of the key criteria in identifying the sample. They have all graduated and, with the exception of Ent02F, all of the participants started work after graduation. There are differences between the male and female entrepreneurs, in that both male participants are unmarried, while both females are married. Both male entrepreneurs are yet to break-even, though this may also be connected to the type of business they have adopted. By and large, all entrepreneurs are from well to do families; this is in contrast with the employee sample, who are all from moderate income families.

Some themes emerged from this brief overview: for example, the importance of family was a common thread. The next section focuses on identifying factors that influence Emirati graduates to become entrepreneurs or seek employment. It also focuses on identifying the challenges and barriers faced by aspiring Emirati entrepreneurs. Identifying concrete themes and analyzing the experiences of graduates who had recently started a business and those who could not manage to do so helped to develop a better understanding of the gap between entrepreneurial intentions and new business start-up rates in the UAE. These factors are highlighted in the form of themes that emerged from the interview data.

This book provides an exploration how entrepreneurship can be advanced in the UAE, specifically from an Emirati entrepreneur's perspective. This chapter focuses on Emirati entrepreneurs, their journey with start-ups, and their perception of entrepreneurship in the UAE. Based on the interviews collected from a purposefully selected sample of ten research participants, this chapter offers insights into the key factors that govern entrepreneurship for this stratum of the UAE population. These interviews exposed five distinct themes. Family, culture, personal characteristics, perceived behavior control, and the role of government emerged as the dynamic yet interrelated tenets that most significantly influenced entrepreneurship in the UAE.

Family and culture are closely related; however, both have been considered separately to develop a deeper understanding of these highly personal facets. The theme of family details the intimate and highly personal facets and the interconnected relationships that affect Emirati entrepreneurs, whereas culture helps separate the wider social elements that shape entrepreneurial intentions and action in the UAE context. The theme of personal characteristics highlights personality traits that appeared most often, or were most apparent during the interviews. The interconnected nature of these themes means that these personal characteristics were inevitably shaped by family influence and culture.

Entrepreneurship, even in free market economies, is heavily influenced by government. However, for Emirati entrepreneurs government came across as one of the strongest influencers. It plays a multifaceted role in shaping the Emirati context at different stages; this was an unexpected finding. The theme of government has been discussed in a separate chapter in detail. PBC highlights key elements that affected the samples' belief in succeeding. A mix of personal characteristics, perceptions and relationships with other external factors are used to define the Emirati entrepreneurs in the next chapter.

Five major themes that emerged from interviews also led to a number of sub-themes. The first theme of personal characteristics included the sub-themes of (a) need for achievement (nAch), (b) need for independence, (c) risk-taking propensity, and (d) capacity to innovate. The second theme of family included the sub-themes of (a) family circumstance, (b) family approval, (c) family support, and (d) commitment to family. The third theme of culture included the sub-themes of (a) collectivist nationalism, (b) perceptions of entrepreneurship, (c) religion, (d) tradition, and, lastly, (e) reputation.

The fourth theme, of perceived behavior control, included the sub-themes of (a) access to finance, (b) access to support, (c) competition, (d) education, (e) market knowledge, and (f) time. Finally the fifth theme, role of government, included the sub-themes of (a) political role models, (b) GSPs, (c) government regulations, and (d) expectations of GSPs. All of the themes were supported by direct quotations from the participants themselves.

Later sections of the book further analyze and summarize these themes and draw out their relevance to the main research questions. These sections confirm some of the complexities in exploring the phenomenon of entrepreneurship which is bound in individual experiences and context (Creswell 2009). This also highlights the interconnected nature of themes, their roles at different stages of the entrepreneurial process, and how individuals interacted with them as they endeavored to realize their entrepreneurial intentions.

Themes

Five interrelated themes emerged from the interview data. The emerging themes were interconnected because of the complicated web of personal and cultural dependencies that constitute the UAE social make-up. Supported by direct quotations from the interview data, this section provides a detailed description of the themes and related sub-themes that consistently appeared in interviews. Further analysis of the themes and their implications is carried out in later chapters. The detailed description includes all significant elements of the interview data and codes that help develop a better understanding of the main themes. As mentioned in the previous chapter, it is important to note that careful attention has been taken not to manipulate direct quotations from participants. This along with the fact that English was not the first language for any of the participants means that, at times, quotations do not adhere to grammar rules.

Theme One: Personal Characteristics

In the last two decades, use of personality traits in studying entrepreneurship has experienced a steady decline because they failed to differentiate between entrepreneurs and managers (Gartner 1988; Shane et al. 2003). However, despite this flaw, personality traits can be useful in understanding entrepreneurial behavior (Baumol 2010; Carsrud and Brännback 2011). This theme highlights the individual make-up of the participants and the internal influences that drive them. These personality traits are exemplified by sub-themes, which include need for achievement (nAch), need for independence, risk-taking propensity, and capacity to innovate.

Need for Achievement

McClelland (1961) identified the achievement motive or need for achievement (nAch) as the main predictor of entrepreneurial intentions (Alschuler 1967; Carsrud and Brännback 2011; Estay et al. 2013). The achievement motive pursues actions that lead to excellence (McClelland 1961). In pursuing excellence, individuals are more likely to undertake tasks that require higher levels of skill, individual responsibility, recognition and impact of outcomes. Taking on the role of an entrepreneur meets all of these criteria (Shane et al. 2003). Thus, a career in entrepreneurship is the most likely outcome for individuals who possess a high need for achievement (McClelland 1961).

Ent01M: I think if people do what they are passionate about they will succeed whatever the challenges... yes I was happy, satisfied, but I see myself I can do more... because the job was not allowing me to express myself as I believe I could....

Ent02F: I am strong and I have a lot of ideas... I was planning for three years till I know exactly what to do... I had this ambition since I was sixteen years old... my business lets me do more, expand maybe open another branch or shop, not just going from kiosk to kiosk... I see myself gaining a PhD I want to be a role model for Emiratis....

Ent03F: Actually I started my business about 1 year before graduation ... because in my last year I only had to do two courses so I had free time... this is my character to be honest with you I like to lead... I just wanted to progress in business life... I was looking forward to have my own business my own income my own employees....

Ent04M: It's nothing to with the dollar sign or the prestige of being a business owner but I think it was more about the feeling that I should do something for myself, something different if I had the freedom to do it and I did not have the freedom to do this at work... for me it was the passion, emotional pride, I always had the fantasy that I will have my own business... the main driver behind it is not really that I just want to be my own boss but that I will be able to make more creative decisions that the office/work box won't allow....

The sample of entrepreneurs (Ent) displayed a deep-rooted need for achievement, which at times spilled over into the need for independence. Ent01M, "I see myself I can do more". Ent02F, "I had this ambition since I was sixteen". Ent03F, "I just wanted to progress in business life". Ent04M, "I think it was more about the feeling that I should do something for myself". As highlighted by McClelland (1961), the achievement motive seems to instill ambition and pushes these Emirati entrepreneurs to identify actions that lead to excellence. Why a career in entrepreneurship was identified as an appropriate avenue to satisfy this ambition was not wholly clear at this stage. Participants who opted for employment also displayed similar traits.

Emp01F: Well, first of all it comes from me I am a very productive person... this work (current job) does not seem enough it is not satisfying... I want to be productive to self-development and gain self-confidence... I want to be a successful business woman or a leader...but I know I needed to do something for myself (own business) in order to become someone... that someone is not best defined in my head... but I just wanted to do my best....

Emp02M: I wanted to start (business) for self-achievement, get another income and be able to help my family (financially).... It's my nature maybe, because other guys can be satisfied with their certification but I wanted more... I think the man have to do as much as he can... to have self-confidence, self- worth (reputation)... to achieve something that is important for me... to have a good reputation? to build something that I build from zero when I don't have time or funds...hmmm, this comes from my father he was always encouraging me to do something more....

Emp03F: I think no one wants to stay at the same level I think everyone is trying to do better? I think it's in our nature, because we want self-esteem, if you want to satisfy yourself, satisfy a motive inside you... Maybe when I see my brothers and sisters, older than me, I don't want to end up like them...I want to be better than them, when my younger sister looks at me she should want to be like me....

Emp04M: I want to be successful so I can get married have kids because until now I could not because I have to look after my brothers and sisters... I have to think about their future....

The sample of employed Emiratis also displayed tendencies toward a need for achievement and added weight to this sub-theme. Emp01F, "Well first of all it comes from me I am a very productive person". Emp02M, "to achieve something that is important for me". Emp03F, "I want to be better them". Emp04M, "I want be successful". Both sample sets displayed a need for achievement and an ambition to achieve beyond their current scope. However, seeds for this need for achievement were different; some highlighted this as a part of their nature, and thus internal, whereas others linked it to external factors such as family needs or social standing. The need for achievement as an individual characteristic is a better predictor of entrepreneurial intentions rather than entrepreneurial action (Shane et al. 2003). Nevertheless, it is a predictable characteristic in most entrepreneurs (Baumol 2010). The sample of incubator managers corroborates the need for achievement among young Emiratis.

Inc01F: *They want to pursue something they are interested in, so for example, even if they are working they will start a business to do what they are interested… so it's like following their passion… another source of income, getting experience of managing their own business, to gain confidence and improve their personality… yes I think the leadership, our belonging to the country, culture, religion it's connected… they want to achieve for the UAE… this is the place we need to build….*

Inc02M: *I think some simply have it in their blood they want to do their own thing, they don't want to work for the government, they want to create something they can do on their own in their own companies… a lot of them have a special wish or the ability to be an entrepreneur… it's simply just a driver….*

Incubator managers suggested that the need for achievement exclusively stemmed from an internal drive and manifests as an ambition, a passion, or simply to do more for themselves. Clearly, there are other influences at play here that connect the need for achievement with starting a business. There are subtle differences in the way the different sample segments express their need for achievement. For entrepreneurs, it seems to be rooted deep in their psyche; however, for some of the employees, the need for achievement is linked with another goal. For example, Emp04M may feel the need to achieve to get married and have kids, whereas Emp03F, simply does not want to end up like her brothers and sisters. These aspects will be explored in greater length in the discussion section.

Need for Independence

The need for independence is closely linked with the need for achievement as individuals seek more autonomy over different variables and assume responsibility for their actions (Carsrud and Olm 1986; McClelland 1961). The need for independence motivates entrepreneurs to pursue actions expected to return financial independence and enhance self-determination (Wagner and Ziltener 2008). In two separate studies carried out in the UAE, Erogul and McCrohan (2008) and Estay et al. (2013) found the need for independence as a key predictor of entrepreneurial intentions and highlighted the antecedents of motivations for established entrepreneurs.

Ent01M: *I did not want to take a loan… I wanted to depend on myself… I thought I can do things from myself… I thought if I am doing this giving my time, effort and knowledge and things to the company then why not for myself… maybe it's human nature, the freedom to be your boss yourself….*

Ent02F: *I am not only a mother that has to stay at home… raising babies is not our only job… we have to study if I have education my babies will have education I will be different than a mother who is not educated so I think I want to change something in women to motivate them.*

Ent03F: *So I thought maybe you can do something to help yourself… I like being self-sufficient, to be independent… I just wanted my own income since I can remember… I did not like asking my mother, father, and now my husband, I wanted to do things for myself build things for myself I don't like asking people for anything….*

Ent04M: *I was asking my father for money and I hated that I needed to have something for myself… If you say to me why you don't go and get normal job or why you love this it's because you can do everything (in this business), its unstructured but you know the structure, but when you go to work you are restricted you have to do things their way… I don't want to be tied in a box….*

Similar to the need for achievement, the sample of entrepreneurs demonstrated a strong need for independence. In line with McClelland's (1961) work, all entrepreneurs associated the need for independence with autonomy, self-sufficiency and financial independence. Ent01M, "the freedom to be your boss yourself". Ent02F, "I am not only a mother that has to stay at home". Ent03F, "I just wanted my own income". Ent04M, "it's because you can do everything... work you are restricted". Apart from Ent02F, each participant seemed to want more control over different aspects of their lives and starting a business seemed to cater to this need for independence.

Emp01F: You have to start your business, you cannot just depend on the salary... it will be enough for maybe just last for one month... if you really want to start saving or if you really want to do something for yourself then you have to start doing something extra.

Emp02M: Because I had to work to help my family... and to achieve self-goals... I thought here finding a proper job is a little bit difficult... so if I could maintain the job before starting the business it will be more secure... If I have a job then I can pay the bills and cover some costs if needed.... Better than starting a business without any experience or funding....

Emp03F: Because you have full control... you can put through the actions that suit you, do things your way, you can have your own income you can make changes without thinking of others... securing my future, financially, I cannot guarantee I will be working for long so I need to be able to prepare for that... I don't want to accept my current situation and I don't want to quit when things get hard and I don't want to listen to people that demotivate me....

Emp04M: I have to do something from them not just for me... for me if the family is fine then it's fine for me I will be happy....

The employee sample seems to recognize the role of entrepreneurship in gaining independence; however, it does not demonstrate strong tendencies toward self-sufficiency. There is also an observable difference between the male and female participants. Interestingly, the male participants associated autonomy with catering for their family rather than for personal or self-interest. For example, Emp02M, "if I have a job then I can pay the bills and cover some costs if needed". Emp04M, "for me if the family is fine then it's fine for me I will be happy". Female participants demonstrate stronger need for independence Emp01F, "you have to start your business, you cannot just depend on the salary segment". Emp03F, "have full control actions that suit you, do things your way, you can have your own income". Differences in the need for independence between male and female participants may also have cultural connotations. For example, males are traditionally responsible for the family's financial security. This element is supported by the male participants' responses as they flag family needs before their own.

Inc01F: *Some say ok I will start my business because at one point I will be leaving my job… also for some it is about flexibility the need for independence, so if they have children they can do things according to their life style, but if they are working then there are some restrictions… they feel happy they can implement things without limitations….*

The sample of incubator managers confirmed some of the motivations behind the need for independence among Emiratis. Although income is a factor, the main motivation is autonomy and more control over their future. Inc01F, "do things according to their life style implement things without limitations". This is in line with recent findings that the need for independence as an entrepreneurial motivation is more common in resource rich contexts (Stephan et al. 2015).

Risk-Taking Propensity

Historically, risk bearing has been seen as a key function of the entrepreneur. For both Atkinson (1957) and McClelland (1961), the individual with high need for achievement was almost risk averse, opting for medium risk propositions. This is in line with the notion that entrepreneurs need a balance between risk aversion and high risk propensity to succeed

(Wagner and Ziltener 2008). The propensity to take risk has highlighted stark differences between the two main samples.

Ent01M: *I am risking my funds, time that I am spending here and not at work, trust of the market (reputation), these are big things to risk but it makes me aggressive in business it motivates me to do well because I am sure I believe whatever is good can be successful.*

Ent02F: *I am very safe in taking any steps... I did not start with a shop I started with a kiosk to know the demand and customers... I had orders in big quantities and I opened accounts in Thrifty, Ali Baba, I have customers, that's why it was a little bit safer.*

Ent03F: *I was afraid no one would take this because they have a lot of shops here in the same categories... I was scared nobody would buy it, but I also believed (in my product) if anyone would buy they would be happy.*

Ent04M: *I'm risking my finance, a normal life and reputation, I had a good job then I was nothing but I don't have any regrets... First and last is how to pay back the loan... I thought this was a big responsibility... calculating the return and the uncertainty of if I am going to be able to do it... we are not only looking for financial benefit but also looking to raise the UAE flag.*

The entrepreneurs highlighted they knew they were taking risks which involved finance, opportunity cost and, interestingly, reputation. However, risking these factors also seems to motivate them; Ent01M, "makes me aggressive in business it motivates me to do well". Ent02F, "I am very safe in taking any steps... I started with a kiosk to know the demand and customers". Ent03F, "I was scared nobody would buy it, but I also believed (in my product) if anyone would buy they would be happy". Ent04M, "I'm risking my finance... calculating the return and the uncertainty of if I am going to be able to do it... looking to raise the UAE flag". The reasons for adopting risk may be diverse among these entrepreneurs, but it is clear they have a healthy risk-taking propensity, which is balanced to manage the impact of risk.

These entrepreneurs are not blindly accepting all risks; rather risk taking seems to be based on careful calculation and the entrepreneurs gear risk to their strengths. This showcases elements of perceived behavior control, as opposed to locus of control, because entrepreneurs evaluate each option (Ajzen 1991). There is also a clear recognition and willingness to accept uncertainty. Again, as Ent01 and Ent03 demonstrate, this is balanced with the belief they will succeed. Lastly, as Ent04 highlights, there is also an element of nationalism which emerges at this stage, suggesting risk taking is rationalized with a sense of higher purpose. On the other hand, risk taking for the employee sample seems to be hampered by finance.

Emp01F: *Finance was the number one reason… I thought based on the list of items we had on our list somehow we needed a big budget… and probably people wanted to get money out of things they did not want and we thought the responsibility would be very overwhelming….*

Emp02M: *… without experience, without money liquidity in your bank account, it was risky to start a business after graduation…*

Emp03F: *The main issue was time and budget and risk because with starting a business you would not know if you would have a stable income every month but then work guarantees a stable income, for me this is the main reason I did not start a business….(with… finance ..time) I did not want the risk of borrowing money from people or the bank because I cannot guarantee that my business is going to succeed….*

Emp04M: *I have some plans… to buy land and rent it… or build shops and rent them… for me it is quite safety (low risk), I know it will take longer but it's safer for me, rather than doing some businesses wasting my money here and there with no guarantee of customers and maybe there will be a competitor this will be a headache for me… This is what I believe… some people want to have adventure – they would put themselves in jeopardy – they will take a loan if I win I win if I lose I lose – so this kind of people sometimes it works sometimes it does not – it's very risky… I cannot do this if I did not pay back the money then*

> *they will put me in jail… and all my reputation will go down in the water….*

In stark contrast to entrepreneurs, the employees demonstrated a lower risk propensity, interestingly all participants seem to rationalize risk in regard to finance. For the employee sample, the sense of a higher purpose did not emerge from the interview data. The importance associated with finance and the fact that the employee sample was largely made of moderate income families would suggest social class also has an impact on entrepreneurship in the UAE context. Emp01F, "finance was the number one reason". Emp02M, "without experience, without money liquidity in your bank account, it was risky to start a business". Emp03F, "work guarantees a stable income, for me this is the main reason I did not start a business". Emp04M, "some people want to have adventure – they would put themselves in jeopardy – they will take a loan if I win I win if I lose I lose – so this kind of people sometimes it works sometimes it does not – it's very risky". However, a deeper exploration also revealed undertones of an unwillingness to accept uncertainty.

The literature review revealed one of the key differentiators between entrepreneurs and managers, which is the entrepreneur's ability to accept uncertainty (Knight 2006; Langlois and Cosgel 1993; Praag 1999). Emp01F, "probably people wanted to get money out of things they did not want and we thought the responsibility would be very overwhelming". Emp03F, "I cannot guarantee that my business is going to succeed…". Emp04M, "doing some businesses wasting my money here and there with no guarantee of customers and maybe there will be a competitor this will be a headache for me". The inability of the employee segment to accept risk under uncertainty was the biggest divide between the two sample segments thus far. Most of the sample also highlighted the impact of government regulation in heightening the sense risk as financial failure in the UAE can lead to real jail time.

Inc01F: …*they are risking money, time, and also the reputation of the person.*

Inc02M: *Entrepreneurship is a lot about mitigating risks so it mean you know how minimize risk, to plan, research the market so you*

> *don't run your head against the wall... entrepreneurs accept risk and a true entrepreneur knows how to handle that risk....*

The sample of incubator managers corroborates what Emirati entrepreneurs are risking. The concept of risking reputation is particularly interesting because of its social and cultural connotations. Although reputation does not contain monetary implications, it does hold importance within the Emirati context, which was emphasized as further themes emerged.

Capacity to Innovate

From Bentham (1748–1832) to Schumpeter (1934), the most endearing quality of the entrepreneur is the ability to innovate. Innovation is a key criterion for distinguishing entrepreneurs from business owners. For Schumpeter (1934), only innovative entrepreneurs initiate start-ups, whereas organizers or managers effectively run established firms. Both of these can be the same people but their functions are inherently different. The ability to innovate not only separates entrepreneurs from managers, it also represents an avenue through which entrepreneurs can succeed in the face of adversity (Baumol 2010; Schumpeter 1934).

Ent01M: *I then defined what I wanted to do and chose the augmented reality business, this the SMART business, I have chosen a field which will be successful in 2020 so it's hard for the time being... we are trying to play it smart and bought some online learning platforms from Saudi Arabia and we are saying we are international company which is true because we have an agreement with the company... this is also a unique product in the UAE... I am renting out the office at different times in the week so this covers at least half of the cost of the rent....*

Ent02F: *I decided to do something new, here and in the GCC we are wearing these jellabiyas for special occasions and we don't like to repeat our clothes and this is costly, so I decided to do jellabiyas two in one, so by adding one more piece you can wear it twice when no one will know, this is a new idea… social media is very important even in my account I am putting my details and that's one of the main ways to get my customers we would not have had the same success by using the traditional methods of marketing… each six months you have to create something new so this is challenge for me bringing new ideas to the market….*

Ent03F: *I made a photo shoot and put it on Instagram from the first two weeks I sold the whole collection… I was dealing with some printing companies for writing on the boxes I wanted to show people that my products are unique… I was making with some good smell, high quality perfume, all garments are sent to the laundry before they are delivered to the customer, I was searching how I can be a luxurious style, unique….*

Ent04M: *Image, it was very important to build a certain image that we are a sports company different from others, going against the flow….*

These entrepreneurs demonstrated an innate ability to innovate, especially in the face of competition. Ent01M, "bought some online learning platforms from Saudi Arabia and we are saying we are international company…. this is also a unique product in the UAE". Ent02F, "I decided to do jellabiyas (Arabic Dresses) two in one… this is a new idea… each six months you have to create something new". Ent03F, "I was searching how I can be a luxurious style, unique". Ent04M, "we are a sports company different from others, going against the flow". This ability to innovate enabled them to get a foothold in the market, survive and compete. The employee sample segment, however, told a very different story.

Emp01F: *I talked to a lot of people who had variable income and this would have been useful for them, there is nothing like this in the UAE and there is also demand for antiques… what would happen to the inventory I will be buying, would I be able to sell everything, so the 50–50 element….*

Emp02M: *…it came for me the idea… after studying about business… (But did not start because) it's my makeup I don't know, I can't think about two major things at a time….*

Emp03F: *You cannot expect or guarantee that your business will be very successful there is a time line involved…we cannot make people like your idea or accept your business, we cannot guarantee that….*

Emp04M: *…if you don't have a new creative business then they will not accept it (government funding). You have a to have an idea that no one has done it, innovative, you know like this, how can you create these kind of ideas, very hard…*

The employee sample segment demonstrated an unwillingness or an inability to either act on their innovative ideas or accept the uncertainty associated with innovation. Emp01F, "nothing like this in the UAE… would I be able to sell everything, so the 50-50 element". Emp02M, "I can't think about two major things at a time". Emp03F, "we cannot make people like your idea…we cannot guarantee that". Emp04M, "how can you create these kind of ideas, very hard". There may be other factors at play which hindered the employee sample from innovating. For example, Emp01F and Emp03F did not seem to have the confidence to innovate. Whereas, Emp04M, had a perception that new business ideas may not be supported by government programs. In any case as Emp04M highlighted, being innovative did not seem to come easy. Nevertheless, the capacity to innovate further distinguishes the line between entrepreneur and employee segments.

Inc01F: *I think it's not about the idea it depends on her passion sometimes you can come up with a new idea and even if their idea was not rejected they would just disappear, the main reason is to continue working on it, so it's not just about the idea but level of commitment and their ability to take feedback….*

Inc02M: *Emiratis (younger generation) love what is new, a lot of them look very deep into what is new and then create something new by themselves so I think there is a level of innovation going on, it's just not the norm, it is still a very small portion of (Emirati) society… They do what they do, not just because they see it as an achievement but because they want to create and be creative, because it's exciting….*

The sample of incubator managers provided a mixed response on this sub-theme. Inc01F, "so it's not just about the idea but level of commitment and their ability to take feedback". Inc02M, "I think there is a level of innovation going on, it's just not the norm". They acknowledged the low levels of innovation in the UAE. However, Inc01F also emphasized the value of commitment above innovativeness in the UAE context. As outlined earlier, entrepreneurs were more likely to act on their innovative ideas. This is most certainly linked to their ability to take risks, but could also be linked to their levels of confidence. For example, the entrepreneur evaluation of innovative task, or perceived behavior control, was more positive because they were more likely to accept the risks and uncertainty involved. However, the proposition was perceived as low or acceptable risk because the entrepreneurs were also more confident of success.

Competencies developed by learning directly affect confidence (Lundstrom et al. 2013). This notion highlights a link between internal and external factors affecting UAE entrepreneurs, in that personality traits of risk-taking propensity, capacity to innovate and confidence are directly influenced by external inputs such as education and relevant experience that develop key competencies. This notion is supported by other studies that emphasize the role of competency based entrepreneurial education and its impact on entrepreneurial action (Lans et al. 2008; Mojaba et al. 2011). This study argues, as competencies increase confidence, they positively affect the entrepreneur's PBC and increase the likelihood of entrepreneurial action.

Theme Two: Family

Previous studies in the Middle East highlight lack of family support as the main barrier for female entrepreneurs (Mutairi and Fayez 2015; Sadi and Al-Ghazali 2012). However, the UAE presents an enigma because the family is perceived as a positive motivational or support factor for female entrepreneurs (Haan 2004; Hossan et al. 2013; Itani et al. 2011). The second theme of family is supported by sub-themes of family circumstance, family support, family approval, and commitment to family. The emerging themes partly supported the finding from previous studies in the UAE and the family emerged as a multifaceted factor that can have positive or negative effects on Emirati entrepreneurs.

Family Circumstance

As the literature review revealed, levels of motivation are bound in context (Graham and Weiner 1996; Murray 1938). Although, there were other environmental factors that influenced behavior and defined family circumstance (Eccles and Wigfield 2002; Nuttin 1984), interviews revealed that the main constant in the Emirati context is largely defined by this sub-theme. This finding is supported by previous studies in the UAE that highlighted family circumstance as a major influence on Emirati life (Erogul and McCrohan 2008; Sowmya et al. 2010).

Ent01M: *When I was a child and going to bed I was thinking of being a business man having my own business… my father had business in construction over 25 years, I was always going with my father to Majlis (sitting area for men) all his friends were doing business, maybe this is one of the reasons because I thought I want to be like them when I grow up… my father said be yourself, act yourself, be ready for the day when you are doing things for yourself, be free, job is good but you cannot be free these words echo in my head you understand these word 15/20 year after, when you are young they don't mean much because you think I am still young why should I listen to him….*

Ent02F: *…actually I forgot to mention that I am a mother of 2 children… I got married 6 years ago… my father and my sister also have their businesses… I remember I was in the Arabic class and we talked about Shaikh Zaid when he said women are half of the society, Shaikh Zaid is the one who inspired me… it directly came to mind because my dad had his own business…. So I was like I will do it!! Sat in my mind.*

Ent03F: *To be honest I got married a little bit early, I was nineteen… I came from a high income family to a low income family… my father is already having a business he is in real estate, my brother*

	has a business... I was thinking I would like to have a business because my father... I thought at the moment I have my father to look after me but later what might happen....
Ent04M:	*I am the eldest boy... I don't have my own family (not married) this was one of the sacrifices I made... I don't have financial responsibility to the family but I contribute... actually my father has his own business and he had never been an employee... and I think this is one of the influences on me... my uncle and both my grandfathers they all had their own businesses... I always use to go with my father when he use to travel, I was 12/13 years old I enjoyed that experience so maybe that also influenced me....*

This sub-theme revealed intimate details about Emirati entrepreneurs, their specific context and the range of factors that influenced them. Ent01M, "I was always going with my father to Majlis (men's sitting area)... I thought I want to be like them when I grow up... job is good but you cannot be free these words echo in my head". Ent02F, "I remember I was in the Arabic class... Shaikh Zaid is the one who inspired me". Ent03F, "I was thinking I would like to have a business because my father". Ent04M, "I always use to go with my father when he use to travel, I was 12/13 years old I enjoyed that experience so may be that also influenced me". The participants essentially revealed early influences that arguably developed different facets of their personality and made them who they are. Interestingly, every entrepreneur had a deep-rooted history of entrepreneurship in their family. This also seems to inspire them, instilling a need for independence and achievement.

Emp01F:	*One of my aunts also has a business she sells Abayas... my uncle, who is a business man, he still actually encourages me from time to time... I had a different opportunity but I could not go for it because my dad got sick and in that case family takes priority... family is a major factor but it depends... actually this was one the main reasons I did not start because I had to look after my dad... I would give up my job and go for business if I had to only look after myself... or if the family was doing well... or if*

	I was the youngest child… I am the eldest I am tied to responsibility (to family)….
Emp02M:	*…family would get affected if I failed in business and I was thinking it will have a higher chance of failure than succeeding… and some businessman can get help (financial) from their family but I could not get this at the time… within my family there are no business man… I am the eldest I had financial responsibilities and had to get another income to be able to help my family….*
Emp03F:	*I am in the middle I have 6 older and younger brothers and sisters…. there is no one in the family that owns a business… may be when I see my brothers and sisters, older than me, I don't want to end up like them, I want to be better than them, when my younger sister looks at me she should want to be like me….*
Emp04M:	*I have to work to support my family this was my first priority… I have financial responsibility I am the eldest in the family so I have to take care of them until they grow so I have to sacrifice something of myself….*

Circumstances faced by the employee sample segment are clearly quite different. Financial responsibility seems to be a prevailing issue that has arguably hampered their likelihood of new venture creation. Emp01F, "actually this was one the main reasons I did not start because I had to look after my dad". Emp02M, "I am the eldest I had financial responsibilities and had to get another income to be able to help my family". Emp03F, "may be when I see my brothers and sisters, older than me, I don't want to end up like them I want to be better them". Emp04M, "I have financial responsibility I am the eldest in the family so I have to take care of them". Unlike the entrepreneur sample, family largely had a negative influence on employees in regard to starting their business. It was also interesting to observe that there was no significant history of entrepreneurship in their families. Income or class may also play a role in this context.

Inc01F:	*Then there is also the issue that most of them are in a very comfortable situation, 80% of the Emiratis work for the Government*

> today where they have short working hours, good salaries and a safe working environment (job security)… it depends on the situation and the person's personality and their passion, ambition, persistence… the family can be positive and negative it depends on the family situation for everything… depends on the family… the more traditional the more strict… their background and their own family culture….
>
> Inc02M: *The family is probably supporting in the initial stages, especially when they are boot strapping, and they give them the encouragement to start and try it out so it does not matter if you fall of you (on your) face, we will pick you up so it takes away some of the stigma….*

In regard to circumstances, although insights into financial situation were lacking, the incubator managers did confirm the role of family as a positive or negative influence. Inc01F, "depends on the family situation for everything". Inc02M, "The family is probably supporting in the initial stages… they give them the encouragement to start and try it out so it does not matter if you fall on your face". Interestingly, employment was also highlighted. Well paid and secure government jobs have also been highlighted by previous research as they influence levels of motivation and intentions of potential Emiratis entrepreneurs (Horne et al. 2011; Sowmya et al. 2010). However, the lure of government jobs did not seem to hold back Ent01M and Ent04M, both of whom gave up lucrative government jobs and took a huge pay cut to start their businesses. The key difference here was variations in family circumstances and their financial position, which defined priorities and influenced how they perceived risk.

Family Approval

A number of studies carried out in the region have revealed the difficulties for female entrepreneurs in gaining family approval (Erogul and McCrohan 2008; Hossan et al. 2013; Itani et al. 2011). However, the interview data has produced some conflicting findings. While gaining approval is important, female entrepreneurs did not see this as a major barrier. The differences in findings may be explained by the fact that the sample involved in this study was made up of graduates and their family culture had already permitted them to participate in the world of work. Thus, gaining family approval was not a major concern for female participants in this study. Nevertheless, the fact that they mentioned it and the male participants did not, indicated this issue does affect female entrepreneurs in the UAE to some extent.

Ent02F: *…family is important… I would have started even if I had no support, but if they said what you are doing is wrong and it does not give society any benefit… If I got my support from my husband I don't care about anyone else… I think it's the same for most people that they only need the approval of their husband or their father. If the father said yes then they will not care ….*

Ent03F: *…my father is trusting about me and what I can do… my father decided with my husband because he cannot do anything without telling my husband… my husband he told me you can do whatever you can….*

For the entrepreneurs' sample segment, family approval only seemed to affect the female participants. Ent02F, "I think it's the same for most people that they only need the approval of their husband or their father". Ent03F, "my father decided with my husband because he cannot do anything without telling my husband". The approval is akin to permission in this context; whether the family supports the idea and the entrepreneur will be discussed in later sub-themes. However, it is important to make the distinction between permission and support at this juncture. The role of the male as the head of the family is also noteworthy.

Emp01F: *Yes (I discuss ideas) always with my mum… I like to take different perspectives I like to ask different people, my mum's opinion is important it may not change what I want to do but I might adjust… family is important but it depends mum's opinion vs someone sick (life and death) in the family is different..*

Emp03F: ...*my family would encourage me.... mum was the first person I talked to about the business....*

The employee sample confirmed that, although family played an important role for female participants, they did not need approval to take certain actions. They also highlighted the role of the mother in the approval process, as opposed to only the male family figure head. It was also encouraging to observe that although female participants clearly required some sort of approval from the family, mainly the male head of the family, they were not discouraged and were able to gain approval.

Inc01F: ...*maybe sometimes family and friends, actually most of the time, are barriers. Some families discourage to start their own businesses, it's like saying ok you have a job you are getting an income why do you need to do extra work. So they would rather have them in a job, it's also more secure....*

Only one of the incubator managers could provide insights into the family approval dynamic, highlighting the family as a discouraging element. Inc01F highlighted that although, if persistent enough, approval could be obtained, the family may initially discourage. The level of initial support or later approval may also rest on whether there is a history of entrepreneurship in the family. Otherwise, the family member responsible for granting approval may not understand the need to undertake additional risk or, indeed, additional work; Inc01F, "you have a job you are getting an income why do you need to do extra work?"

Family Support

Previous studies in the UAE have highlighted the importance of family support in determining success for entrepreneurs (Bahrami 2014; Erogul and McCrohan 2008). The interview data revealed family support mainly affected female participants positively. Unlike other countries in the region (Mathew 2010), family has been identified as a positive support mechanism for female entrepreneurs within the UAE (Bahrami 2014; Erogul and McCrohan 2008). Interview data also confirmed these findings. A crucial role of the family is linked to providing emotional and practical support (Krueger and Brazeal 1994). Along with practical support with children, the female entrepreneurs highlighted emotional support as the most important benefit. The importance of emotional support has also been recognized by previous studies in the UAE (Erogul and McCrohan 2008).

Ent01M: I had my work, my studies and my family, that was enough for me... not sure if that was a barrier.

Ent02F: My husband support me a lot he is taking care of the babies when I am not there, my family and my mother in law also help, they give me their opinion on the styles, garments, with the website whenever I need anything they will be there.... family is one of the reasons for my success, without them I would not be able to do all these things, actually if I did not get the support from my family I would not even finish my education....

Ent03F: I showed my husband everything he said OMG how did you do this... now you should do it (start-business) he helped me a lot because I was pregnant with my third baby... my sister helped me compare prices... My father was helping me and advising me on what I can do, different options....

Ent04M: ...the family is an enabler and a black hole because they want me to become like a normal person because I could have a big responsible position, but at the same time they are pushing me when they see my picture in the newspaper....

Similar to approval, family support mainly seemed to affect female entrepreneurs in the sample. Ent02F, "my husband support me a lot he is taking care of the babies... family is one of the reasons for my success". Ent03F, "I showed my husband he helped me a lot because I was pregnant with my third baby". Family support to establish and run the business was clearly very important to the female entrepreneurs. While family played an important role for male entrepreneurs, for example, Ent01M, "my family that was enough for me... not sure if that was a barrier". Ent04M, "the family is an enabler and a black hole". The family seems to weigh down the male entrepreneurs. In contrast, female entrepreneurs seem to benefit from the practical and emotional support provided by the family.

Emp01F: *When I told my mother she said the Emirati society is different from the international society so she said people are going to think this is ridiculous because people (Emirati) normally just give away their clothes and they don't seek money for these....*

Emp03F: *...maybe they see me differently, they see me as someone with more capability because I was an A student I don't need to be reminded of doing things and can count on me....*

Emp04M: *I have support from my family they are saying one day you will retire so do you want to live on the pension alone?*

Because the employee sample had not started a business, it was not possible to demonstrate the family support dynamic in this context. However, the participants did highlight the importance of family support. Emp01F, "when I told my mother she said people are going to think this is ridiculous". Emp03F, "maybe they see me differently… they can count on me". Emp04M, "I have support from my family. This suggested the level of perceived family support may encourage or discourage Emiratis to start the business". Emp03F, "also highlighted emotional support and possible impact on confidence derived from family support".

Inc02M: *The family is probably supporting in the initial stages, especially when they are boot strapping, and they give them the encouragement to start and try it out so it does not matter if you fall of you face, we will pick you up so it takes away some of the stigma....*

One of the incubator managers also highlighted the importance of emotional family support at different stages of the entrepreneurial process. As approval from a male figurehead in the family seemed to cancel out some of the negative cultural elements, it would seem the emotional family support also tended to pacify some of the social constraints placed on Emirati entrepreneurs.

Commitment to Family

In line with other sub-themes discussed thus far, commitment to family encompasses the importance Emiratis associate with family. This is also affected by the social roles assigned by traditional cultural and religious structures. The types of commitment toward the family were mainly expressed as emotional and financial. However, the level of commitment was determined by an individual's position among siblings and the family's financial health or social class. These factors also seemed to affect how individuals perceived risk and evaluated business propositions.

Ent01M: *I had my own issues, my father passed away in 2009... I had my younger brothers and sisters to look after, below 18, now after 6 year they are married and working so at that time... there were lots of possibilities and I had to choose, take care of the family or start a business.... actually I knew I postponed it I could have started in 2008... but you know how it is there are things you want and Allah wants....*

Ent02F: *...that's why I decided to leave my job... to find a better work life balance ... I was scared that I would not be able to manage (she took a pause here – her eyes watered - this is clearly an issue) – but I tried my best to balance but I don't think I lost that balance... may be sometimes it is normal but I am trying....*

Ent03F: *...but you know we are in the UAE and we are not telling our husbands that I want and I want, if he can do it then he will... but I know that I cannot ask him to buy me the things I'm used to, So I thought maybe you can do something to help yourself...*

Ent04M: *...it could mean having your own family, wedding, the nice cars, and I did sacrifice all these things... the business was one of the reasons I did not get married... because you know how expensive is it to get married here....*

Commitment to the family revealed some interesting aspects about the motivation of Emirati entrepreneurs. Again, the family seemed to act as a barrier or an enabler for entrepreneurs. Ent01M, "lots of possibilities and I had to choose, take care of the family or start a business". Ent03F, "I know that I cannot ask him to buy me the things I'm used to, so I thought maybe you can do something to help yourself". Commitment to family can also affect the way entrepreneurs work once they have started. Ent02F, "find a better work life balance I was scared that I would not be able to manage". Lastly, entrepreneurs may not see compatibility between business and family in regard to spending enough time with them. Ent04M, "it could mean having your own family, wedding I did sacrifice all these things… the business was one of the reasons I did not get married". Ent01M, "I had to choose take care of the family or start a business". In other words, they were unwilling to do both at the same time; this notion is also supported by responses from the employee sample.

Emp01F: *I don't come from a rich family so I wanted to have a different sources of income for myself and for my family… I actually did study accountancy to get a good job otherwise I wanted to be an artist.…*

Emp02M: *…within my family there are no business man I want to be the first one… it will help my family (non-financial) enhance them (socially)… it's important to help because they are my family I want to do good for them, help them ….*

Emp03F: *…when my younger sister looks at me she should want to be like me…Emp04M: Honestly if I want do business then I cannot do both work and business you cannot have time for both of them, especially you have to take care of your family also, three responsibilities.. Obviously something will be damaged, either the business, your work or your family…*

The incubator managers did not have much to say in regard to this sub-theme. However, it is clear from the account of the employee sample segment that commitment to the family and acting in accordance with their benefit is a major influence on the way Emiratis behave. Emp01F, "I actually did study accountancy to get a good job otherwise I wanted to be an artist". Emp02M, "it's important to help because they are my family I want to do good for them". Emp04M, "then I cannot do both work and business you cannot have time for both of them, especially you have to take care of your family".

Comments from the employee sample demonstrated that young Emiratis, whether choosing employment over starting a business, choosing a certain degree program over another or simply intending to achieve more, are heavily affected by their commitment to the family. This sub-theme suggests young Emiratis are firmly committed to putting their family's needs above their own.

In summary, the two themes described thus far highlight some of the key factors that affect Emirati entrepreneurs. These factors influence their intentions and the strength of their conviction in acting upon their intentions. This chapter also highlights the strength of closely related external factors such as family, what Liñan (2011) calls closer valuation. However, it would seem for the Emirati entrepreneur the closer environment is deeply rooted and has far reaching consequences for their personal ambition and decision making.

References

Ajzen, I. (1991). The theory of planned behaviour. *Organizational Behaviour and Human Decision Processes, 50*(2), 179–211.

Alschuler, A. (1967). *The achievement motivation and the development project: A summary and review.* Center for Research and Development on Educational Differences. Harvard University press.

Atkinson, J. W. (1957). Motivational determinants of risk-taking behavior. *Psychological Review, 64,* 359–372.

Bahrami, S. (2014). Entrepreneurship intentions and perceptions in the UAE: A study of moderating effects of gender, culture and family. *International Journal of Small Business and Entrepreneurship Research, 2*(4), 37–50.

Baum, R., Locke, E., & Smith, K. (2001). A multidimensional model of venture growth. *Academy of Management Journal, 44*(2), 292.

Baumol, W. J. (2010). *The Microtheory of innovative entrepreneurship. The Kauffman Foundation Series on Innovation and Entrepreneurship.* Princeton University Press. ISBN: 1400835224.

Carsrud, A., & Brännback, M. (2011). Entrepreneurial motivations: What do we still need to know? *Journal of Small Business Management ProQuest, 49*(1), 9–26.

Carsrud, A., & Olm, K. (1986). The success of male and female entrepreneurs, a comparative analysis of the effects of multidimensional achievement motivation and personality traits. In R. Smilor & R. I. Kuhn (Eds.), *Managing take-off in fast-growth companies* (pp. 147–162). New York.

Creswell, J. (2009). *Research design: Qualitative, quantitative, and mixed methods* (3rd ed.). Newbury Park: Sage.
Eccles, J., & Wigfield, A. (2002). Motivational beliefs, values, and goals. *Annual Review of Psychology ProQuest Central, 53*, 109–132.
Erogul, M., & McCrohan, D. (2008). Preliminary investigation of Emirati women entrepreneurs in the UAE. *African Journal of Business Management, 2*(10), 177–185.
Estay, C., Durrieu, F., & Akhter, M. (2013). Entrepreneurship: From motivation to start-up. *Springer Science+Business Media New, 11*, 243–267.
Gartner, W. (1988). Who is an entrepreneur? Is the wrong question. *American journal of small business, 12*(4), 11–32.
Graham, S., & Weiner, B. (1996). *Theories and principles of motivation*. London: Prentice Hall.
Haan, H. (2004). *Small enterprises: Women entrepreneurs in the UAE*. Centre for Labour Market Research & Information (CLMRI).
Horne, C., Huang, V., & Al Awad, M. (2011). *Entrepreneurship in the United Arab Emirates*. The Global Entrepreneurship Monitor (GEM). Retrieved from http://www.gemconsortium.org/docs/2626/gem-uae-2011-report
Hossan, C., Parakandi, M., & Saber, H. (2013). Entrepreneurial knowledge, preferences and barriers of female business students in the Middle East. *Journal of Business and Policy Research, 8*(2), 83–99.
Itani, H., Sidani, S., & Baalbaki, I. (2011). United Arab Emirates female entrepreneurs: Motivations and frustrations. *Equality, Diversity and Inclusion: An International Journal, 30*(5), 409–424.
Knight, F. (2006). *Risk, uncertainty and profit*. Cosimo, Inc. ISBN 1602060053.
Krueger, N., & Brazeal, D. (1994). Entrepreneurial potential and potential entrepreneurs. *Entrepreneurship Theory and Practice, 18*, 91–104.
Langlois, R., & Cosgel, M. (1993). Frank Knight on risk uncertainty and the firm: A new interpretation. *Economic Inquiry, 31*, 456–465.
Lans, T., Hulsink, W., Baert, H., & Mulder, M. (2008). Entrepreneurship education and training in a small business context: Insights from the competence-based approach. *Journal of Enterprising Culture, 16*(4), 363–383.
Liñan, F. (2011). Regional variations in entrepreneurial cognitions: Start-up intentions of university students in Spain. *Entrepreneurship & Regional Development, 23*(3–4), 187–215.
Lundstrom, A., Zhou, C., Friedrichs, Y., & Sundin, E. (2013). *Social entrepreneurship: Leveraging economic, political, and cultural dimensions*. Springer Science & Business Media. ISBN: 3319013963.

Mathew, V. (2010). Women entrepreneurship in Middle East: Understanding barriers and use of ICT for entrepreneurship development. *Journal of International Entrepreneurship & Management, 6,* 163–181. Springer Science+Business Media.

McClelland, D. (1961). *The achieving society.* Van Nostrand: Free Press Paperback.

Mojaba, F., Zaefarianb, R., & Azizi, A. (2011). Applying competency based approach for entrepreneurship education. *Social and Behavioral Sciences, 12,* 436–447.

Murray, H. A. (1938). *Explorations in personality.* New York: Oxford University Press.

Mutairi, A., & Fayez, F. (2015). Factors motivating female entrepreneurs in Kuwait. *Journal of Applied Management and Entrepreneurship, 20*(1).

Nuttin, J. (1984). *Motivation, planning, and action: A relational theory of behavior dynamics.* Hillsdale: Erlbaum.

Praag, M. (1999). Some classic views on entrepreneurship. *De Economist. ProQuest Central, 147*(3), 311.

Sadi, M., & Al-Ghazali, B. (2012). The dynamics of entrepreneurial motivation among women: A comparative study of business women in Saudi Arabia and Bahrain. *Asian Academy of Management Journal, 17*(1), 97–113.

Schumpeter, J. (1934). *The theory of economic development: An inquiry into profits, capital, credit, interest, and the business cycle.* New Brunswick/London: Transaction Publishers. ISBN: 0878556982.

Shane, S., Lockea, E., & Collins, C. (2003). Entrepreneurial motivation. *Human Resource Management Review. Elsevier Science Inc, 13,* 257–279. https://doi.org/10.1016/S1053-4822(03)00017-2.

Smith, J., Flowers, P., & Larkin, M. (2009). *Interpretative phenomenological analysis theory, method and research.* London: Sage Publications. ISBN: 9781446203897.

Sowmya, D., Majumdar, S., & Gallant, M. (2010). Relevance of education for potential entrepreneurs: An international investigation. *Journal of Small Business and Enterprise Development, 17*(4), 626–640.

Stephan, U., Hart, M., and Drews, C. (2015). Understanding Motivations for Entrepreneurship; A Review of Recent Research Evidence. Enterprise Research Centre. Retrieved from https://www.enterpriseresearch.ac.uk/.../2015/.../Understanding-Motivations-for-Entreprenurship

Wagner, K., & Ziltener, A. (2008). *The nascent entrepreneur at the crossroads: Entrepreneurial motives as determinants for different type of entrepreneurs.* Discussion Papers on Entrepreneurship and Innovation.

6

Entrepreneurship in the UAE (II)

Part two of entrepreneurship in the UAE reports on the research results, outlining the major themes of culture and perceived behavior control. These themes emerged from interviews conducted with young Emiratis that all reported to have entrepreneurial intentions as undergraduates, but not all of them were able to act on these intentions. These themes help explain the entrepreneurial gap and related challenges and opportunities for entrepreneurship within the UAE. The theme of culture includes the sub-themes of collectivist nationalism, perceptions of entrepreneurship, religion and tradition, and, lastly, reputation. The theme of perceived behavior control includes the sub-themes of access to finance, access to support, competition, education, market knowledge, and time. As with the previous chapter, all of the themes were supported by direct quotations from the participants themselves.

Some of the sample's demographic information is repeated here for the benefit of the reader. The phenomenon of entrepreneurship is inextricably bound in individual experience and context, which makes its study more complex. In addition, this chapter also provides the individual context of the main sample which should provide the reader with a more intimate view of the sample, without compromising individual privacy. The real names of participants have been omitted. The sample of four graduates that managed to start a business is represented as, for example, "**Ent01M**". The "Ent" indicates they are entrepreneurs, the number indicates the sample count and M or F indicates whether they were male or female. Similarly, "**Emp**" is used to represent the sample of graduates who are employees and in effect failed to start a business but found employment. In the same way, "Inc in **Inc01F**" represents the smaller sample of two incubator managers.

The demographic statistics in part (I) highlights that an equal number of male and female participants were used in interviews. Excluding the incubator manager sample, participants' age ranged from 24 to 36 years, with an average of 28.75 years. With the exception of two participants, each graduate was from a different subject area. Subject areas have been omitted but they ranged from Accounting to Mechanical Engineering. With the exception of one participant who graduated five years ago, the sample had graduated within the last two years. All of the participants were Emiratis, UAE nationals working in Sharjah or Dubai. However, their permanent residence is located in a range of different Emirates. For the incubator managers sample, the "(Bus)" highlighted in Table 5.1 under "number of employees", indicates the number of businesses currently under incubation.

Interestingly, when comparing the average age of each sample group separately, there was a noticeable difference. For example, the average age of entrepreneurs was 30.75 years whereas the employees' average was 26.75 years. The four-year difference may indicate that these entrepreneurs did not jump into starting a business straight away and waited after graduation. This notion is supported by the fact that nearly all entrepreneurs interviewed were previously employed for a short while and some continued to post-graduate education.

Further attention to the entrepreneur sample also highlighted that all of the businesses were nascent businesses. The number of employees ranged from 7 to 4 and the average age of these businesses was 2.25 years. This had positive implications for the study as the participants were able to provide the latest insights into the experience of opening a business from an Emirati perspective.

Individual Context

This section provides a narrative of the individual context of each participant from the main sample of entrepreneurs and employees. Despite having written consent of participants to use their real names, codes have been used to ensure privacy and to avoid any potential situation that may compromise the participants' position due to implications of the analysis section. Ent01–04 represent the sample of entrepreneurs, whereas Emp01–04 represent the sample of employees.

Ent01M is a single Emirati male who had been interested in starting a business since an early age. As an undergraduate he had dabbled in real estate but never actually opened an official real estate business. After initially graduating with a Bachelor's degree he worked for a public sector organization for a few years. During this time, he also completed his Master's degree, but left his high ranking position as a government employee to start his business. Ent01M is passionate about technology and that is one of the reasons he started an IT business. He is the eldest of four children and from a well-to-do family that has a history of entrepreneurship, extending from his grandfather to his father. However, Ent01M's chosen field of business is very different from that of his father and grandfather. Ent01M is yet to break-even but explained that income streams were improving.

Ent02F is a married Emirati female who married at an early age and is now a mother of two children. She had always wanted to own a business. She is passionate about advancing female leadership and this is also the topic of her Master's degree. After initially graduating with a Bachelor's degree she worked for a bank, but left to complete her Master's, and it was during the Master's program that she was able to take advantage of a government funded program to initiate her business in the fashion industry. Ent02F is from a well-to-do family with a history of entrepreneurship, as her father and sister also own businesses. However, Ent02F has opened her business in an entirely different sector. Her business is profitable and succeeding in a competitive market and Ent02F is in the process of scaling up her business this year.

Ent03F is a married Emirati female who married at an early age and is now a mother of three children: she always wanted to own a business. In fact, after receiving a small loan from her father, she started her business in the fashion industry as an undergraduate. After graduating, she focused on the business but now Ent03F also works for a public sector organization. Ent03F is from a well-to-do family. There seems to be no history of entrepreneurship in the family as both her parents and husband are working in the public sector. Ent03F runs a luxury fashion business that is profitable. She seems to be content with keeping the business small, although her customer base extends across the UAE.

Ent04M is a single male who is passionate about motor sports. His business is a sports marketing company, one of only a few in the region. After graduation, Ent04M worked in the public sector for a few years before leaving his job to start his business. During this time, he also completed his Masters. Ent04M is from a well-to-do family. There is a strong history of entrepreneurship in the family, with his father, uncles and grandfather all owning successful businesses. However, Ent04M has opted for a very different sector to open his own business. Ent04M is yet to break-even.

Emp01F is a single female who wanted to start a business but, due to a range of reasons, she had to find employment. She is from a moderate income household. Emp01F is the eldest of three children and, due to unforeseen events; she is partially responsible for generating an income for the family. After graduation, Emp01F started working in a public sector organization, which she feels is rewarding but not challenging her enough. She has a strong academic background and is still planning to open her business one day.

Emp02M is an Emirati male who has recently got married. He is the eldest of six children and has financial responsibilities for the extended family. Emp02M is from a moderate income household. He had always wanted to own a business, but after graduating with a Diploma he had to start work as soon as possible; so he started work in a public sector organization. He has been working there for a few years, during which time he has gone back to University to finish his BA, which he completed this year. Emp02M has a very distinct business idea, in the food and beverage sector, which he wants to implement.

Emp03F is a single female who wanted to start a business but, due to a range of reasons, she chose to find employment. She is the fourth in a family of six children. She has a strong academic background and works for a well-known multinational company. Emp03F is from a moderate income household but she does not have any financial obligations to the family. Emp03F would like to open a café but for the time being she is inundated with a heavy work load and cannot see this happening in the near future.

Emp04M is a single male who came close to starting a business many times in his life, but has not managed to do so for a range of reasons. He is from a moderate income family. Emp04M is the eldest out of four children and, due to unforeseen circumstances, he has full financial responsibility for the household. Therefore, when he graduated with a diploma, he had to find employment and start working for a public sector organization. In this time he has finished his Bachelor's degree.

Theme Three: Culture

Culture can shape an individual's motivation, self-concept, personality, and cognition (Bandura 1977; Urban 2010). Principally considering the US context, Schein (1983, 2004) argued that cultural influences shaped entrepreneurs' assumptions and outlooks on how their firms should operate; therefore, social culture largely directed organizational culture. However, in regard to specific cultural influences on starting a business, although some studies in the United States found that culture indirectly affected individual attitudes and perceived success in certain actions, they did not find direct links between entrepreneurial intentions and culture (Krueger and Brazeal 1994; Krueger et al. 2000). In the Middle East, culture plays a stronger role in predicting entrepreneurial action and studies conducted in the region indicated stronger correlations between culture and entrepreneurial intentions (Erogul and McCrohan 2008; Itani et al. 2011). Within the theme of culture, sub-themes of collectivist nationalism, perceptions of entrepreneurship, religion and tradition, and, lastly, reputation appeared most consistently in the interview responses.

Collectivist Nationalism

In a study of Emirati and non-Emirati youths in the Emirate of Ras al Khaimah (UAE), Jones (2011) found Emirati youths to have high nationalist tendencies. A sense of nationalism can instill higher purpose and spur individuals to achieve more: countries such as China and South Korea exemplify this notion well (Christiansen & Koeman 2015; Jones 2011). Furthermore, the previous theme of family pointed to a collectivist culture within the UAE. Along with family, responses from the entrepreneurs' sample outlined a clear sense of duty toward country and community. Although some have argued that collectivism can have a negative effect on entrepreneurship (Zeffane 2014), for the entrepreneurs in this study, collectivism and nationalism combined point to a powerful source of motivation that drives them to better themselves and their society.

Ent01M: …at the same time you put something to the community and that's good because if you do something good you are helping so many people… I will give something from myself and do something for the country… I understand the people, the area the culture…because you want to feel like you have left something good for the community…

Ent02F: I feel like the government gives us everything so when I finish my MBA I have to do something in return… so having a business is not only for myself this is something I have to do for my country…

Ent04M: I would say the UAE is like my family I have to raise the flag as much as I can the UAE flag is important to us… it's like something that you belong to… for the national feeling the Emirati feeling… When it comes to the sports business I want to show the people that we have Emirati Talent, we have the Heroes, this is what I have been working for, it really means something because I belong to this country this is also everyone's duty, because the UAE given us a lot you know… not many people can say they were cheering on an Emirati in the middle of the desert, I don't want to give this up and go behind the desk…

All but one of the entrepreneurs exhibited strong nationalistic and collectivist tendencies. Ent01M, "something to the community… something for the country". Ent02F, "I feel like the government gives us everything… I have to do for my country". Ent04M, "I would say the UAE is like my family I have to raise the flag as much as I can…this is also everyone's duty, because the UAE given us a lot". While religion and culture also played a role, the sense of nationalism and community seemed to pour out a sense of obligation linked to the benefits provided by the country and political leadership.

Emp01F: …people around the world have a negative view of the middle east but the UAE gave me so much, like free education free health care so perhaps somehow if I started this business and it made it locally, regionally and if it goes international, then perhaps we can show the world a different perspective about us, that if we are given the opportunity we have the potential we have ambition we are more than what is usually shown on the TV or media…

Emp02M: I can help them (other family members) open businesses as well, it will also help the country grow in terms of the economy, because it affect back towards us on other levels… having more local businesses will enhance the UAE income and it will contribute to general conditions like education etc.

Emp03F: …when they talk to the younger generation they say that you are the country's leaders, you are the ones that will drive the country to be ambitious, try to succeed in your life we will support you with whatever you need…

The response from the employee segment was similar to the entrepreneurs and it confirmed that Emiratis' ambition was influenced by a sense of nationalism, which mainly stemmed from the political leadership. Emp01F, "the world have a negative view of the Middle East but the UAE gave me so much, perhaps we can show the world a different perspective about us". Emp02M, "having more local businesses will enhance the UAE income". Emp03F, "younger generation they say that you (the young generation) the country's leaders, you are the ones that will drive the country to be ambitious, try to succeed". Similar to the entrepreneur segment, arguably, the sense of nationalism for female participants in the employee segment came from the political leadership and an obligation to the country. A notion of needing to prove themselves to the world was also interesting.

Inc01F: …they want to start a business to contribute to the UAE economy? Like prove to the world that Emiratis can run their own businesses… they want to build the UAE brand and market the UAE to the outside world… most of the people here are attached to the UAE and we want to give something back to the UAE… because you know our leaders provided us with a lot of facilities like education and healthcare, so we are blessed in this country so we feel it's the time to give something back contribute back to the UAE…

Inc02M: …they are following a vision of being the number 1, I think that is something that is very much pushed and emphasized through the ruler's office…

The sample of incubator managers captured the sub-theme of collectivism and nationalism well. Inc01F, "they want to start a business to contributing to the UAE economy… prove to the world… give something back to the UAE… our leaders provided us with a lot of facilities". Inc02M, "they are following a vision of being the number 1… emphasized through the ruler's office". The sense of nationalism seemed to drive Emiratis and instill a sense of ambition and the achievement motive. The role of government in promoting nationalism was also noteworthy.

Perceptions of Entrepreneurship

Previous studies in the UAE have highlighted positive perceptions of entrepreneurship, especially among Emirati undergraduates (Sowmya et al. 2010). These positive perceptions also explain high levels of entrepreneurial intentions among Emirati undergraduates (Bahrami 2014; Itani et al. 2011; Sowmya et al. 2010). The interview data confirmed largely positive perceptions of entrepreneurship. Furthermore, the data also revealed that positive attitudes toward entrepreneurship mainly derived from GSPs and political leadership. Participants expressed positive attitudes toward entrepreneurship: for example, they saw it as a worthwhile task and a valuable career option that was well supported. However, one female participant did highlight negative cultural perceptions of entrepreneurship.

Ent01M: …one of the factors is the country is pushing me… the country is saying our people we are supporting you, the leaders are pushing us, the rules and regulations every year,

	they are pushing so now were are confident when we know we have a leader that support and pushes us… so that is a big push you feel it inside…
Ent02F:	…culture can be negative but I had the support from my husband… culture in general is not supportive not too much because culturally people don't want people to be better than them… I had to go to a networking event to market, I found there a lot of negative questions like, oh you still have time you are still young… when locals (Emiratis) get all this support they know they will pay different than others, quarter of the amount, they will dream big… they imagine that everything will be very fast, they will get this and this…
Ent03F:	Culturally Emiratis looks at businessmen and women more favorably…
Ent04M:	…we need to change the stereotypes about Emirati… to start something creative innovative that can go to international level… most of the businesses here are like restaurants, laundries etc we want to change the stereo type not just for the international community but also for the local people… because some people think we are lazy… but we are capable…

The entrepreneur sample's perceptions toward entrepreneurship were slightly mixed. They were either positive or identified with a need for positive change. Ent01M, "now we are confident when we know we have a leader that support and pushes us". Ent03F, "culturally Emiratis looks at businessmen and women more favourably". Ent04M, "we need to change the stereotypes about Emirati… to start something creative innovative". One of the female participants did identify with a negative cultural perception of entrepreneurship. Ent02F, "culture in general is not supportive not too much because culturally people don't want people to be better than them". However, this might be explained through her personal experience of trying to break into a male dominated industry as a young female entrepreneur. Nevertheless, participants' perceptions of cultural support for entrepreneurship and entrepreneurial opportunities were largely positive.

Emp01F: Cultural does effect, but I had many experiences at college that sort of created a bullet proof vest that I don't really care... as long as it is serving a good purpose then it's fine... actually like this country motivates me... whenever you open the news every day you see successful people you see the number of people who are going after what they like...

Emp02M: For myself in the UAE there are a lot of opportunities they are pushing people to start... I have read quite a lot about it in newspapers about Khalifa Fund also there are a lot of accounts on Instagram which supports these business ideas...

Emp03F: General culture in Sharjah, UAE is supportive of entrepreneurship, I just feel like from the new businesses that young people started, they are supported because they want them to do well... may be the older generation is less supportive... because they say to start the business you have to be a certain age you cannot start when you are too young and there are certain types of businesses that you cannot go into (religious reasons) all of my friends are ambitious, they all want to start a business...

Emp04M: ...culture is important but it depends on their family – the rich families are encouraging their kids to do something with business, but some families for example me... they have the family responsibility I have to work to support them so they can have a decent life... my friends motivating me they have their own real estate business, especially in Dubai, they are recommending me to buy a land so that is pushing me...

Comments from the employee sample segment explained some of the variations identified in the entrepreneurs' responses. As with the entrepreneur sample, the responses from the employee sample were largely positive. Emp02M, "in the UAE there are a lot of opportunities they are pushing people to start". Emp03F, "general culture in Sharjah, UAE is supportive of entrepreneurship. However, as one of the female participants alludes to, there may be some less obvious deficiencies". Emp01F, "culture does affect, but I had many experiences at college that sort of created a bullet proof vest that I don't really care".

More importantly the participants also highlighted a complicated web of influences that develop participants' cultural perceptions about entrepreneurship. Emp03F, "they are supported because they want them to do well… maybe the older generation is less supportive… you have to be a certain age you cannot start when you are too young, certain types of businesses". Emp04M, "culture is important but it depends on their family". There was an observable difference in the way entrepreneurs' and employees' perceptions toward entrepreneurship were developed. For entrepreneurs, government support and political leadership were the main influencers. However, for employees this field extended to include friends and family.

Inc01F: …it's an international city so it's like grabbing that opportunity, rather than being a normal employee and a consumer for other business may be you can start your own business and take this opportunity of being a National… this is what I hear, even me if I have a new idea they say why are you wasting your time or ok there are risks involved in the business why you want to take that risk, this discourages people…

Inc02M: Absolutely culture is changing, I can see huge steps forward in just the last 3.5 years that I have been here. I would say generally there are not many people that start something and then close it down because it did not work out and then start again, people try to make sure they move forwards in a responsible way and not in this. com way, so it seems there is a lot of sensibility in start-ups here… Emiratis are used to a high standard of living today compared to any other country especially here in Dubai and AD, so boot strapping your way to a start-up you must be quite committed anyway and really believe in what they are doing…

Comments from the incubator managers support this sub-theme as Emirati perceptions of entrepreneurship were largely positive and aligned with perceptions of entrepreneurial opportunity. Inc01F, "maybe you can start your own business and take this opportunity of being a National". Inc02M, "people try to make sure they move forwards in a responsible way and not in this. com way". Incubator managers also highlighted the complex nature and origins of these perceptions. Inc01F, "they say why you are wasting your time or ok there are risks involved in the business why you want to take that risk". This confirmed that while cultural perceptions about entrepreneurship were largely positive, there were elements that discouraged and even discriminated against risk, which could ultimately play a negative role in developing Emirati perceptions. Interestingly, incubator managers also highlighted that positive perceptions of entrepreneurship were linked to high levels of perceived opportunity. This notion is supported by previous studies in the UAE and beyond (Dayan et al. 2013; Berglund 2007).

Religion and Tradition

Webber's work on the protestant work ethic highlights the historical recognition of the role that religion can play in influencing individuals and the economic decisions they make (Kim 2012). More recently, in a study of over 90,000 Indian workers, Audretsch (2007) found religion to significantly affect the likelihood of starting a business. Religion plays a big role in the UAE and encompasses tradition and culture to a large extent. Previous studies in the UAE have highlighted that Emirati entrepreneurs are strongly affected by religion and tradition (Erogul and McCrohan 2008). Therefore, although these two constructs may have been highlighted separately in studies carried out in different regions, a decision was made to combine these two aspects. The interview data supported findings from previous studies that emphasized the importance of religion and tradition in the UAE society (Erogul and McCrohan 2008).

Ent01M: The main thing was I did not want to start with a loan… I did not want to pay interest because of religious reasons, this feeling of obligation to help the country is from first our teacher (Prophet) Mohammad (PBUH) then from family my parent have taught me to do good things, then

	outside the home today and before we had great leaders who were really pushing their own people to do good and they were helping, providing them with the opportunity... for example when Shaikh Zaid said we don't create countries without men...
Ent02F:	When I started the business I have to meet suppliers many different people, a lot of guys, this is not really allowed... for example we changed the color of the Abaya (type of everyday clothing) culturally this is not accepted, but change is happening this young generation is really strong so we will change it...
Ent04M:	This sense of family I think its general feeling in the UAE... the way we are raised the way we are close to the UAE I think... from day one when Dubai was a small family everybody used to help each other and it's grown from there... it's my duty to make sure the one next door is living as happy as I am... This sense of duty & responsibility comes from our religion maybe and also the way we have been raised...

The sample of entrepreneurs placed high value on religion and tradition. These factors were inseparable and interwoven into the cultural tapestry of the UAE. However, religion and tradition seemed to affect entrepreneurs in different ways. For some, they were clearly a source of inspiration. Ent01M, "this feeling of obligation to help the country is from first our teacher (Prophet) Mohammad (PBUH)... family... then outside the home today and before we had great leaders". Ent04M, "this sense of duty & responsibility comes from our religion maybe and also the way we have been raised". Other entrepreneurs saw tradition as a barrier but also highlighted change. Ent02F, "I have to meet suppliers many different people, a lot of guys, this is not really allowed... change is happening this young generation is really strong". As outlined by Ent02F, religion and tradition can also restrict entrepreneurship. However, as highlighted in the earlier themes of family, these only seemed to affect female entrepreneurs. Furthermore, religion and tradition also seemed to affect access to finance, more specifically interest based finance.

Emp01F: I feel like it's an obligation (to give something back to society) it's just part of being a good citizen... it's just general moral to be a good citizen... it's part of our religion...

Emp04M: ...religion has an effect for example we cannot buy and sell pork because we are Muslims it will not be acceptable for us, so it restricts the type of business but that's it...

The employee sample's responses to religion and tradition were similar to the entrepreneurs' responses; however, it did not register as a major factor. Similar to the sub-theme of family support, the lack of importance employees associate with religion and tradition, in starting a business, may be due to the fact they have not started a business. Nevertheless, it did come across as an important behavior moderator. Emp01F, "to be a good citizen... its part of our religion". Emp04M, "religion has an effect... so it restricts the type of business but that's it". Thus, religion and tradition seemed to either inspire Emiratis or at times pose challenges. These challenges seem to be more prevalent for female Emiratis; nevertheless, they are overcoming these challenges and perceive positive change.

Inc01F: ...this is how we feel? You know this is coming from the love we have for the country and for the leaders also our life style... we are attached to our country... this is the place where we belong.

Inc02M: ...well I think the traditional culture is not really speaks for trying out something new but I think this is what the ruler is successfully trying to change...

Although the incubator managers did not mention religion, they did corroborate the multifaceted effects of tradition. On the one hand a sense of belonging, lifestyle and love for the country, with nationalistic undertones, seemed to inspire Emiratis and guide their moral compass. On the other hand, tradition (pressure from older generations) deterred them from trying out something new (Inc02M). However, positive change was also highlighted by different segments.

Reputation

Although research on reputation and its effects on entrepreneurship is lacking within the UAE, studies conducted in related disciplines, for example, business to business relationships, found that Emiratis placed a high value on reputation and the consequences of injured reputations were highly damaging (Houjeir and Brennan 2014). The sub-theme of reputation was gender specific as none of the female participants mentioned it as an issue. On the other hand, all male participants highlighted the importance of reputation or social standing.

Ent01M: I am risking funds, time that I am spending here and not at work and trust of the market, my reputation.

Ent04M: I'm risking reputation I had a good job then I was nothing, but I don't have any regrets…

Emp02M: I mean something that will maintain for me my self-confidence, have enough money and also a good reputation in front of people…

Emp04M: …reputation is very important in every country… if I will lose my own money and I will go to the prison and my family reputation will go down especially if I have sisters then this will affect them when they want to get married, because one family members reputation extends to the rest of the family…

The key difference between entrepreneurs and employees seems to be that entrepreneurs were able to risk their reputation. Ent01M, "I am risking… my reputation". Ent04M, "I'm risking reputation". Conversely, the employees were not willing to risk their reputation. Emp02M, "I mean something that will maintain… good reputation in front of people". Emp04M, "reputation is very important… my family reputation will go down". There were strong links with risk-taking propensity and fear of failure; however, reputation was a strong influence on male Emiratis, maybe because, as Emp04M highlighted, one family member's reputation extends to the rest of the family.

Inc01F: Emiratis feel they have to prove themselves to their colleagues, family, customers and the world... starting a business and the success of the business ... will automatically translate that if the business is successful the owner is also a successful person.... this related to the UAE culture, for example, if one person tried to start and failed then maybe her friends will talk, so it's like the word of mouth that will be spreading about that person (reputation) like sometimes that will scare the person... Obviously there is this fear of failure so they think if they fail people will remember this about me and its like that will be stopping them from starting a business...

Inc02M: Risk of losing their image, the stigma of failure which a lot of them try to avoid which stops them from even starting... its culturally not acceptable to fail and a high number of start-ups will fail, simply it's the name of game for each hot area where there are a lot of entrepreneurs there will be a lot of failures because obviously not all of them can be successful...

Incubator managers confirmed the importance of reputation in the UAE context; however, they also asserted that it is not a gender specific factor. Inc01F, "they will say look at this person she tried to start a business but she failed... so it's like the word of mouth that will be spreading about that person's reputation". Inc02M, "Risk of losing their image, the stigma of failure which a lot of them try to avoid which stops them from even starting... it's culturally not acceptable to fail". In a close-knit society such as the UAE, losing one's reputation or social standing is clearly a strong influence; although it may have stronger connotations for male Emiratis, incubator managers suggested it is not limited to them but also affects the females. Furthermore, risk to reputation also seems to add to the fear of failure.

Theme Four: Perceived Behavioral Control

PBC is a key construct of an individual's intentions and one of the best predictors of behavior (Ajzen 1991). Related to an individual's confidence and perceived capabilities of undertaking and succeeding in certain tasks, PBC equates closely with Bandura's (1997) concept of self-efficacy (Ajzen 1991; Shane et al. 2003). These two constructs are important in developing an individual's understanding of the entrepreneurial process and are widely used in entrepreneurship research (Krueger et al. 2000). Studies in Europe and the Middle East have found PBC to be the best predictor of entrepreneurial intentions and behavior (Almobaireek and Manolova 2011; Liñan 2011).

Unlike the generalized locus of control, which relates closely with an individual personality trait, PBC assesses the likelihood of success in each task based on its own merit (Ajzen 1991; Rotter 1966; Shane et al. 2003). This is an important insight as it emphasizes an individual's ability to make calculated decisions to choose one task over another. The sub-themes related to perceived behavior control were access to finance, access to support, competition, education, market knowledge, and time. These sub-themes outline the range of factors that Emiratis seem to use in weighing the decision to start a business or find employment. The presence of these factors seems to be key in determining whether Emiratis have the confidence to start their business.

Access to Finance

A number of studies in the region have highlighted difficulties in access to finance (OECD 2013; Rocha et al. 2010). In a study of bank lending to SMEs in the Middle East and North Africa (MENA) region, Rocha et al. (2010) found that, globally, UAE had one of the lowest percentages of finance loaned to SMEs. The same study also found only 20% of SMEs had access to finance. This is considerably lower than other parts of the world; for example, in Latin America 40% of SMEs had access to finance (Rocha et al. 2010). Some of these difficulties can be attributed to limitations posed by the regulatory framework; for example, bankruptcy carries jail time.

However, as the study by OECD (2013) highlights, limitations of access to finance may be further aggravated by the entrepreneurs' unwillingness to use formal sources of finance. Organizing finance was highlighted as a challenge, but despite the apparent difficulty in accessing finance, the entrepreneur sample did not highlight this as a major issue.

The entrepreneurs either used their own savings or received help from family members. This is in line with findings from previous studies in the region, which show that entrepreneurs in the UAE generally financed their own start-up or received help from family members (OECD 2013; Rocha et al. 2010)

Ent01M: I did not want to start a business with a loan and start in the negative… I reached a point when I had enough money (from job savings)…

Ent02F: …finance was the main challenge… because whatever I saved from my job I used all the money for the business and Alhamdulillah we were getting special rates (SME) this is what helped me a little bit…

Ent03F: …so one day my father and my husband decided to give me around ten thousand AED and said if you can do anything with this then go ahead, this is your money and you can do whatever you want…

Ent04M: I had to invest my own money and bring in people that shared the same values and understood what they were doing… but also had to make many other sacrifices like stability, time, 16 hour days…

The sample of entrepreneurs saw finance as a challenge but one they were able to overcome. Ent01M, "I had enough money (from job savings)". Ent02F, "finance was the main challenge… I saved from my job". Ent03F, "so one day my father and my husband decided to give me around ten thousand AED". Ent04M, "I had to invest my own money". Entrepreneurs were able to finance their business mainly through their own savings, apart from Ent03F, who received a loan from her father. In contrast, the employee sample saw access to finance as a bigger challenge and one which they could not overcome.

Emp01F: space was an issue my home is not that big (for storage) and actually the inventory would have cost… oh I did not say the budget (finance) was probably the first and biggest reason because to buy the inventory we did not really have

	the budget… based on the list of items we had somehow we needed a big budget… the responsibility would be very overwhelming…
Emp02M:	I did not start a business because I had no available funding, no experience and lack of knowledge about the procedures…
Emp03F:	I did not have my own money and even now I have expenses I need to pay… I did not want the risk of borrowing money from people or the bank because I cannot guarantee that my business is going to succeed… starting a business you would not know if you would have a stable income every month but then work guarantees a stable income, for me this is the main reason I did not start a business…
Emp04M:	but if you want to start a business you need money so you need to have a good budget you cannot get a lot of government support these days… for example I want to do a business now this shop (in the mall) will cost me 100 or 200 thousand ok where is the location most of them are very bad, perfect places the rent is too high, how can you afford the rent and your equipment….

Access to finance was a dividing factor for the sample of employees. Emp01F, "I did not say the budget (finance) was probably the first and biggest reason… the responsibility would be very overwhelming". Emp02M, "I did not start a business because I had no available funding". Emp03F, "I did not have my own money… I did not want the risk of borrowing money… work guarantees a stable income, for me this is the main reason I did not start a business". Emp04M, "you need money… you cannot get a lot of government support these days… how can you afford the rent and your equipment". There is something more here than just the unavailability of finance: the employee sample seems to shy away from the risk of investment. As Emp03F stated, the employee sample would rather opt for the security of a stable income.

There is a clear unwillingness to take on the risk of securing finance. This may be amplified by harsh UAE bankruptcy laws and the fact that the employee sample did not have savings. Bankruptcy or failing to pay a legal debt leads to jail time in the UAE. The lack of savings also highlights class and the family's financial background as a factor. Arguably, the entrepreneurs were able to save because they were not financially committed to their families, whereas the employees were financially committed to their families, precisely because they were from low to moderate income families. Once again, a range of interconnected influences emerged from this sub-theme, highlighting the complex nature of entrepreneurship in the UAE.

Inc01F: I think most have good salaries so can put aside some money and save for the business. Also we have programs for SMEs, Like Dubai SME offers discounted license so this will encourage…

Inc02M: I think there are a lot of funding schemes so the usual financial barriers don't really exist here…

Incubator managers corroborated the use of personal savings as a likely source of finance for Emirati entrepreneurs. Inc01F, "most have good salaries so can put aside some money and save for the business". However, they also repudiated the perception of lack of government funding. Inc02M, "financial barriers don't really exist here". Interestingly, other than benefiting from discounted business services, entrepreneurs did not access government funding schemes. This falls in line with empirical evidence from the region which suggests that new entrepreneurs, especially graduates, prefer self-finance or family loans to bank loans or equity finance (Rocha et al. 2010).

Access to Support

Previous studies in the UAE have indicated that Emirati entrepreneurs are able to bring together a wide range of stakeholders, such as family, friends, government agencies, and formal and informal mentors, to organize an effective support network (Goby and Erogul 2011; Haan 2004; Kargwell 2012). Interview data confirmed this finding from previous studies. However, GSPs appeared most consistently in the interviews. These will be explored further in later themes.

Ent01M: I went to the Mohammad Bin Rashid foundation the Dubai SME that time I was still looking… I did not succeed to come up with something… I felt I had the knowledge and money and now I need a partner not for funding but someone to work with me I needed people to give me their time I tried my friends but did not have much luck they were not really interested, some wanted to do it but did not have the passion…

Ent02F: I had support from SME and I was member of the impact HUB (incubator) as well… SME gave all types of support, like special rates… I had a partner, I depended on my partner for knowledge because he had a business like this back in the UK… important to have a good coach (mentor)… you need the support but if it is not there you have to carry on and you will find it somehow… I had a lot of support from my family…

Ent03F: …so I was talking to the ministry and they asked if I want a shop…. My husband, father and sister were helping… one of my friends was working at the ministry and she was helping me a lot…

Ent04M: SME were supportive, but I think the idea was new for them… it's not like we got it from the sports federation or someone else who believe in us, we said no let us go and fight the fight… If you talk about this year, even though we did well I would say we failed… but that did not stop us it made us stronger…

On the surface, it would seem yet again there is a gender divide when it comes to access to support; the female entrepreneurs seemed to access a wide support network whereas the male entrepreneurs could not. However, the reason for this may not be gender specific and instead relate to the type of business. Both male entrepreneurs are involved with non-traditional businesses and this may have hampered support from government entities, friends and potential financers because they could not fully comprehend the business. As one of the incubator managers outlined earlier, the UAE culture is still relatively uncongenial to innovation.

Ent01M, "I went to the Mohammad Bin Rashid Foundation… I tried my friends but did not have much luck". Ent02F, "I had support from SME and I was member of the impact HUB… I had a partner… important to have a good coach… support from my family". Ent03F, "I was talking to the ministry… my husband, father and sister were helping… one of my friends was working at the ministry". Ent04M, "SME were supportive, but I think the idea was new for them". Female entrepreneurs highlighted an increased awareness and access to a network of support.

Whether male entrepreneurs lacked effective support due to the newness of their idea or lacked awareness of organizing support networks, support seemed to fall short of expectations for them. Family as a possible avenue of support was also not mentioned by the male entrepreneurs. However, whether the entrepreneurs accessed support or not was less important at this stage than their awareness of its existence. This factor arguably played a role in their perceived success in starting a business. This sub-theme also highlighted potential differences in the way male and female entrepreneurs might perceive the entrepreneurial environment within the UAE.

Emp01F: No I did not try them (government support), I did not know there were any … I knew Khalifa Fund, there is a lot of competition for their support … the process takes a long time… I think it's difficult to reach out to them, some of my friends actually tried with a better business idea than ours, but they did not get any funding or support at the time, so I did not reach out…

Emp02M: I know about government support for Nationals but you have to apply and make a file and cover all different aspects of your business or idea… so you have to have the experience and knowledge to cover these to get it right and I did not have these at the time… some businessmen can get help (financial) from their family but I could not get this at the time…

Emp03F: maybe they don't have wasta as well to get the government support.

Emp04: To be honest we live in a country where we use so much wasta (who you know)… you know some influence for recommendation from some high positions to say this is my good friend or something, we recommend him, this is happening a lot if you don't have wasta then it will be very difficult… you cannot get rid of wasta it's like the corruption in India…

This sub-theme also draws a dividing line between the employee and entrepreneur samples. Emp01F, "I did not know they were any … I knew Khalifa Fund etc… but I think it's difficult to reach out to them". Emp02M, "I know about government support for Nationals, but you have to apply and make a file… I did not have these at the time". Emp03F, "maybe they don't have wasta". Emp04, "to be honest we live in a country where we use so much wasta… if you don't have wasta then it will be very difficult". Although the employees were largely aware of support, government or otherwise, it was not seen as a viable option and perceived as unattainable. The concept of Wasta, or 'who you know', was also important as it seemed to affect confidence in attaining support. The employee sample highlighted a low level of perceived access to support.

Although the incubator managers did not specifically highlight entrepreneurs' perceptions about the access to support, they confirmed the availability of a wide range of support mechanisms. Inc01F, "like the Chamber of Commerce, Dubai SME etc". Inc02M, "there is Khalifa Fund, there is the ICT fund, DTEC… Incubators… family". One of the incubator managers also highlighted the challenges of accessing support. These will be discussed further in later sections.

Competition

Previous studies in the UAE highlight an intensely competitive SME sector (Goby and Erogul 2011). Although GSPs for Emirati nationals help reduce the impact of competition (Haan 2004), they do not fully compensate for disproportionate competition faced by Emiratis from a large expat community which represents over 85% of the population

(Ryan et al. 2011), even though GSPs are designed for positive discrimination in favor of Emirati nationals. The entrepreneurs did not perceive competition through the national and non-national lens, which is arguably a healthy outlook. However, they did highlight an intensely competitive market place and overwhelming competition from large multinationals.

Ent01M: Ejari (a government tendering platform for contracts) has lots of companies there… competition from large multinationals is hurting, I don't know if you can even call it competition, when you compete on price and quality its competition, but competition when customers don't even look at you because you are too small, no one said it but we felt it….

Ent02F: There is huge competition especially in the garment industry… so I decided to do something new… something unique to be better than the competition…

Ent03F: I was afraid no one would take this because they have a lot of shops here in the same categories… I was searching for something unique I started with ribbons on boxes…

Ent04M: …teams we are competing against come as factories and we entered as private with our own money… we are fighting with sharks, we have first time entrepreneurs fighting with large multinationals… but competition can make you faster, for example there are so many people that are doing the same thing but there not many like us in the market…

The entrepreneurs' sample revealed they face intense competition, especially from larger firms. However, they mainly seemed to use innovation to overcome competition. Ent01M, "competition from large multinationals is hurting… when customers don't even look at you because you are too small". Ent02F, "huge competition especially in the garment industry, so I decided to do something new". Ent03F, "lot of shops here in the same categories… I was searching for something unique". Ent04M, "we have first time entrepreneurs fighting with large multinationals, but there not many like us in the market". Interestingly, the two entrepreneurs that mention competition from multinationals are also the ones that are yet to break-even. As highlighted in previous themes, these entrepreneurs also lacked effective support; yet again the main factor here may be the type of business. Nevertheless, entrepreneurs are facing up to competition to survive and as in the case of Ent02F and Ent03F making a profit.

Emp03F: …to be honest with you there are a lot of shops that have new ideas so I think it would have been difficult to compete…

Emp04M: I know it will take longer but it's safer for me (buying and selling land), rather than doing some businesses wasting my money here and there with no guarantee of customers and maybe there will be a competitor this will be a headache for me…

Understandably, the employee sample did not have much to say on the subject of competition because they were not in business. However, two employees did reveal that the perceived threat of competition may have deterred them from starting the business. Emp03F, "I think it would have been difficult to compete". Emp04M, "there will be a competitor this will be a headache for me". This indicates that the threat of competition affects entrepreneurial intentions and actions before and after start-up. There was also something more here; it seems that employees were unwilling to accept the uncertainty posed by the threat of competition. Yet again, this unwillingness to accept uncertainty may represent one of the most important differentiators between employees and entrepreneurs.

Inc02M: …very often we find that start-ups have not done enough research… so run into the problem that there are 3 or 4 companies that are doing something very similar and may be they are better than you? With larger companies competition is often underestimated so direct or indirect competition can have a big effect on the success of the company…

The incubator managers did not have much to say on this sub-theme, but did corroborate the threat of larger firms. Interestingly, lack of research into potential competitors was also highlighted as an issue by the incubator manager sample. This points to deficiencies in effective entrepreneurial education or experience.

Education

Previous studies in the UAE highlighted the importance Emiratis place on entrepreneurial education. Young Emiratis expect universities to play a leading role in facilitating education and also helping as incubators to create new ventures (Sowmya et al. 2010). However, these studies also highlighted deficiencies in the entrepreneurial education programs offered by universities in the UAE (Erogul & McCrohan; Itani et al. 2011; Sowmya et al. 2010). Findings from the UAE were echoed elsewhere and went further to highlight negative effects on entrepreneurship caused by ineffective entrepreneurial education (Fayolle 2006). However, participants revealed mixed experiences of education.

Ent01M: …the effect of education was huge, not just a certificate but real learning, learning from others… knowledge is very important, I also continued with studying because I thought I needed to get more knowledge, because I thought I would be better prepared. I was prepared but not prepared that I have everything… this was time when I first thought I want to start my own business… preparation for my business, honestly 50% and 50% from my own knowledge…

Ent02F: I decided to open my business whilst I was doing my Master's because, when I started actually the first time when I opened a kiosk… I was studying things in my university and doing things in the real world as well… it helped me a lot because it focused on what I was doing, it's coming in the same time… (Parallel) actually MBA is what really changed me…

Ent03F: …you know after studying the foundation of business… I got a lot (of) papers and started to write my mission and vision, I do not know why I did that maybe because I did not have the trust in myself (self-belief) I thought to myself why don't you start writing maybe something will help you… so I started writing my business plan… I remember it was project on this when I was studying so I started putting together different things the mission, target logo etc… for

	financial calculations I was searching for these on Google as well… but I remember doing them in college I was studying it and I have a lot of copies about that so it was easier…
Ent04M:	…education is what you want from it when you want it… when I studied engineering it structured my brain then my MBA helped me in the business side… the business model we learnt really helped me understand the structure what I am doing now…

The sample of entrepreneurs revealed a heavy influence from education. At times education seems to indirectly impact the process of entrepreneurship and serve as an aid to build confidence, Ent01M, "I also continued with studying because I thought I needed to get more knowledge". Ent03F, "I do not know why I did that maybe because I did not have the trust in myself". At other times, it seems to have a direct impact on entrepreneurs, preparing them for business or representing the key ingredient in the start-up process. Ent04M, "the business model we learnt really helped me understand the structure of what I am doing now". Ent02F, "I decided to open my business whilst I was doing my Master's". The responses from entrepreneurs highlight the multifaceted role of education within the entrepreneurial process. It not only instills confidence, but provides practical support and guidance before and after the start-up process. As Ent02F revealed, entrepreneurial education was most effective when amalgamated with real world practical input.

Emp01F:	I was part of many activities and programs we won one of the competitions, these activities strengthen my intentions to some extent… they gave us a clearer general idea of how a business plan should look like…
Emp02M:	I thought of becoming a businessman after high school… the idea came to me after studying about business…
Emp03F:	When we did a business course about a business plan here I thought about starting a business, because I thought we had a unique idea… preparation for business, may be kind of in terms of the finance calculations and so on I am not sure…

Emp04M: I was working I also continued with my study so I could gain the knowledge and experience to start my own business… we have learnt from the college a lot but we did not really get any real knowledge, it should involve real life even for the small things, like this kiosk, I think you can do these kind of small things in the beginning…

The sample of employees confirmed the multifaceted role of education. Employees highlighted the importance of education in developing entrepreneurial intentions. Emp01F, "I was part of many activities and programs we won one of the competitions, these activities strengthen my intentions". The employee sample also identified education as a source of inspiration and confidence. Emp02M, "the idea came to me after studying about business". Emp03F, "when we did a business course about a business plan here I thought about starting a business". However, there was also dissatisfaction with education. Emp04M, "we did not really get any real knowledge, it should involve real life even for the small things, like this kiosk". This last comment also highlighted the diverse range of educational offers available to Emiratis.

Participants in both sample segments suggested education prepared them for business. In the case of Ent02F, it was instrumental because her MBA program was geared toward different stages of her start-up. However, others, for example, Ent01M and Emp04M also highlighted its limitations. Differences in the way participants viewed the impact of entrepreneurial education may relate to their diverse experiences and interactions with education. This also highlights inconsistencies in approach and the way universities deliver entrepreneurial education.

Inc01F: …in general education is positive, it's good but if they want to focus more on entrepreneurship then there should be a major in entrepreneurship… so they can be better prepared… there should be more public private partnership for it to be more effective…

Inc02M: …here are some good entrepreneurial programs that eliminate a lot of myths associated with entrepreneurship… we have been at all of the Emirati universities what we have found is that in the region they tend to think of businesses that are either to do with clothes or food and that seems to be the focus I have seen very few IT based business I think it probably has something to do with Education…

The incubator managers partly corroborated what was said by the sample of entrepreneurs and employees. However, they were more critical and suggest education had a bigger role to play. One of the incubator managers touched on the subject of public and private partnerships to improve the effectiveness of entrepreneurial education. This is an important point because most of the entrepreneurs that managed to start a business had benefited from public and private partnerships. These partnerships also highlight the most effective way forward in integrating practical real life aspects within entrepreneurial education.

Market Knowledge

In a study of UAE graduates and the factors that influence first generation entrepreneurs, Kargwell and Inguva (2012) highlighted the lack of effective market knowledge as one of the key barriers to entry and a cause of failure for Emirati entrepreneurs. For potential entrepreneurs, market knowledge also related to perceived behavior control (Sommer and Haug 2010). As effective market knowledge increased, so did the perceived likelihood of success in undertaking entrepreneurial action (Ajzen 1991; Krueger and Brazeal 1994). The entrepreneurs largely confirmed they had at least some market knowledge. However, the interviews also highlighted entrepreneurs' efforts to gather additional market knowledge. This emphasized the importance of market knowledge to Emirati entrepreneurs and how they applied it to manage risk and make effective decisions.

Ent01M: I started in technology because I am in technology, I am a technology person… In the market there are technology platforms in education… I thought to research the market I did research for two years… I learnt and understood a lot,

	the fast changes in the market, I saw that all technologies are becoming SMART… I even went abroad to get more knowledge and share business information…
Ent02F:	I saw demand for huge quantity because I got a lot of requests when I started the first one… so when I started to second one… again I got request for big quantities… Deira is a central place where all the nationalities come and they buy specially big quantity… so we found the demand and we bring more staff… they are only going around to get the requirements from others and now we are bring over huge quantities, he found a lot of demand for the wholesale as well, so this was the third step…
Ent03F:	I started to think about what I should do, I started looking for a tailor because I cannot do everything at the same time, like have a tailoring shop as well as, the cost would have been too high if I did everything so I decide that in the beginning maybe I can go to someone to do this for me… my sister helped me to check and compare prices…
Ent04M:	…this is a complicated business… I had to research so many things to understand the market, this was very important for us…

The entrepreneurs placed great importance on market knowledge and the need to understand the market. Ent04M, "I had to research so many things to understand the market". More importantly, entrepreneurs relied on market knowledge to make calculated business decisions. Ent01M, "I did research for two years… I even went abroad to get more knowledge and share business information". Ent02F, "he found a lot of demand for the wholesale as well, so this was the third step". These entrepreneurs seemed to take a step by step approach to gathering information and market knowledge before exercising judgment. This also highlighted the role of market knowledge in making calculated decisions.

Emp01F:	…nothing like this in the UAE… there is also demand for antiques… I felt society was going towards this direction… I talked to a lot of people who had variable income and this

	would have been useful for them… hygiene was an issue… we did not want to get into health issues and we did not know the process behind it perhaps this one the reasons we did not start…
Emp02M:	…yes opportunities in the market many… a lot of government support and lots of different types of business that were in fashion… especially online businesses but did not pursue at the time because of lack of knowledge about the market in the UAE…

Although the employee sample segment recognized the entrepreneurial opportunity, they did not seem to possess, or were unable to obtain, all the relevant market knowledge required to start the business. Emp01F, "there is also demand… we did not know the process behind it perhaps this one the reasons we did not start". Emp02M, "yes opportunities in the market many… did not pursue at the time because of lack of knowledge about the market in the UAE". This is an important factor to consider when trying to understand the differences between samples of entrepreneurs and employees. Both recognized opportunity and started with limited knowledge of the market: however, the entrepreneurs demonstrated a strong commitment to gather additional market knowledge, to make calculated decisions.

Arguably, this was also one means of minimizing risk and may be a reason entrepreneurs were able to accept higher degrees of uncertainty and risk. Furthermore, on the surface it may seem Emp01F and Emp02M did not start a business because they did not have effective market knowledge; however, there is also a link with their original ambition and motivation. The entrepreneurs were in a similar position before they took entrepreneurial action. Arguably, they were able to take entrepreneurial action because of stronger ambitions and motivation, which led to stronger entrepreneurial intentions.

Inc01F:	Some people have discovered their real interest what they want to do for the rest of their life, others have to find it… it depends on the situation and the person's personality and their passion…

Inc02F: …funds needed are miscalculated, it's almost always takes longer than you think… so the practical business knowledge… because you cannot calculate into the plan the unforeseen problems… then there is also a lot of emphasis on the product and not the other things that affect your business…

The incubator managers confirmed the need for effective market knowledge and also highlighted that gathering effective market data may depend on levels of motivation and the strength of entrepreneurial intentions.

Time

There is insufficient empirical data on the relationship between time and its impact on entrepreneurs. The way participants perceived time and its relationship to undertaking additional tasks consistently appeared in interviews and emerged as a sub-theme. This sub-theme closely connected with the need for achievement, but also contained distinct elements. For example, although allocating free time efficiently may have related to the need for achievement, the perceived availability of extra time indicated the availability of an extra resource. Thus, if an individual believed they had free time, then they were more likely to undertake additional tasks. Furthermore, this sub-theme also highlighted the individual's perception of the right time. This related to the individual's self-confidence or the alignment of relevant resources required by him/her to undertake additional tasks.

Ent01M: I could have studied (doubled my Master's) worked and started a business … but I did not want to do all these at the same time… being rational and logical I thought there would be a right time to start… it was suitable because fitted in with my studies…

Ent02F: Yeah because just quit my job to do my masters… I was free so I have a chance to do something so I decided to open a business because I really wanted to do it… it was the right time to do it…

Ent03F:	I had free time I decided I should do something with this money… I found something to do in my free time… mostly in my free time you can see I am a little bit sad a little bit nervous… since I was a child I was helping my mother to take care of my brothers and my sisters… I think it depend on this life style of your family… so I saw that my parents were not getting any free time…
Ent04M:	…free time is uncomfortable I feel like lost… I feel like I am not doing anything beneficial and I question my benefit…

The responses from entrepreneurs highlighted a perception of a right time to carry out new or additional tasks. Ent01M, "I did not want to do all these at the same time… being rational and logical I thought there would be a right time to start". This may also indicate an alignment of resources and circumstance which make it possible to start a business. Arguably, the interview data thus far indicates slight differences in circumstances can make the difference between starting a business or not.

The perceived availability of extra or free time is also important in calculating the likelihood of success in a given task. Ent02F, "I was free so I have a chance to do something so I decided to open a business… it was the right time to do it". Ent03F, "I had free time I decided I should do something with this money". Ent04M, "free time is uncomfortable I feel like lost". Thus, if individuals felt they had extra time and additional situational factors such as family, work and education were aligned, then their perceived success in a given task was higher, making it more likely for them to engage in additional tasks.

Emp01F:	I have extra time but I always find something to re-use the time… I am writing no its serious, I want to be productive… sometimes I think about start a business… but sometimes rather than just thinking and thinking I like to do something productive….
Emp02M:	I always want to do something (small vacation is good) but otherwise I am confused… I need to achieve something and manage my time…my nature maybe but I wanted more although I did not have time I think the man have to do as much as he can….

Emp03F: The main issue was time and budget and risk… for me it more about focusing on one thing so when I was at college I would rather focus on my studies than starting a business. When I thought of starting a business I looked at all the options and thought working was the best option at the time, but now I don't want to start a business whilst I am working… I did not want to do two things at the same time… now I am working so I don't have time for anything else… it takes my whole day so I cannot do more… also my time, because if I start a business then I would have to give up my time with my family or the time that I allocate for myself…

Emp04M: Honestly if I want do business then I cannot do both work and business you cannot have time for both of them, especially you have to take of your family also, three responsibilities… Obviously something will be damaged, either the business, your work or your family, there will be some cost.

Inc01F: …time, I have some students that are studying, working and want to start a business…

This sub-theme also highlights key differences between the two samples. Clearly, participants faced similar challenges of managing time between work, family, themselves and the potential business. This was corroborated by one of the incubator managers. However, the employee sample demonstrated a clear unwillingness to divide their time to entertain a possible venture. Of course there were a number of factors that fed this unwillingness, some of which have already been highlighted. However, as with market knowledge, the reluctance to allocate extra time to a possible business venture clearly highlights differences in levels of motivation and arguably strength of entrepreneurial intentions.

In summary, the two themes described thus far highlight some of the key factors that affect Emirati entrepreneurs. These factors influence their intentions and the strength of their conviction in acting upon their intentions. This chapter also highlights the strength of closely related external factors such as family, what Linan (2011) calls closer valuation. However, it would seem for the Emirati entrepreneurs, the closer environment is deeply rooted and has far reaching consequences for their personal ambition and decision making. The third and fourth major themes are discussed in the next chapter. The fifth theme "role of government" is an example of an environmental factor that does not seem closely related, but has far reaching consequences for the participants. Government forms part of the social framework that heavily influences Emirati and helps shapes them as individuals. This theme has been discussed separately in Chap. 7, which then leads onto defining the Emirati entrepreneur.

References

Ajzen, I. (1991). The theory of planned behaviour. *Organizational Behaviour and Human Decision Processes, 50*(2), 179–211.

Almobaireek, W., & Manolova, T. (2011). Who wants to be an entrepreneur? Entrepreneurial intentions among Saudi university students. *African Journal of Business Management, 6*(11), 4029–4040. https://doi.org/10.5897/AJBM11.1521.

Audretsch, D. (2007). *The entrepreneurial society.* Oxford University Press. ISBN: 978-0-19-518350-4.

Bahrami, S. (2014). Entrepreneurship intentions and perceptions in the UAE: A study of moderating effects of gender, culture and family. *International Journal of Small Business and Entrepreneurship Research, 2*(4), 37–50.

Bandura, A. (1977). *Social learning theory.* New York: General Learning Press.

Bandura, A. (1997). *Self-efficacy: The exercise of control.* New York: Freeman.

Berglund, H. (2007). Opportunities as existing and created: A study of entrepreneurs in the Swedish mobile internet industry. *Journal of Enterprising Culture, 15,* 243–273.

Christiansen, B., & Koeman, J. (2015). *Nationalism, cultural indoctrination, and economic prosperity in the digital age.* Hershey: IGI Global. ISBN 9781466674936 1466674938.

Dayan, M., Zacca, R., & Benedetto, A. (2013). An exploratory study of entrepreneurial creativity: Its antecedents and mediators in the context of UAE firms. *Creativity and Innovation Management, 22*(3), 223–240.

Erogul, M., & McCrohan, D. (2008). Preliminary investigation of Emirati women entrepreneurs in the UAE. *African Journal of Business Management, 2*(10), 177–185.

Fayolle, A. (2006). Effect and counter effect of entrepreneurship education and social context on Student's intention. *Estudios de Economica Aplicada, 24*(2), 509–523.

Goby, V., & Erogul, M. (2011). Female entrepreneurship in the United Arab Emirates: Legislative encouragements and cultural constraints. *Women's Studies International Forum, 34*(4), 329–334. https://doi.org/10.1016/j.wsif.2011.04.006.

Haan, H. (2004). *Small enterprises: Women entrepreneurs in the UAE*. Dubai: Centre for Labour Market Research & Information (CLMRI).

Houjeir, R., & Brennan, R. (2014). *Cultural influences on the antecedents of trust in B2B relationships: A study of Financial Services in the United Arab Emirates*. Paper presented at 30th Annual IMP Conference, Bordeaux.

Itani, H., Sidani, S., & Baalbaki, I. (2011). United Arab Emirates female entrepreneurs: Motivations and frustrations. *Equality, Diversity and Inclusion: An International Journal, 30*(5), 409–424.

Jones, C. (2011). *Economic, social, and political attitudes in the UAE: A comparison of Emirati and non-Emirati youth in Ras al Khaimah*. Paper prepared for the Gulf Comparative Education Society (GCES) Symposium, United Arab Emirates.

Kargwell, A. (2012). Comparative study on gender and entrepreneurship development: Still a male's world within UAE cultural context. *International Journal of Business and Social Science, 3*(6), 44–55.

Kargwell, S., & Inguva, S. (2012). Factors influencing the first generation entrepreneurs: An analytical study on the graduates of UAE universities. *International Journal of Business and Social Science, 3*(7), 143–149.

Kim, S. H. (2012). *Max Weber. The Stanford encyclopedia of philosophy*. Retrieved from http://plato.stanford.edu/archives/fall2012/entries/weber

Krueger, N., & Brazeal, D. (1994). Entrepreneurial potential and potential entrepreneurs. *Entrepreneurship Theory and Practice, 18*, 91–104.

Krueger, N., Reilly, M., & Carsrud, A. (2000). Competing models of entrepreneurial intentions. *Journal of Business Venturing, 15*(5–6), 411–432.

Liñan, F. (2011). Regional variations in entrepreneurial cognitions: Start-up intentions of university students in Spain. *Entrepreneurship & Regional Development, 23*(3–4), 187–215.

OECD. (2013). *Competitiveness and private sector development new entrepreneurs and high performance enterprises in the Middle East and North Africa OECD*. International Development Research Centre, OECD Publishing. ISBN 9264179194.

Rocha, R., Farazi, S., Khuori, R., & Pearce, D. (2010). The status of bank lending to SMEs in the Middle East and North Africa Region: The results of a joint survey of the Union of Arab Banks and the World Bank. *The World Bank & The Union of Arab Banks*. Washington, DC, and Bruit.

Rotter, J. B. (1966). Generalized expectancies for internal versus external control of reinforcement. *Psychological Monographs, General and Applied, 80*, 1–28, American Psychological Association.

Ryan, J., Tipu, S., & Zeffane, R. (2011). Need for achievement and entrepreneurial potential: A study of young adults in the UAE. *Education, Business and Society: Contemporary Middle Eastern Issues, 4*(3), 153–166.

Schein, E. (1983). *The role of the founder in the creation of organizational culture*. Cambridge, MA: Alfred P Sloan School of Management.

Schein, E. (2004). *Organizational culture and leadership* (3rd ed.). Hoboken: Jossey-Bass. ISBN: 0-7879-6845-5.

Shane, S., Lockea, E., & Collins, C. (2003). Entrepreneurial motivation. *Human Resource Management Review, 13*, 257–279. https://doi.org/10.1016/S1053-4822(03)00017-2. Elsevier Science Inc.

Sommer, L., & Haug, M. (2010). Intention as a cognitive antecedent to international entrepreneurship—Understanding the moderating roles of knowledge and experience. *International Entrepreneurship and Management Journal, 7*(1), 111–142.

Sowmya, D., Majumdar, S., & Gallant, M. (2010). Relevance of education for potential entrepreneurs: An international investigation. *Journal of Small Business and Enterprise Development, 17*(4), 626–640.

Urban, B. (2010). Antecedents of entrepreneurship, with a focus on culture in an emerging country context. *Problems and Perspectives in Management, 8*(1), 114–126.

Zeffane, R. (2014). Does collectivism necessarily negate the spirit of entrepreneurship? *International Journal of Entrepreneurial Behaviour & Research, 20*(3), 278–296.

7

Role of Government

There is an academic divide on the role government should play in managing entrepreneurship (Baumol 2010; Hayek 1968; Mazzucato 2013). According to Austrian economists, such as Mises (1949) and Hayek (1968), any attempt to control market forces or interruption to economic transactions reaching their natural ends poses a direct threat to their integrity. Thus, any form of intervention, whether subsidies to support entrepreneurs, or rent controls to protect customers, is ultimately harmful to entrepreneurship. In sharp contrast to the Austrian view, Keynesian or antitrust thought calls for government intervention to rein in unruly market forces that cannot be left to their own devices (Audretsch 2007; Steele 2001).

However, government interventions to support entrepreneurship are not simply related to the Keynesian notion of managing demand or controlling the unruly powers of capitalism (Mazzucato 2013; Steele 2001). As Mariana Mazzucato (2013) points out in "The Entrepreneurial State", governments need to go beyond the traditional scope of creating infrastructure and regulation. Indeed, in the most successful economies, governments play a leading role in fostering innovation. By proactively creating conditions conducive to innovation and by making strategic investments, governments can help entrepreneurs manage the most difficult part of the entrepreneurial process, uncertainty (Mazzucato 2013).

The non-interventionist view on the role of government is largely based on the pillar that upholds free market principles. These have been discussed at length in Chap. 2 under the Austrian perspective. However, in regard to innovation it would be useful to highlight a few conclusions from Chap. 2. The traditional notion of competition as a regulatory force is obsolete. Oligopolies best represent almost every industry, where a select few firms dominate the market to such an extent that any new entrant is forced to settle for a sector that has either been discarded by the existing firms or does not represent sufficient long-term opportunity. When the few market sectors not yet discovered are cultivated, large firms are quick to buy out entrepreneurs.

It is then unsurprising to see that the ambitions of some nascent entrepreneurs do not extend beyond being bought out by one of the major players in their market. This leads us to a reality where innovation, the main weapon of entrepreneurs, is hijacked by large firms. This helps maintain status quo, dilute the destructive nature of innovation and help integrate it within dominant firm's existing timetable to release, or drip feed, innovation into the market. In this reality nascent entrepreneurs have little to no competitive advantage, but worse still is the realization that success will inevitably lead to assimilation into one of the large firms that controls the market. At first this notion may not seem so bad; regardless, the market process continues to flourish. However, one would argue that in the long run these practices lead to decrease in productivity, demand, and most importantly innovation, ultimately, causing inefficiencies in the market process that are beyond repair. The pronounced bouts of cardiac arrest in most western economies in the last three decades or so can arguably be traced back anti-competitive practices that have been allowed to take root. Therefore, it is crucial for governments to intervene not just to curb unfair competition but also to help bolster nascent entrepreneurs in regard to their capabilities, access to opportunity, and start-up support that goes beyond financial support (Mazzucato 2013).

The role adopted by the UAE government is not very different from the one envisaged by Mazzucato (2013). Strategic investments in large scale technological research projects such as Masdar City and establishment of a range of entrepreneurship support programs such as the Khalifa Fund or Dubai SME provide a clear focus on entrepreneurship and are a testament to the proactive nature of the UAE government (El-Sokari et al. 2013; Dubai SME 2011; Government of Abu Dhabi 2008). Thus it was not surprising to see the role of government emerge as a major theme in interviews.

The role of government as a theme was supported by four sub-themes of GSPs, government regulation, political leadership as role models, and perceptions and expectations of government support. GSPs highlighted the experiences of participants in relation to the many specialist government funded organizations, such as Khalifa Fund and SME Dubai, set up to develop young Emiratis and foster entrepreneurship (Government of Abu Dhabi 2008). The sub-theme of government regulation detailed how participants have been affected by government regulations and its impact on their entrepreneurial intentions. The sub-theme of political leadership as role models was unexpected; this sub-theme highlighted the experiences and perceptions of Emiratis and how political leaders, past and present, had a profound effect on young Emiratis' motivation and ambition. The sub-theme of expectation of government support detailed what young Emiratis expect from GSPs and their perceptions about how these programs apply to their context.

Government Support Programs

A number of comprehensive GSPs exist within the UAE. Studies conducted in the UAE recognize the importance of these programs and their impact in promoting entrepreneurship within the UAE (El-Sokari et al. 2013). However, some studies also highlighted criticisms relating to the level of support, specifically in regard to insufficient training and capacity building (Itani et al. 2011; Sikdar and Vel 2011). The entrepreneurs provided a very similar picture to this narrative.

Ent01M: *frankly it's a very good initiative, I am happy there is a SME (Dubai) which supports startups, but unfortunately it's not the way I thought about it… ok they reduce the license price so you save 6000, they register you in the government procurement website Ejari, good… what they do is good it helps with the basic the infrastructure, they give funds but not to everyone, they give contacts, but I can get these myself,*

Ent02F: *SME (Dubai) gave me a lot of chances, they helped me with the legal side and licensing… I was able to open a free kiosk in Wafi Mall for 4 days… SME (Dubai) created more opportunities to grow with networking, they put me in impact hub… we are getting a VIP number in the DED so it's easier and faster, special rates… if we did not get this support I don't think I will easily start my business….*

Ent03F: *…after 7 months I decided to have my own shop and with my own tailor, I talked to Khalifa Fund they said they can provide for me some opportunities they came to see my shop and they said they can put me in Galeries Lafayette… put me in a fashion show….*

Ent04M: *SME were supportive but I think the idea for them was new and they did not know how to deal with it… I think SME is now more of an umbrella for those who want to start and not really for those who want to operate and expand….*

GSPs are clearly a crucial component within the entrepreneurial process in the UAE. They also contribute toward creating a positive institutional environment conducive to entrepreneurship (Gupta et al. 2012). The fact that each participant from the entrepreneur sample and some from the employee sample benefited from GSPs is a testament to their success. However, the level and effectiveness of support varied among different entrepreneurs. Ent01M, "what they do is good it helps with the basic the infrastructure…". Ent02F, "SME gave me a lot of chances… opportunities to grow… if we did not get this support I don't think I will easily start my business". Ent03F, "Khalifa Fund they said they can provide for me some opportunities… put me in a fashion show". Ent04M, "SME were supportive but I think the idea for them was new and they did not know how to deal with it". These passages acknowledge the benefit of GSPs but also highlight their limitations. Interestingly, female entrepreneurs involved in traditional businesses seem to be more satisfied with the level of support than their male counterparts who were involved in non-traditional businesses. For example, for Ent01M and Ent04M the support was limited to basic infrastructure and overlooked support opportunities for guidance or growth.

Emp01F: *I was part of many activities and programs we won one of the competitions ... there is a lot of competition for their support... the process takes a long time (experience learnt from when friends were doing it) and so I thought the process will be less complicated and be quicker if we started by our own savings....*

Emp02M: *...it help us with more facilitation for business, with funding maybe so it is important... and actually they are also encouraging the locals to start the business.*

Emp03F: *When I joined the Shaikh Mohammad bin Rashid program (scholarship program from SME) I was an average student I did not get involved in many activities, did not really have any idea about business, but then the people who were with me they were really talented and ambitious and when I met them I wanted to be just like them....*

The employee sample did not pursue their business ideas, and thus did not have experience of GSPs for start-ups. However, the employee sample highlighted an awareness of GSPs and their experiences of interactions at different levels. Emp01F, "I was part of many activities and programs... there is a lot of competition for their support". Emp02M, "they are also encouraging the locals to start the business". Emp03F, "when I joined the Shaikh Mohammad bin Rashid program... the people who were with me they were really talented and ambitious and when I met them I wanted to be just like them". GSPs not only focus on entrepreneurs, they also offer a range of opportunities to raise awareness and foster a culture of entrepreneurship (Dubai SME 2011). Even though this sample did not pursue their business ideas, these comments suggest that GSPs are raising awareness of entrepreneurship, inspiring young people, and expanding opportunities for personal growth.

However, as Emp01F highlighted, there were perceived difficulties in accessing support; this issue will be explored further in a later sub-theme. Furthermore, although the entrepreneurs knew of these programs, they did not have a good understanding of what they entailed. This suggests opportunities for improvement in communication, a notion that is also supported by other studies conducted in the region (Itani et al. 2011; Sikdar and Vel 2011).

Inc01F: ...*we have programs for SMEs, Like Dubai Chamber is running some workshops... SME ok we have discounted license... actually I think the support depends on the type of business because if it was something common it would be easy for them to get the support, but if they came up with a new idea or concept then they would get the support but it will take some time and the entrepreneurs they don't like to waste time....*

Inc02F : *There is Khalifa Fund there is the ICT fund, (Government support and funding bodies) DTEC we support Emiratis, it's a Semi Government, Incubators that are private and public, Dubai SME.*

Both incubator managers confirmed the wide range of support networks available to Emirati entrepreneurs and potential entrepreneurs. However, limitations of the support in its current form were also highlighted. As the entrepreneur, employee, and incubator manager samples suggested, these support programs might be less successful when it comes to dealing with entrepreneurs, especially when they have started the business. Inc01F also highlighted that businesses in new or non-traditional sectors were less likely to gain support. This notion could be justified in a target based culture, such as the one adopted in the UAE in recent years (Government of Abu Dhabi 2008). If support organizations are measured by the number of business started, then it is easier to achieve this target by focusing support in businesses that fit well within the existing framework. While this may work in the short-run, it does not help create impactful enterprises that the UAE needs to achieve its long-term targets.

Government Regulation

Government regulation and laws pertaining to entrepreneurs are stringent within the UAE and lag behind most Western countries (Gupta et al. 2012). As mentioned earlier, bankruptcy carries a jail sentence, which adds to how entrepreneurs evaluated the risk of starting a new business or securing finance (Rocha et al. 2010). Interviews produced mixed results on this sub-theme. Interestingly, entrepreneurs were somewhat positive about government regulation, whereas the employees tended to focus on the negative elements.

Ent01M: ...*the rules and regulations every year they are pushing... things have changed ... 20% business in government contracts going to Emirati companies... were are confident when we know we have a leader that support and pushes us....*

Ent02F: ...*my paper work was not finished, but if I had finished it then I would have had much lower rates it took long about 2 weeks to have everything completed because my issue was a little bit complicated, I should remove my partner, because it should only be locals on the license....*

Ent04M: ...*licensing was a struggle, first off they did not really understand my business, what it is, so they did not make any special license ... they used what they knew and gave me a general marketing, sports management and consultation license...*

The entrepreneurs sample suggested that while the nature of government regulations may be changing, they may be creating unintentional limitations due to increased bureaucracy. These limitations related to increased waiting time and difficulties in obtaining business licenses for non-traditional businesses. These notions were highlighted in the earlier theme of government support. Ent01M, "rules and regulations every year they are pushing... things have changed". Ent02F, "it took long because my issue was a little bit complicated". Ent04M, "licensing was a struggle... first off they did not really understand my business". Therefore it can be argued that some of the limitations in government support stem from the regulatory framework. Furthermore, rigidity of the regulatory framework may be stifling innovation or at best it is slowing down the entrepreneurial process.

Emp03M: ...*above all municipality regulation are the biggest barriers stopping me from starting now... because they don't have a category for my business idea....*

Emp04M: ...*a business for men's there is a criteria, different criteria for women, but if I want to do both, it's not so simple, there are a many restrictions... don't want to end up in Jail you know, new regulation now you cannot hire Bengali people, these are the cheapest labor in our country, if you want to hire Filipino they have their own rules, rules costs....*

Inc01F: ...*because they would need new approvals, maybe they would not have an activity matching that concept so they would have to create a new activity for them... maybe it would take years... there is a home license but apart from the price (1000 AED) there is not any other benefits you are getting... I had a client who was interested in starting a business but she needed financial support... they agreed... by the time she got the approval it was two and half years already... she did not want to do it, the market, competition had changed....*

The effects of government regulations were less prevalent than some of the other sub-themes highlighted thus far. However, participants that mentioned government regulation as an issue were significantly affected. Emp03M, "above all municipality regulation are the biggest barriers". Emp04M, "it's not so simple, there are a many restrictions... rules costs". Government regulation is either stopping entrepreneurs from obtaining a license to trade or stopping them from trying. The incubator manager also confirmed some of the apprehensions highlighted by entrepreneurs and employees. Inc01F, "create a new activity for them, maybe it would take years... by the time she got the approval, she did not want to do it, the market, competition had changed".

The lack of responsiveness and inability of the regulatory framework to cater to innovation was highlighted by each sample segment. This is a serious issue for a country aiming to build a knowledge based economy. Any support for entrepreneurs has to be matched with existing regulations; ultimately a sluggish regulatory framework has a knock-on effect on support programs and undermines government's efforts to foster a culture of entrepreneurship.

Political Role Models

The impact of political role models on entrepreneurship is largely unexplored in the UAE and beyond. However, this construct emerged as a consistent theme from the interviews. Participants, especially entrepreneurs, highlighted a deep rooted affiliation with political role models, past and present. Some participants attributed their original ambition and motivation specifically to political role models, whereas others identified the impact of political role models as the key contributor to taking entrepreneurial action. Thus, political role models' influence could be observed at different stages of the entrepreneurial process within the UAE.

Ent01M: *The leaders are pushing us, for example when Shaikh Zaid said we don't create countries without men… we have a leader that support and pushes us … this gives the confidence that ok now this is the time to push yourself….*

Ent02F: *I remember I was in the Arabic class and we talked about Shaikh Zaid when he said women are half of the society… he opened a special university for them get them on board. If he did not do this small step we would not be where we are today… because I felt I have to mention that Shaikh Zaid is the one who inspired me, sat in my mind… so I was like I will do it!!*

Ent04M: *When we have these great rulers like Shaikh Mohammad, Shaikh Zaid saying come on Emirati, then what we can do is to say ok here we go, so he has this sense of responsibility and he spreads that to us its part of our inside duty. Mohammad Bin Rashid is saying that we want to make everybody happy… you know Shaikh Mohammad is an entrepreneur, he created Dubai in this vision… what he has created cannot be created by someone who just wants to be a ruler….*

The phenomenon of political leaders as role models was a surprise sub-theme. Almost all participants from the entrepreneur sample identified with a political role model and were able to trace the origins of their inspiration to a specific experience in their life. Ent01M, "Shaikh Zaid said we don't create countries without men… we have a leader that support and pushes us". Ent02F, "I remember I was in the Arabic class and we talked about Shaikh Zaid… Shaikh Zaid is the one who inspired me". Ent04M, "great rulers like Shaikh Mohammad, Shaikh Zaid saying come on Emirati… he has this sense of responsibility and he spreads that to us its part of our inside duty". Literature on the role of political leadership driving effective economic policy is widespread (Persson and Tabellini 2002; Roseland 2012; Rosenau and Czempiel 1992). However, empirical evidence of political leaders as role models who inspire the general population to achieve more and become entrepreneurial was difficult to obtain. The literature review could not identify any studies in the region that reported on this phenomenon. The entrepreneurs revealed political leaders were sources of inspiration, instilled confidence, and a sense of duty. This may well highlight one of the origins of a need for achievement, while also increasing perceived levels of success in undertaking entrepreneurial action.

Emp01F: Shaikh Mohammad Bin Rashid saying that I am always number one, so this gives you motivation it tells you that this country is a land of opportunity… if you give it sometime if you are ready to take the risk, but to take these risks I myself have to be in a suitable condition… Shaikh Mohammad Bin Rashid said that we should all try to give our best, I think it does drive you to give your best when you hear inspirational people.…

Emp02M: …leaders in our country are inspiring us, they now have government funding, this is a huge support for people who want to start a business, even the banks offer very low interest, because these are instructions from the leaders… like Shaikh Mohammad Bin Rashid, Shaikh Mohammed bin Zayed, when they talk to the younger generation they say that you are the country's leaders, you are the ones that will drive the country to be ambitious, try to succeed in your life we will support you with whatever you need.…

The above vignettes are relatively long, however, they contain valuable insights into the experiences of young Emiratis and the different ways they are affected by political role models. Emp01F, "Shaikh Mohammad Bin Rashid saying that I am always number one, so this gives you motivation… it does drive you to give your best". Emp02M, "leaders in our country are inspiring us… they say… you are the ones that will drive the country to be ambitious". The employee sample confirmed political role models as sources of inspiration that also implanted a sense of duty.

However, Emp01F, revealed an important factor that arguably differentiates the two sample segments. Emp01F, "to take these risks I myself have to be in a suitable condition". Most participants in both samples were inspired by political role models. However, arguably, the employee segment did not perceive the right conditions to risk a business venture. This goes beyond risk-taking propensity and links with perceived behavior control, because Emp01F did not find suitable conditions that would increase the likelihood of success. Furthermore, the suitable conditions also relate to family circumstances. As highlighted earlier, Emp01F's family circumstances were not conducive to undertaking risk and starting a business.

Inc01F: …*leaders of our country they are close to us, every year they encourage… it's like a vision of our leaders they want to have more Emirati to start their own business so it's like the continues support they are providing and encouragement.…*

Inc02M: *They (Emirati entrepreneurs) are following a vision of being the number 1, I think that is something that is very much pushed and emphasized through the ruler's office… he is the drive, he wants to drive innovation drive entrepreneurship because he know that mean Emiratis are creating the future not just accepting the future.…*

The sample of incubator managers corroborated the sample of entrepreneurs and employees to identify political leaders as role models. Inc01F, "it's like a vision of our leaders they want to have more Emirati to start their own business". Inc02M, "they (Emirati entrepreneurs) are following a vision of being the number 1, I think that is something that is very much pushed and emphasized through the ruler's office". Interestingly, both incubator managers identify entrepreneurship with the leadership's vision. This is in line with government papers set out in 2008, for example, the Abu Dhabi 2030 Plan and the Abu Dhabi 2021 Vision (Government of Abu Dhabi 2008). Arguably, young Emiratis aligning their goals with government ambitions demonstrates, at least in part, government success. However, this also alludes to the existence of significant weaknesses with the UAE entrepreneurial ecosystem that are causing the entrepreneurial gap (Bhat and Khan 2014).

Expectations of Government Support Programs

Previous studies in the UAE indicate Emiratis have high expectations from GSPs (Erogul and McCrohan 2008; Sowmya et al. 2010). However, to some extent, this sub-theme revealed a mismatch between the expectations of Emirati entrepreneurs and what GSPs deliver. As the earlier themes suggested, these high expectations may be linked to participants' perceived ambitions of political role models. This mismatch between the perceived expectations of political role models and what government supports deliver was best articulated by Ent01M when he talked about political role models "the leaders are pushing us". However, when he mentioned GSPs, "you don't feel they push you to start".

Ent01M: *…you don't feel they push you to start… if you want to help young people they need money but not just money they need guidance… maybe like a partnership, for example if I am working with Dubai SME and I go to another Government department then they should choose me… of course I would have to offer the right product good prices…help them growth, push them in the market… if you take on an entrepreneur they should make sure they survive….*

Ent04M: *I asked them to open doors for me in terms of sponsors and to exploit different opportunities… but I think SME (Dubai) is now more of an umbrella for those who want to start and not*

> *really for those who want to operate and expand... I was expecting they evaluate your business and say what have you achieved that are your needs and how we can support you... my expectations are not to get the discount, but let's looks at how we can support how we can cooperate... SME have the power because Shaikh Mohammad (Ruler of Dubai) gave them that power... as an entrepreneur you expect to knock other people's door but I would like them to knock our door and say what they can do... I would not say partner but more like our godfather, our advocate....*

Again the above two passages are lengthy, but they do provide a detailed insight of the entrepreneurs' perceptions of and expectations from GSPs. Ent01M, "not just money they need guidance... maybe like a partnership... I go to another Government department then they should choose me". Ent04M, "my expectations are not to get the discount, but let's look at how we can support how we can cooperate... because Shaikh Mohammad (Ruler of Dubai) gave them that power... I would not say partner but more like our godfather". Ent02F and Ent03F did not express further expectations from GSPs, arguably because they were content and the level of support had reached their expectations.

Ent01M and Ent04M expressed disappointment with the level of government support in the earlier sub-theme of government support. Therefore, a variation in the received and expected support was not surprising. These entrepreneurs clearly expected more from government support, almost a partnership with government bodies that would enable them to get a foothold in the market. There was also a sense of entitlement and an expectation for government agencies to play an active role. Arguably, these expectations, whether reasonable or unreasonable, also result from the sense of collective duty instilled by political role models.

Inc02F: *...not really happy with the level of support entrepreneurs get, I think there are a lot of things that need to be done... ok so they are supporting by giving discounts for 3 years, for the license... they are offering some workshops but there is still a lot that needs*

> to be done, like networking events, work closely with small owners to give them better opportunities, offer them a practical place to offer their services or conduct business… special license for small businesses on social media so they can be trusted, providing mentors (coaches), not just providing the rent space but helping them grow… a lot of private companies would be happy to help… The companies (private sector) can do it as part of their CSR or as part of giving something back to society….

Unlike the entrepreneurs, the employee sample did not access GSPs, hence did not express expectations relating to this sub-theme. One of the incubator managers corroborated deficiencies in the expected support levels provided by GSPs. There was a clear expectation for government support to go beyond monetary benefits. Inc02F, works closely with small owners to give them better opportunities. Similar to the entrepreneur sample, there was an expectation that the GSPs should work more closely with the entrepreneurs to help them survive and grow their business. There was also an expectation for public private partnerships to support entrepreneurs. This strategy has been called for and adopted elsewhere in the world with positive results and may offer an effective way forward for government support agencies to improve their offering to Emirati entrepreneurs (Groenewegen and Steen 2007; Grossman 2008; Nelson 2007; Patrinos et al. 2009).

This short chapter highlights the importance and impact of the government on Entrepreneurship in the UAE. The influence of government in the UAE comes across as the single most important factor that can advance and support entrepreneurship. The various GSPs have clearly inspired and supported entrepreneurs. This chapter also points to a number of challenges and opportunities that can further improve support mechanisms for entrepreneurs. At the time of this writing, some of these issues were being studies by the UAE government. For example, in regard to government regulation, bankruptcy laws in particular have received significant reforms. Under the Federal Decree No 9, as of December 29, 2016, bankruptcy in the UAE was decriminalized. Although this law reform does not apply to private individuals and still requires commercial entities to meet several conditions, it is a significant step forward in increasing the UAE's international competitiveness and benchmarking the UAE's regulatory framework with advanced economies. Ultimately these changes are creating a safer and more transparent environment for entrepreneurs when it comes to securing finance (KPMG International 2017; UAE Ministry of Finance 2016).

These recent changes to the UAE bankruptcy laws will be discussed further in Chap. 9, Emirati Model of Entrepreneurship: Critical Success Factors. While changes in financial regulation signify a positive forward, there are significant opportunities ahead to further improve the entrepreneurial ecosystem within the UAE. An important factor to consider here relates to business licensing. New business licensing regulation in the UAE still varies from one Emirate to another. Some elements of regulation relating to business licensing come under the federal law whereas other elements are covered by the local Emirate regulation, specific to each Emirate. For example, when acquiring a new business license in any of the seven Emirates, an entrepreneur would have to adhere to regulation of the specific Emirate. These can range from the type and scope of business activity to the minimum investment requirements and terms and conditions relating to leasing and trading. Whereas, when it comes to employment, health and safety, finance, and a host of other important legal requirements, the entrepreneur has to comply with the UAE federal regulation. Most of these regulations are covered in the Federal Law No. 2 of 2015, which was an update to the 1984, 1983 legal framework for commercial companies. In many respects issues for entrepreneurs trying to negotiate this complicated legal terrain is overshadowed by the lack of integration. This is a worldwide issue where local and federal authorities are vying to address their primary stakeholder concerns, and trying to find a balance between national interest and regional integrity. However, from an entrepreneur's point of view, a simple coherent regulatory framework is needed, especially when embarking on an uncertain new venture. This is where GSPs can play an essential role.

References

Audretsch, D. (2007). *The entrepreneurial society.* Oxford University Press. ISBN: 978-0-19-518350-4.

Baumol, W. J. (2010). *The Microtheory of innovative entrepreneurship* (The Kauffman Foundation Series on Innovation and Entrepreneurship). Princeton: Princeton University Press. ISBN: 1400835224.

Bhat, S., & Khan, R. (2014). *Government policy ecosystem for entrepreneurship development in MSEs sector.* Munich University Library, Germany: MPRA.

Dubai SME. (2011). The role of government in supporting entrepreneurship & SME development. *Dubai Department of Economic Development.* Retrieved from http://www.oecd.org/mena/investment/47246782.pdf

El-Sokari, H., Van Horne, C., Huang, Z., & Al Awad, M. (2013). *GEM UAE: Entrepreneurship—An Emirati perspective.* Retrieved from http://www.gem-consortium.org/docs/2892/gem-uae-entrepreneurship-an-emiratiperspective.

Erogul, M., & McCrohan, D. (2008). Preliminary investigation of Emirati women entrepreneurs in the UAE. *African Journal of Business Management, 2*(10), 177–185.

Government of Abu Dhabi. (2008). *The Abu Dhabi Economic Vision 2030.* Retrieved from https://www.ecouncil.ae/PublicationsEn/economic-vision-2030-full-versionEn.pdf

Groenewegen, J., & Steen, M. (2007). The evolutionary policy maker. *Journal of Economic Issues. ProQuest Central, 41*(2), 351.

Grossman, S. (2008). The case of business improvement districts: Special district public-private cooperation in community revitalization. *Public Performance & Management Review, 32*(2), 290–308.

Gupta, V., Yayla, A., Sikdar, A., & Cha, M. (2012). Institutional environment for entrepreneurship: Evidence from the developmental states of South Korea and United Arab Emirates. *Journal of Developmental Entrepreneurship, 17*(3). https://doi.org/10.1142/S1084946712500136.

Hayek, F. A. (1968). Competition as a discovery procedure. *Quarterly Journal of Austrian Economics, 5*(3), 9–23.

Itani, H., Sidani, S., & Baalbaki, I. (2011). United Arab Emirates female entrepreneurs: Motivations and frustrations. *Equality, Diversity and Inclusion: An International Journal, 30*(5), 409–424.

KMPG International. (2017). *KPMG Insights, UAE Bankruptcy Law.* Retrieved from. https://home.kpmg.com/ae/en/home/insights/2016/12/uae-bankruptcy-law.html.

Mazzucato, M. (2013). *The entrepreneurial state: Debunking public Vs. Private sector myths*. London: Anthem Press. ISBN 0857282522.

Mises, L. (1949). *Human action: A treatise on economics*. New Haven: Yale University Press.

Nelson, J. (2007). *Building linkages for competitive and responsible entrepreneurship*. The United Nations Industrial Development Organization (UNIDO) and the Fellows of Harvard School. Puritan Press. https://www.unido.org/sites/default/files/2008-06/Building_Linkages_for_Competitive_and_Responsible_Entrepreneurship_0.pdf

Patrinos, H., Osorio, F., & Guaqueta, J. (2009). *The role and impact of public-private partnerships in education*. World Bank Publications. ISBN 0821379038.

Persson, T., & Tabellini, E. (2002). *Political economics: Explaining economic policy*. Cambridge, MA: MIT Press. ISBN 0262661314.

Rocha, R., Farazi, S., Khuori, R., & Pearce, D. (2010) The status of bank lending to SMEs in the Middle East and North Africa Region: The results of a joint survey of the Union of Arab Banks and the World Bank. *The World Bank & The Union of Arab Banks*. Washington, DC, and Bruit.

Roseland, M. (2012). *Toward sustainable communities. Solutions for citizens and their governments* (4th ed.). Gabriola Island: New Society.

Rosenau, J., & Czempiel E. (1992). *Governance without government: Order and change in world politics*. Cambridge, MA: Cambridge University Press. ISBN 0521405785.

Sikdar, A., & Vel, P. (2011). Factors influencing entrepreneurial value creation in the UAE-an exploratory study. *International Journal of Business and Social Science*, 2(6), 77.

Sowmya, D., Majumdar, S., & Gallant, M. (2010). Relevance of education for potential entrepreneurs: An international investigation. *Journal of Small Business and Enterprise Development*, 17(4), 626–640.

Steele, G. R. (2001). *Keynes and Hayek, the money economy*. London: Routledge.

UAE Ministry of Finance. (2016). *The Final Draft of the Federal Bankruptcy Law*. Retrieved from: https://www.mof.gov.ae/En/Media/News/Pages/06092016.aspx

8

The Emirati Entrepreneur

This chapter summarizes major themes and sub-themes and highlights important outcomes of the interviews to establish a coherent picture of the nascent Emirati entrepreneur. In line with the methodology, this section provides brief interpretations and starts the meaning-making process. The themes were established by comparing the entrepreneur sample responses with those of the employee sample. In a bid to triangulate, responses from incubator managers were used to corroborate or confirm the themes. Triangulating in this way not only helped validate findings but also developed a deeper understanding of key issues, which added to the strength and rigor of the study (Denzin 2006; Denzin and Lincoln 1994). Each major theme was supported by relevant sub-themes that connected experiences of participants. Major themes that emerged from interviews were interconnected and affected Emirati participants at different stages of the entrepreneurial process. For example, the theme of family was heavily connected with culture and affected a range of other themes such as personal traits and perceived behavior control.

Family came across as a major theme in the study; it played a major role in the UAE context. The interviews revealed that family affected almost every aspect of the participants' lives. Family circumstances, support, approval, and commitment to the family were major influences on whether Emiratis started a business or found employment. Family circumstance, for example, participants' position among siblings, responsibilities, the history of entrepreneurship within the family, and the family's financial situation came across as major behavior modifiers.

Family circumstance influenced risk-taking propensity, which had a direct effect on the strength of participants' entrepreneurial intentions. For example, if participants were the eldest within the family and had financial responsibility, they were less inclined to take risks and were more attracted toward the security offered by employment. Furthermore, all but one of the employee sample highlighted financial responsibilities or commitment toward the family and identified this as the defining factor for a choice between starting a business and finding employment. In comparison, none of the entrepreneurs felt they were currently responsible for the financial security of the family. This emphasized the role of the family in shaping individual character, moderating behavior, and guiding actions. In the early stages, participants identified family as a source of inspiration and positive role models, and the encouragement and values learnt within the family environment contributed to the development of personality traits, specifically the need for achievement. Although the need for independence is influenced by a range of factors, family circumstances also helped shape this trait. For example, the achievement motive, coupled with a sense of responsibility, enabled participants to develop associations with leadership. These two factors and the family's financial situation led to the development of the need for independence.

Comparison between male and female responses revealed a gender difference in the way family affects Emirati entrepreneurs. All participants identified parental influence, especially from their fathers, as a major factor. Parents were identified as a source of inspiration and guidance. Female participants highlighted the need to gain permission from the male family head in order to work or start a business, while male participants associated family with a sense of responsibility. The influence of family went beyond developing character and intentions; interview data also revealed the importance of family approval as a key enabler for the female participants to act on their intentions.

Similarly the level of support, emotional and practical, may also determine the level of success once a business has been started. Female entrepreneurs attributed their success in business heavily to the level of family support. In comparison the male participants, both entrepreneurs and employees, did not need family approval and did not see family as a source of support. Instead, the male participants largely identified family as a barrier to starting a business. Interestingly, the female employees also identified commitment to family as a barrier to starting a business.

Commitment to family, not just in regard to financial responsibility but also responsibilities toward their younger siblings and the need to spend time with their family were important for participants, especially the employee sample. Male entrepreneurs seem to recognize this as a conflict and highlighted they did not get married for this reason, sacrificing family life for the sake of their business. The sample of employees did not seem to be prepared to make similar sacrifices and identified family life and its wellbeing as their main priority.

In summary, family seemed to seed early ambitions and build key characteristics among these Emirati graduates. It moderated behavior and guided their actions. However, the impact of family was determined by the individual context. Financial situation, commitment toward the family and the history of entrepreneurship came across as the most important elements in this context. The importance of family was closely linked to the UAE culture and religion; nevertheless, family played a major role when it came to Emiratis determining who they were and what they did.

The UAE culture is heavily influenced by religion and affects every aspect of Emirati life. Research participants made a number of different references to culture, which were developed as sub-themes. In a predominantly religious country, references to religion and tradition were expected; however, reputation and social standing were also flagged, which was unexpected. Much like family, culture affected Emirati graduates at different stages. Participants identified with a collectivist culture, as there was a strong sense of community and civic duty. This sense of duty was also developed by nationalist tendencies, which seeded early ambitions to undertake tasks that ultimately improved society.

Similarly, religion also instilled a sense of duty to do the best they could to make a difference to the family and wider society. This also accounted for the achievement motive in many participants and revealed a deeply intimate aspect of their psyche. Culture seeded a deep ambition in participants to succeed, not just for themselves but for others. None of the entrepreneurs cited profit as their main motive; instead, all of them linked their entrepreneurial motivation to making a difference.

However, culture is also dependent on other factors. For example, while entrepreneurs saw entrepreneurship as a viable vehicle to achieve their ambitions, the employee sample did not. This may be because the employee sample saw a greater and more immediate need to improve their family situation: almost all members of the employee sample identified with this need; hence family took priority over the wider society and employment became more desirable than entrepreneurship. Comparatively, the entrepreneur sample was not restricted by family circumstances and they were able to accept greater risk to achieve social change.

Cultural perceptions about entrepreneurship produced conflicting opinions. While some participants, mainly female, identified negative cultural perceptions about entrepreneurship, most of the participants felt the UAE culture appreciated entrepreneurship and entrepreneurs. It is important to highlight two points at this juncture. First, apart from one female entrepreneur who had personal experience of discrimination, which she associated with cultural factors, all other negative accounts were based on perceptions. Participants who highlighted negative perceptions toward entrepreneurship associated them with tradition, and also said that things were changing and saw the overall UAE culture as largely positive. Second, again for female participants, the impact of cultural factors was nullified if there was family approval, especially from the male head of the family. Thus, although cultural perceptions may play a role in moderating behavior, they did not have a strong influence on these Emiratis when it came to starting a business.

Reputation or social standing came across as a vital component in the decision-making process, but this only seemed to affect male participants. Just as family approval only seemed to affect female participants, gender differences were highlighted by this sub-theme of reputation. The stigma of losing one's reputation because of bankruptcy was highlighted not only by male participants, but also by incubator mangers. The effects of this fear were deemed so strong that they could potentially stop male

Emiratis from ever trying to open a business. It has to be said that although in theory bankruptcy before December 2016 was covered by criminal legislation, in practice there were very few cases which affected the local Emirati population.

This book looks at Emirati entrepreneurs as the sole owners of their businesses, rather than the commonly found silent partners in foreign enterprises. Therefore, apart from serious cases of neglect or fraud, which are few and far between, the number of Emiratis facing jail time for bankruptcy is negligible. Nevertheless the stigma of not being able to pay ones debt is real in Emirati society. Losing reputation or social standing becomes significant in a tightly knit community such as the UAE. It does not affect Emiratis just on an individual level, but, as one participant from the employee sample explained, loss of reputation extends to the whole family. Thus, the consequences are far more severe, further harming reputation and amplifying the fear of failure.

In summary, culture is a significant influence on Emirati entrepreneurs. It affects male and female Emiratis differently, but largely has a positive impact on developing individual ambition. Cultural impact on actual behavior is less positive and while female Emiratis are able to overcome negative elements by counterbalancing them with family approval, the male participants do not have this option. However, it should also be highlighted that the stigma of failure is outweighed by the rewards of success. Therefore, if conditions are suitable, mainly the financial circumstances of the family, then male participants may risk the loss of reputation. Thus, while the impact of culture is significant, it is superseded by other factors, such as family.

The role of government was prevalent in the lived experiences shared by Emirati graduates and emerged as a major theme from the interviews. Government played a vital role at different stages of participants' lives. The sub-themes of GSPs, government regulation, political role models, and expectations of start-up support were drawn out of the experiences shared by participants and how they were affected by different aspects of government. For example, there are a wide range of GSPs that focus on developing young Emiratis. These range from skill development to supporting start-ups. Most participants had either experienced developmental programs as undergraduates or start-up programs after graduation.

These were largely positive experiences which built confidence and seeded ambition.

Government regulation was identified by the employee sample as a direct or indirect barrier to starting a business. The entrepreneur sample also highlighted government regulation as a barrier; however, changes in regulation were also a source of encouragement. The importance of government regulation was also flagged by the incubator sample which emphasized some limitations, such as the lack of responsiveness and inability of the regulatory framework to cater to innovation. These aspects were discussed in detail in Chap. 7.

Conversations on the expectations of government start-up programs were limited to entrepreneurs, specifically the male segment of the entrepreneur sample. This was not a surprise because the employee sample had not experienced start-up support directly. Furthermore, the female entrepreneurs were largely satisfied with the level of start-up support. Therefore, expectations of start-up support were mainly highlighted by the male entrepreneurs, who were not satisfied with the current level of support available after starting their business. Interestingly, the female level of satisfaction with GSPs may be related to their choice of business which the support programs were better equipped to support. An incubator manager also highlighted this as a key area for improvement. Within this sub-theme, research participants highlighted valuable insights into how government support may be developed to become more responsive to the needs of Emirati entrepreneurs.

By far the most common sub-theme within the role of government was the impact of political role models. UAE political leaders, past and present, were perceived as role models and a source of ambition. Participants revealed specific moments in their lives which inspired them to do better for themselves and others. These moments represented the origins of entrepreneurial motivation and ambition, a facet often lacking in entrepreneurial research. The influence of political role models also developed individual characteristics, such as the need for achievement and independence and encouraged risk taking in the pursuit of entrepreneurship. This is in sharp contrast to most governments around the world, who may be able to encourage entrepreneurship through policy, but can seldom be accredited with inspiring the masses to be entrepreneurial. Political role models deeply affected Emiratis and seeded a sense of duty in Emiratis to do the best they could for their country. Arguably, this also influenced entrepreneurs' expectations of government start-up programs.

Political role models also instilled confidence, which was further enhanced by the perception of government support. As mentioned earlier, there are a wide range of support programs and competitions that develop Emiratis at the undergraduate level and promote support available to start-ups after their graduation. The combination of these factors highlighted entrepreneurship as a feasible and desirable avenue for Emiratis because these programs increase the levels of perceived success in undertaking entrepreneurial action.

Thus, government plays an integral role in developing and strengthening entrepreneurial intentions among Emirati graduates. But there are opportunities for improvement. For example, the employee sample highlighted perceived unavailability or the difficultly in accessing government support as one of the main reasons for not trying to gain start-up support. In sharp contrast, the entrepreneur sample revealed they had strong perceptions about the availability of government support and start-up programs. Arguably, the fact that none of the employee sample tried to access start-up support highlighted their weak entrepreneurial intentions, which could have been one of the main reasons for inaction.

Whether intentions were translated into actions depended on a range of factors, some of which have been discussed already. However, in regard to government's influence, entrepreneurial intentions only seem to translate into action if perceived levels of support are reinforced by actual government support. The male entrepreneurs in particular highlighted some of the difficulties in accessing different support mechanisms. Responses from female entrepreneurs would suggest that access to government support is relatively straightforward for traditional businesses. In other words, if the entrepreneur's business idea or sector already exists, then it is relatively easy for them to access government support.

However, if the idea is new in the market, as was the case with the male entrepreneurs, then support is more difficult to access; it certainly takes longer and the process becomes more complicated. These issues relating to traditional and non-traditional businesses were also confirmed by the incubator managers who highlighted deficiencies in the current support mechanism to cater to innovation. This marked a significant divide between the ambitions of political leadership and current capabilities of GSPs.

It is also important to consider that GSPs depend almost entirely upon government regulations that approve business activities and their scope, and govern types of business licenses granted to entrepreneurs. As the incubator sample revealed, a new type of business activity, not listed as a pre-approved business activity, has to be approved by the specific Emirate's Department of Economic Development, which, in effect, brings it into law. This process takes a long time, and, as markets move quickly in new sectors, this time lapse has suffocating effects on innovation and the opportunities available to entrepreneurs. Therefore, while start-up support programs certainly have the potential to improve, the challenges posed to innovation mainly stem from ineffective and sluggish regulation.

There is also something to be said about the expectations of entrepreneurs and to some extent the incubator sample. Entrepreneurs expected GSPs to become partners, or as one of the entrepreneurs expressed "godfathers". Thus, the role of GSPs was not expected to diminish after the establishment stage; instead, there was an expectation to work hand in hand to actively help establish and grow new Emirati businesses. Entrepreneurs expected support programs to be actively involved in securing sales and to be given priority in the awarding of government contracts.

These are unreasonably high expectations, especially from the free market viewpoint, and could be interpreted as meaning that Emirati entrepreneurs have an unreasonable sense of entitlement. However, this would be an over simplification. High expectations stem directly from the encouragement of political role models and the initial promise of GSPs. Furthermore, as discussed earlier there are other external factors that instill a sense of duty and responsibility within Emiratis. Thus, instead of a false sense of entitlement, the high expectations among Emiratis are a reflection of what they perceive as a common endeavor between them and the GSPs established by their political role models.

In summary, the UAE government plays an overwhelmingly strong role at different stages of the entrepreneurial process, especially when compared with Western free market economies. Political role models are a source of inspiration and instill a sense of duty among Emiratis, which leads directly to an ambition to improve themselves and the country. GSPs provide a vehicle that highlights a career in entrepreneurship as a viable option to realize these ambitions. This leads to high expectations of GSPs. However, there are deficiencies in start-up programs that are amplified by ineffective regulation, which is also counterproductive to innovation. This highlights a mismatch between the government's strategic aim of fostering a knowledge-based economy driven by entrepreneurship and the tools established to help achieve this aim.

Interview data also point to a number of personality traits that consistently featured in both samples. The need for achievement was the most common personality trait, closely followed by the need for independence. However, there were significant variances in other traits such as the risk-taking propensity and capacity to innovate. These variances were, arguably, the key differentiators between entrepreneurs and employees. Almost all participants from both samples displayed personality traits of the need for achievement and independence. However, it was their ability to accept risk and uncertainty that determined whether they chose employment or entrepreneurship to fulfill their ambitions. If a career in entrepreneurship was chosen, it was the entrepreneur's capacity to innovate that determined success in starting and surviving in business.

Participants revealed that the need for achievement was developed early in their lives. Although influences of other factors such as family, culture, and political role models could be observed, in their own words, most participants identified the need for achievement as an inbuilt quality, something that was always a part of their character. On the other hand, the need for independence seems to directly result from family circumstances and the need to generate an income for themselves. Both of these traits had a direct effect on the individual's desire: as some participants revealed, they felt they had to do something for themselves and for others. However, this desire or ambition was not given direction and although participants felt they had to achieve, they did not necessarily understand what or how.

It is important to point out that some entrepreneurs were the exception in this regard as the need for achievement, independence, and entrepreneurial motivation all seem to originate from one inspirational experience in their lives. Nevertheless, for most participants, the need to improve their family circumstances, positive cultural perceptions about entrepreneurship, and optimistic perceptions about government support developed entrepreneurial intentions. These intentions were then evaluated through a complex process, whereby individuals appraised the prospect of starting a business against a number of different factors, which were again linked with different aspects of family, culture, and government. In this process, the personality trait of risk-taking propensity played a vital role.

Whether entrepreneurial intentions equated to entrepreneurial action was largely determined by the individual's propensity to take risk. These personality traits were affected by factors such as the family's financial circumstance, family support and approval, perceived threat to reputation and perceived availability of government support. For example, some participants pointed out that the uncertainty of not generating an income was the main hindrance to starting a business because their family depended on them to provide financial support. In other cases, failing was not an option because of the devastating effects it would have had on the individual's reputation, which would potentially extend to the whole family; thus, this also led to lack of entrepreneurial action. Therefore, different aspects of the individual's context, family, culture, and government moderated the risk associated with certain actions, which formed a vital link between entrepreneurial intentions and actions.

In summary, personality traits are not developed in isolation; they are a product of an individual's environment, developed and influenced by a range of external factors. Traits such as the need for achievement and independence supported and nurtured individual ambition at early stages and called these Emiratis to action. However, although they might have had the ambition to do something, they did not necessarily know what that might be. Again a range of external factors from family to government point to appropriate actions suitable to fulfill their ambition. Crucially, personality traits of risk-taking propensity seem to steer individual choice between entrepreneurship and employment.

Participants consistently talked about certain factors that directly affected their level of confidence and perceived success in developing entrepreneurial intentions and undertaking entrepreneurial action. These were categorized under the theme of PBC. Perceived behavior control was supported by the sub-themes of access to finance, access to support, competition, education, market knowledge, and time. Unlike earlier themes, apart from education, none of these sub-themes were identified as the source of early ambition. Instead, participants felt that these factors directly affected their entrepreneurial intentions and the decision to start a business or opt for employment.

One of the key differences between whether an Emirati started business or found employment was access to finance. All of the entrepreneurs had either saved the capital needed to start their business or were given financial supported by their family. In contrast, the employee sample did not have access to finance and highlighted this as the main reason for not starting a business. In this regard, access to finance came across as one of the biggest barriers to starting a business. Those who had access to finance also felt more confident about undertaking a business venture. Interestingly, although the male entrepreneurs are seeking government funding to further establish their business, none of the entrepreneurs accessed government funding to start their business. The required start-up capital was relatively small and entrepreneurs boot-strapped in the beginning. This in itself came across as a common theme and may allude to a successful start-up strategy for Emiratis.

Participants also talked about their perceived access to support. This was distinguished from family support and mainly focused on how confident participants felt about the likelihood of accessing government support. The entrepreneur's sample shared experiences that went beyond perceptions because, unlike the employee sample, they had accessed government support. Nevertheless, for the entrepreneur sample, perceived access to support increased their confidence in succeeding and played a major role in the final push to start the business.

On the other hand, the employee sample had overwhelmingly negative perceptions of accessing government support. These perceptions revolved around the complicated application process and the time associated with gaining approval for government support. The incubator sample also confirmed these factors. However, it is important to point out that, for the employee samples, these were just perceptions; they had not tried to access government support for themselves. Therefore, the fact that they had not got this far in the start-up process indicates that there may have been other factors at play which did not let the employee sample get beyond their initial entrepreneurial intentions. In the same vein, one should not ignore the fact that negative perceptions about government support place serious limitations on its effectiveness. As the incubator sample pointed out, these negative perceptions were not wholly unfounded.

Within the UAE context, education came across as one of the most important facets of the start-up process. Education was also highlighted as a source of confidence that pushes entrepreneurs to act on their intentions. Employees on the other hand did not have the same confidence. This marks an important divide between the two samples. Some of the entrepreneurs attributed their confidence and success in initiating their start-up directly to education. Other entrepreneurs saw the positive impact of education in preparing them for business but also highlighted some limitations of the general approach used in education. These views were echoed in the employee sample, who also felt more could be done. For example, there was an emphasis on practical knowledge and adopting an experiential learning approach.

Some participants attributed their ambition to education, while others identified the origins of their entrepreneurial intentions as a direct consequence of their educational experience. As mentioned earlier, entrepreneurs revealed that their educational experience prepared them and gave them confidence in their ability to start their business. Therefore, education is one of the few factors discussed thus far that has a direct impact on multiple facets of the entrepreneurial process within the UAE.

The existence and threat of competition also affected the perceived levels of success for Emirati entrepreneurs. However, it was the reaction of the two samples that is of most interest. The employee sample revealed that the threat of competition was either a barrier they could not overcome or a challenge not worth taking on. For the same employee sample, this also related directly to relatively low levels of risk-taking propensity, capacity to innovate, restrictions imposed by family circumstances, and importance of maintaining reputation. On the other hand, the reaction of the entrepreneurs' sample was almost the exact opposite.

Entrepreneurs recognized the threat of competition and saw it as a challenge. However, they were motivated by competition and accredited innovations in their business as a direct consequence of competition. The reaction to competition revealed a stark divide between the two samples in their ability to innovate and accept risk. However, the fact that competition was identified as a source of motivation also highlights the interconnectivity of many other factors discussed thus far. For example, arguably the entrepreneurs were prepared to accept high levels of risk and innovate because their family's strong financial position allowed them flexibility. This also reduced the threat of losing one's reputation, thus minimizing the impact of negative cultural retribution while increasing the probability of improved reputation. Therefore, the complex mix of these factors not only makes the proposition more attractive but also more feasible.

Market knowledge also affected the perceived levels of success associated with starting a business. Most of the participants, from both samples, felt they did not have the right market knowledge to start a business. However, yet again it was how they reacted to this situation that sets them apart. Entrepreneurs recognized limitations in their market knowledge, but took steps to fill these gaps. For example, they were able to build up support networks of family, friends, and business partners to ensure effective market information was in place before they made key business decisions. On the other hand, the employee sample was not able to overcome this barrier, not only because they were not able to establish a support network, but also because of other factors, such as family, that took priority.

Time was an interesting sub-theme because it did not necessarily differentiate between the employees and entrepreneurs. Closely connected with the need for achievement, all of the entrepreneurs felt they had to make effective use of their time and did not feel comfortable with the prospect of free time. While two employees also expressed similar views, others felt they did not have enough time. The employee sample felt that their responsibilities to family and work did not allow them time to take on extra tasks. Hence, the perceived availability of time and the desire to use time most effectively increased the perceived feasibility and desirability of taking on extra tasks.

There were also other factors at play, which highlighted starting a business as an appropriate task to make use of extra time. For example, as one of the employee sample expressed, they felt they had extra time and so took up writing. Therefore, although perceived availability of time has positive implications for the perceived desirability of undertaking additional tasks, whether starting a business is recognized as a feasible task depends on other factors. For example, factors such as access to finance, government support, and family circumstances identified earlier. Nevertheless, Emirati attitude toward time plays an important role within the entrepreneurial process.

In summary, the interview data revealed Emirati entrepreneurs use a number of gauges to assess the likelihood of success in undertaking entrepreneurial action. Access to finance is the best indicator of perceived success in undertaking entrepreneurial action. Education aids ambition, develops entrepreneurial intentions, and has wide ranging effects on the entrepreneurial process that go beyond developing confidence in performing certain tasks. Perceptions of other factors such as access to support, competition, market knowledge, and time are also important and affect the feasibility and desirability of undertaking entrepreneurial action. However, the way different participants reacted to these perceptions was interesting. The employee sample was quick to shrug off the challenges posed by negative perceptions and label them unattainable. On the other hand, entrepreneurs demonstrated an ability to see challenges as opportunities and used these as a source of motivation. Overall, factors that seem to stop employees in their tracks were exactly the same factors that highlighted entrepreneurial action as feasible and desirable to the entrepreneur sample.

The individual context of the two main sample segments provided insights into the origins of their ambition motivation and which external factors influenced and developed certain personality traits. The ambition motivation, in the context of this study, represents the strengths and scope of an individual's achievement motive. This is an important tenet in the proposed EME graduates discussed in Chap. 9, as early influences on personality and motivation affect individual behavior throughout the entrepreneurial process. This book has helped conclude that the individual context of Emiratis is strongly influenced by key external factors such as family, culture, and government. For example, family circumstances, culture, and political role models instilled a sense of nationalism and a moral duty within Emiratis to improve themselves and the community.

These factors not only make up the individual context, but, more importantly, modify behavior and shape personality traits such as the need for achievement and independence. Although personality traits such as risk-taking propensity and capacity to innovate were not involved in the early stages of the model, these traits were also shaped by the individual context. External influences of political role models, family circumstances, nationalism, and a sense of duty to the community cultivated the internal personality traits of the need for achievement and independence. Fused together, these factors are the key ingredients that produce an individual's ambition motivation.

There is a close link between the individual context and an individual's ambition motivation. This book concludes that the presence of an individual's ambition motivation depends on the existence of complex networks of internal and external factors. For example, a family's financial position, a history of entrepreneurship, the individual's position among siblings. These factors, along with a sense of nationalism, moral duty to community, and inspiration from political role models, also determined the strength and scope of an individual's ambition motivation.

For example, most entrepreneurs had a strong history of entrepreneurship within the family. Their families were well off and so they had little to no financial commitment toward the family. These entrepreneurs also demonstrated nationalistic tendencies and a strong sense of duty toward the community. For example, three out of four participants displayed a strong sense of nationalism and commitment to community. Interestingly, this seems to stem from a sense of obligation linked to the benefits provided by the country and political leadership. Furthermore, nearly all of the entrepreneurs themselves were able to identify the origins of their ambition with political role models. These factors equated to high levels of ambition motivation.

The two main sample segments were selected on the basis of possessing entrepreneurial intention; therefore, similarities in their context and ambitions were expected. However, comparatively, most of the employee sample was financially committed to the family's upkeep, which affected their ambition motivation. Although all of the employees demonstrated a need for achievement, arguably the need for independence was more observable in female participants. This highlights that gender and social class have an influence on entrepreneurship within the UAE. Variances in the employee sample also highlight the possibility that some participants from the employees sample are just a few steps behind entrepreneurs in starting a business. The fact that, on average, the entrepreneur sample had a higher average age and had held employment at some stage supports this argument.

Although a number of participants demonstrated high ambition motivation, these did not necessarily equate to strong entrepreneurial intentions. They mostly perceived culture, family, and government to be supportive of their ambitions. However, this ambition was not directed and a career in entrepreneurship was only identified as an appropriate vehicle to achieve ambition motivation if the right balance of external factors were in place. For example, education, interaction with GSPs, existing knowledge of entrepreneurship, along with family circumstances, determined the strength of entrepreneurial intentions. Through the effective use of marketing, entrepreneurship competitions, and educational programs, the role of government was the strongest factor in highlighting entrepreneurship as the best vehicle to achieve personal ambitions at this stage.

Participants with strong ambition motivation also developed strong entrepreneurial intentions. However, the strength of entrepreneurial intentions was influenced by an individual's perceptions of government and family support along with perceived cultural acceptance. Furthermore, an individual's financial commitment toward the family played a role and determined the strength of entrepreneurial intentions. The combination of these factors, along with the individual context, altered the perceived desirability and feasibility of starting a business and determined the strengths of entrepreneurial intentions. Similar to Ajzen's (1991) elements of attitude, social norms, perceived behavior control, Shapero's

(1982) perceived desirability and feasibility highlight the process of evaluating actions. However, specific factors relating to individual context and personal ambition, highlighted within the EME, represent the antecedents of entrepreneurial intentions in the UAE context.

Previous research indicated that intentions are the best predicators of action (Hart et al. 2012; Ismail et al. 2009; Krueger et al. 2000; Liñan 2011). However, within the UAE context a number of factors influence the transition of intentions into action. The study concluded that entrepreneurial action within the UAE depends on strong entrepreneurial intentions. However, strong entrepreneurial intentions are not enough and there are a number of internal and external factors at play, which ultimately determine whether Emiratis are able to start a business or find employment. An individual's personality traits such as risk-taking propensity and need for achievement, along with business and market knowledge and perception of completion, represent internal influences affecting Emirati graduates.

On the other hand, access to government start-up programs, government regulation, access to finance, financial responsibility and commitment toward the family, represent the external factors Emiratis use to evaluate the likelihood of success in undertaking entrepreneurial action. Emiratis also highlighted that their cultural perceptions toward entrepreneurship affected the perceived desirability of undertaking entrepreneurial action. Family is a constant in every step up to entrepreneurial action and those with financial commitments to family are much less likely to start a business. The attraction of the alternative, for example, government jobs, offers a far more secure proposition for Emirati graduates who prioritize family needs above personal ambitions. In this regard, the personality trait of risk-taking propensity assumes command over other traits such as the need for achievement. Similarly, access to finance and government start-up programs also provide a dividing line between entrepreneurs and employees. This disconnect between entrepreneurial intentions and action represents the most significant cause for the entrepreneurial gap within the UAE.

Entrepreneurial success emerged as an unexpected off shoot of the research findings as entrepreneurs were keen to articulate what they perceived were the most important elements in further establishing and delivering success for their business. Internally, some personality traits, such as the need for achievement, were still important; however, an entrepreneur's capacity to innovate came across as a crucial factor in achieving entrepreneurial success once the business had started. Externally, the effectiveness of GSPs and regulation, along with family support and the strength of competition were highlighted as the main determinants of entrepreneurial success.

Entrepreneurs with innovation and technology-based businesses identified deficiencies in government funded start-up support. Indeed, they highlighted expectations of government support that went beyond the start-up stage and focused on establishing and growing Emirati start-ups. Whether expansions in government support are justified needs further investigation. However, there are limitations in GSPs when it comes to dealing with non-traditional businesses. This issue was also emphasized by incubator managers and certainly highlights an area for improvement in GSPs. These changes along with other critical success factors will be discussed further in the next chapter. However, for any support mechanism to be effective it is equally important to recognize the needs of young Emiratis at different stages of their entrepreneurial journey.

This study points to very distinct needs of the nascent Emirati entrepreneur and the different roles support organizations need to adopt to effectively cater to these needs. Accordingly this book proposes five distinct types of young Emiratis who may not be entrepreneurs but have the potential. In doing so, the book provides a better understanding of how more Emiratis may be supported to recognize entrepreneurship as a viable vehicle to realize their ambitions and advance entrepreneurship in the UAE. This taxonomy does not account for newly established entrepreneurs who also have distinct post-commercialization needs. The needs of these newly established entrepreneurs are similar to their counterparts around the world. However, there are some nuances that differentiate them. An in-depth look at critical success factors in provided in the next chapter. This short section defines these entrepreneurs and outlines some support strategies that would be useful in generating a better understanding of fostering entrepreneurship among young people (Fig 8.1).

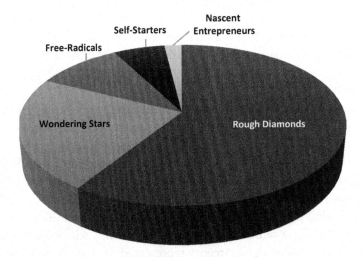

Fig. 8.1 Taxonomy of Emirati entrepreneurs

Type A: Rough Diamonds

This category represents the majority of young Emiratis who may or may not have heard about Entrepreneurship. Either way they do not fully understand what is entrepreneurship. They do know about businesses, people who own businesses, the concept of profit and loss. But they do not understand the mechanisms of starting a business. These young Emiratis do not know what is involved to become, or indeed be, an entrepreneur. Basic concepts of cost and income are also vague to this category. At some point in their life they may have admired an entrepreneur and momentarily wished they had a business. But, they do not have a business idea nor have they thought about it in depth. This category of Emiratis represents the biggest potential for cultivation but it is in need of entrepreneurial inspiration.

Work with Type A: Rough Diamonds is based on promoting entrepreneurship and increasing their knowledge. Crucially we need to inspire them and get them to think about entrepreneurship as a viable career option. These may be through workshops, competitions, specialist events, guest speakers, and other inspirational events. Delivering career workshop and having a real presence at career fairs in schools and universities should be a priority for any organization hoping to promote entrepreneurship. This work will have a dual benefit of increasing awareness and enhancing the skill base and work readiness of these students.

Type B: Wondering Stars
This category represents some Emiratis, especially those that have just graduated. Findings from this study would suggest there are more women in this category than men. These Emiratis have ambition but without well-thought-out ideas about how to realize that ambition. Like Rough Diamonds, Emiratis in this category also do not fully understand the mechanics of starting and running a business. They have been inspired by political leaders past and present, or by someone in their family, or indeed because they have a sense of duty toward the family, wider community, and the UAE. The previous category represented the biggest opportunity to cultivate entrepreneurship, but this category of Emiratis represents the most urgent need for intervention or guidance to inform and promote the possibilities entrepreneurship has to offer and which niche they might fit into. These wondering stars have ambition and a sense of destiny, a desire to achieve something, but without the means. They do not know what or how, but they just want to be successful.

Work with Type B: Wondering Stars is similar to Type A's work, as it mainly focuses on raising awareness about the possibilities entrepreneurship has to offer. Creativity and idea generation are essential components in working with this category. Along with inspiring, the aim here is to inform and promote the possibilities entrepreneurship has to offer and which niche they might fit into. Idea generations workshops, and competitions are the main means at our disposal. Success with this category is measured by how many are able to latch onto an idea and are willing to take it forward.

Type C: Free-Radicals
This category represents a minority of Emiratis who have ideas but are without direction. These Emiratis are ambitious and equipped with an idea or ideas. However, these ideas have to be verified and may need to be developed, improved, or changed all together. These Free-Radicals might

have been passed through the previous two categories: they might have been inspired by an idea or quite likely to have experienced an initiative designed to promote entrepreneurship. Either way, crucially they are ready (in their minds) to start a business. This group represents the most viable category in regard to making an immediate impact and advancing entrepreneurship in the UAE. This category needs acceleration, time, space, and support to verify whether their ideas are truly ready for the challenges of the market place.

Work with Type C: Free-Radicals need to ensure they are truly ready. For this task the work of well qualified mentors, internal and external, is important. It is crucial for these potential entrepreneurs not to lose momentum and need to accelerate their ideas into fruition. Along with mentors there needs to be a lot of individualized support to ensure the idea is commercially viable. The free-radical should be capable of taking the lead here, conducting market research, and testing and proving their concept. The support organization, while working with internal and external partners, should also support in connecting with relevant government bodies, support networks, and service providers to verify and confirm different aspects of their business. Success at this stage is measured by the completion of a commercially viable business plan. If the plan has achieved funding then it is an added bonus.

Type D: Self-Starters

This is a very small minority of young Emiratis ready to establish, manage, and work in their own businesses. These Emiratis have verified business plans and are ready to license, or have obtained a license for their business. There are also some free-radicals in this group that may already be running a small (in most cases) profitable business. But they run it as a hobby and without a license. In these cases tailored support is needed to help take these Emiratis to the next stage. This support may be provided by accelerators or incubators, but essentially it needs to be tailored to the developmental stage of the individual. This category represents a group that is in most urgent need of support, as they are at the cusp of success or failure.

Type E: Nascent Entrepreneurs
This category is very similar to self-starters, if only a little ahead. These entrepreneurs have recently entered the market and their businesses have very specific needs. These may include but not limited to funding, office space, customer access and securing sales, office services support, and professional services. These Nascent Entrepreneurs have taken the brave decision to enter the market, most likely with the support of one or more GSPs. However, they still need extensive help if they are to survive as a small fish in a very big ocean. As one of the entrepreneurs alluded to, these entrepreneurs still need someone to hold their hand, a "Godfather". This idea instinctively goes against the grain. But these instincts have grown out of free market notions of entrepreneurship which need to be reframed in the UAE context.

Work with Type D and Type E: Self-Starters and Nascent Entrepreneurs, respectively, are essentially already entrepreneurs and although their businesses have very specific needs, the support strategy can be quite similar. The essential role of the support organization with these categories is to help establish their business until it has a firm grip on the market. This is a highly individualized and heavy task. In the UAE support organizations will need to establish and make use of effective relationship with their respective departments of economic development to license these businesses. This is a crucial step for entrepreneurs making the first real leap into the work of entrepreneurship. A fully equipped facility is essential for this task. The equipment here does not just relate to hardware but also to support services and access to professional services. These newly hatched businesses may stay with the support organization for a year to 18 months. The emphasis here is on supporting the establishment of a new business in the market, mentorship, corporate governance support, and future planning.

The last three categories are not transfixed and often flux between one category and another depending on their individual needs and stage of development. Therefore, the need for individual tailored support is crucial. This is a key factor that binds these last three categories. In all of these categories, individuals are in need of education and training on key business aspects. These may range from managing finance to completing sales. Scaling the business at an appropriate pace is also a concern. The emphasis here is on supporting these Emiratis as they make the transition into the market. Support mechanisms for these Emiratis need a clear focus on mentorship and corporate governance. These and other support strategies will be discussed in the next chapter.

This chapter reported on the key findings and themes that emerged from interviews. The themes relate to the external and internal factors that were identified by the interviewees most consistently. All themes are interconnected and affect Emirati entrepreneurs at different stages of the entrepreneurial process within the UAE. These have been used to help draw a detailed picture of the Emirati entrepreneur. The next chapter provides a summary of results and proposes a model of entrepreneurship for UAE graduates. The chapter also provides key conclusions drawn out of the findings, and recommendations based on these findings.

References

Ajzen, I. (1991). The theory of planned behaviour. *Organizational Behaviour and Human Decision Processes, 50*(2), 179–211.

Denzin, N. (2006). *The research act: A theoretical introduction to sociological methods.* McGraw-Hill. ISBN 0070163618.

Denzin, N. & Lincoln, Y. (1994). *Handbook of qualitative research.* London: Sage Publications. ISBN 0803946791.

Hart, M., Levie, J., & Shamsul, Karim. (2012). Closing the generational start-up gap. Strathclyde Business School, Hunter Centre for Entrepreneurship. *Report:* Royal Bank of Scotland, Inspiring Enterprise. https://strathprints.strath.ac.uk/41939/

Ismail, M., et al. (2009). Entrepreneurial intention among Malaysian undergraduates. *International Journal of Business and Management, 4*(10), 54–60.

Krueger, N., Reilly, M., & Carsrud, A. (2000). Competing models of entrepreneurial intentions. *Journal of Business Venturing, 15*(5–6), 411–432.

Liñan, F. (2011). Regional variations in entrepreneurial cognitions: Start-up intentions of university students in Spain. *Entrepreneurship & Regional Development, 23*(3–4), 187–215.

Shapero, A., & Sokol, L. (1982). The Social dimensions of entrepreneurship. *Encyclopedia of Entrepreneurship,* 72–90.

9

Emirati Model of Entrepreneurship: Critical Success Factors

This section outlines major conclusions that can be drawn from this book and through these a model of entrepreneurship in the UAE is proposed. Although this model is drawn from the UAE context it has relevance to the wider Gulf region. It can help provide a better understanding of Emirati entrepreneurs, the challenges they face and which support mechanisms can be developed to help advance entrepreneurship specifically among this stratum of the population. While conclusions in this chapter highlight major tenets of the research they are not intended to diminish the developmental conclusions that have already been outlined in this book. The developmental conclusions in this chapter aid understanding of the overall picture of entrepreneurship in the UAE and help explain the entrepreneurial gap within the UAE. The key conclusions outlined in this section focus on the main factors that affect Emiratis in making a choice between entrepreneurship and employment. This also helps add to the limited but increasing range of empirical knowledge in the context of entrepreneurship within the UAE.

Social class has an effect on Emirati graduates' entrepreneurial intentions. There is a widely held misconception that all Emiratis are rich. The glittering sky scrapers and various records for the first, biggest, or best make this an easy buy. Furthermore, there is scant empirical evidence to

© The Author(s) 2018
W. A. Minhas, *Advancing Entrepreneurship in the United Arab Emirates*,
https://doi.org/10.1007/978-3-319-76436-8_9

correct this myth (Jones 2011). Generous government social support programs do maintain Emiratis well above the poverty line. However, large families and an increasing inflation make it difficult to classify all Emiratis in the mid to high income bracket (Kirdar 2010). Emiratis from moderate to low level income families are less likely to engage in entrepreneurship because of the high levels of uncertainty it poses. Emiratis from high income families not only perceive finance as low to medium risk factor, but are also more likely to have access to financial support. Thus, Emiratis from higher income families are more likely to engage in entrepreneurship. In the same vein, the study also revealed that entrepreneurs who have a history of entrepreneurship in the family are more likely to start a business than those who do not.

The importance of family has been recognized in a number of other studies in the region. However, these studies do not provide appropriate depth on its effect on Emiratis (Erogul and McCrohan 2008; Haan 2004; Hossan et al. 2013; Itani et al. 2011). If financial support is not required for the extended family, overall the family has a positive effect on female entrepreneurs because the family is seen as a support mechanism. However, even if the extended family does not require financial support, for male entrepreneurs the family still represents a negative element and ultimately a barrier to entrepreneurship. It is important to clarify the term 'negative element' here. Family is an important and cherished social institution for Emiratis. The head of family, usually a male, is responsible for the family's upkeep and this responsibility takes priority over personal ambitions or risker propositions (entrepreneurship) and superseded by safer propositions (employment). The term negative elements is used to highlight the fact that regardless of family circumstance, for males it is seen as the most important responsibility. This helps explain why the two male entrepreneurs chose not to marry. Thus, it can be concluded that the family is a major factor affecting entrepreneurship in the UAE; however, it affects male and female entrepreneurs differently. This also highlights the importance of gender and its effects on entrepreneurship within the UAE.

A number of studies in the region have highlighted that female entrepreneurs are more proactive and motivated than their male counterparts (Gallant and Pounder 2008; Itani et al. 2011). Although there is a range of reasons for this gender imbalance, following on from the above conclusion it can be argued that the way males and females interact with the family within the UAE's social structure plays a big role. For example, if the family is perceived as a support mechanism instead of a responsibility, then individuals are more likely to accept uncertainty and undertake entrepreneurial action. Interview data from all of the participants highlights the family as the single most important factor for UAE graduates. Therefore, it is understandable how it could contribute to creating a gender imbalance in the way males and females evaluate risk and entrepreneurial action.

Although reputation has not featured in previous studies conducted in the region, this book highlights the way social class and culture combine to emphasize reputation as a major factor affecting levels of new start-up activity in the UAE. Further, gender imbalances can be observed when it comes to reputation. The interview data revealed that loss of reputation due to failure in business was a major concern for nearly all male participants but did not appear as a concern for any of the female participants. In the same vein, government regulation, specifically on bankruptcy and the social stigma attached to financial failure, also came across as a major barrier to entrepreneurship, but again this mainly seemed to concern the male participants. Thus, a combination of responsibility to family and reputation may be the key factors in creating the gender imbalance identified by previous studies. This also helps explain why young female Emiratis appear to be more proactive and motivated in the field of entrepreneurship than their male counterparts.

It is important to point out that motivation and pro-activeness alone are not enough at this stage to propel female entrepreneurs ahead of their male counterparts. In 2013 only 44% of female Emiratis participated in the labor market compared to 92% of males (The Economic Review 2013). Higher levels of entrepreneurial intentions also have not led to better gender equality (Sarfaraz et al. 2014). For example, female entrepreneurs still find it more difficult to open a company in the UAE (Mazrouei and Krotov 2016). Nevertheless, female entrepreneurs are becoming more prominent and more important in the UAE context (Tashakova 2016) and increasingly taking a leading role in the UAE's economic landscape. A point highlighted well by the increase in labor force participation rates from 44% in 2013 to 51.5% in 2014 (Young 2016).

The importance of education in advancing entrepreneurship has been recognized in regional studies and beyond. Studies in the UAE have also revealed that, although young Emiratis recognize the importance and role of education in establishing successful businesses, they do not find appropriate educational programs that would help them achieve this goal (Sowmya et al. 2010). This study corroborates these findings. However, research participants also revealed what they saw as the key components of effective entrepreneurial education. For example, participants from both the entrepreneurs and employee sample recognized the impact of experiential education. Furthermore, participants highlighted that entrepreneurial education was most effective when it was delivered in partnership with other public and private sector organizations. Thus, it can be concluded that an increase in educational partnerships between educational institutes and other relevant public and private sector organizations represents one of the main ways to improve entrepreneurial education within the UAE. In fact an increasing number of higher education institutions in the region are now actively developing their own incubators and innovation hubs to help foster entrepreneurship. This approach has also been successfully adopted in Europe and the United States (Groenewegen and Steen 2007; Grossman 2008; Nelson 2007; Patrinos et al. 2009).

Previous studies in the region have recognized the value of GSPs in advancing entrepreneurship within the UAE (Haan 2004; Sikdar and Vel 2011). However, this study has revealed mixed results. GSPs, in partnership with educational institutions, seem to play a crucial role in creating entrepreneurial intentions among young Emiratis. The entrepreneur sample also credited GSPs as key components in helping them start their businesses. However, entrepreneurs in the technology sector criticized GSPs for not doing enough to aid business survival and growth once the business had started. This was in stark contrast to feedback from entrepreneurs whose businesses were in the more traditional fashion industry. Thus, it can be concluded that while GSPs play an invaluable role in advancing entrepreneurship within the UAE, they may lack capabilities to cater to entrepreneurs who start non-traditional businesses, especially in the technology sector.

A focus on GSPs also revealed an interesting concept of "Wasta", translating to who you know or who you are connected with that works in relevant GSPs, indicating that access or speed of access to GSPs is determined by whether applicants are connected with someone working in these organizations. Participants in both samples commented that access to GSPs was affected by Wasta. As there is little to no previous empirical research on this area, it is difficult to understand the full implications of this factor. Nevertheless, the fact that most participants touched on this issue does highlight that Emiratis at least perceive it as an important factor in accessing government support programs. Therefore, perceptions of Wasta affect an individual's perceived behavior control as it distorts how they evaluate one action over another, which overall, signifies negative implications for entrepreneurship within the UAE.

When comparing the samples of entrepreneurs and employees, the study revealed similarities in personality traits such as the need for achievement and independence. However, these personality traits seem to play a secondary role in determining entrepreneurial action, as other facets of the individual context, such as commitment to family, were the primary concerns of young Emiratis. The ineffectiveness of personality traits as the sole definers of entrepreneurs is in line with previous research (Gartner 1988; Shane et al. 2003). However, the study did reveal stark differences in the way entrepreneurs and employees perceived risk and uncertainty. Arguably, for employees the effect of these traits was enhanced by other external factors, such as family, culture, and class. For example, financial commitments imposed on most of the employees because of their family circumstances increased the impact of risk.

Comparatively, entrepreneurs revealed a very different outlook on risk and uncertainty. This may be largely due to their family's stronger financial position, or family circumstances, but also due to other factors such as family support. For the entrepreneurs, the threat to the loss of reputation also did not have the same significance as it did for the employees. Furthermore, entrepreneurs also demonstrated a capacity to innovate, which enabled them to survive in competitive markets. These factors empowered entrepreneurs to undertake greater risks and rationalize uncertainly. Thus, it can also be concluded that although personality traits cannot fully define Emirati entrepreneurs, their ability to accept risk and uncertainty enables them to start a business, whereas it is their capacity to innovate that enables them to survive and succeed.

One of the most interesting findings in this study focuses on the appeal of political role models in the UAE. Emiratis, whether entrepreneurs or employees, seem to be inspired by past and present political leaders. This is in stark contrast to most parts of the world, where political leaders are a target of public condemnation. Instead, Emiratis are inspired by their political role models to achieve more for themselves and the wider society. Therefore, it can be concluded that although social institutions such as family, culture, and government have an enduring effect on entrepreneurship within the UAE, political role models play a significant role in inspiring Emiratis to excel and find ways of improving themselves and the UAE.

The study concludes that, although a diverse combination of internal and external factors affects the entrepreneurial process within the UAE context at different stages, three constants of family, government, and education affect entrepreneurs, and therefore entrepreneurship, at every stage. Thus, it can be concluded that a combination of these factors, supported by other peripheral factors such as culture and personality traits, make up the individual context and inspire origins of ambition motivation. A combination of these three factors highlights entrepreneurship as a viable career option for Emiratis to achieve these ambitions; therefore, they are also a source of entrepreneurial intentions. In the same way, these factors help Emiratis determine whether they can act on their intentions. Whether Emiratis choose to start a business or find employment, the same combination of family, education, and government enables them to succeed in their choice of careers.

Lastly, this study concludes that the entrepreneurial gap exists within the UAE because Emiratis with entrepreneurial intentions are not able to act upon them because of family circumstances, social class, social stigma attached to financial failure, and financial regulation. These external factors have a knock-on effect on internal factors and affect how Emiratis perceive risk and evaluate entrepreneurial action, while other factors, such as government support programs and effective entrepreneurial education, can potentially improve levels of entrepreneurial intentions and facilitate entrepreneurial action among Emiratis. The external factors mentioned above ultimately act as the main barriers and create the entrepreneurial gap within the UAE. Although these factors explain the entrepreneurial gap, the same factors also explain why Emirati graduates actually start a business. Therefore, slight variations in circumstance could make the difference between entrepreneurship and employment. This highlights significant opportunities to advance entrepreneurship within the UAE which will be discussed in the next section of chapter which outlines an EME.

The research findings outlined in this book also highlight a number of questions which warrant further research in at least five key areas. Entrepreneurs with technology based businesses indicated deficiencies in GSPs. If so, this highlights GSPs as barriers to technological innovation within the UAE. This area needs further investigation because if the entrepreneur's claims are substantiated and strategies to improve support for technology entrepreneurs are identified, then it would mark a major step toward achieving the government's aim of a knowledge based economy. The history of entrepreneurship within the family has a major effect on an individual's likelihood of starting a business. Although this facet is well researched worldwide, there is not enough empirical evidence within the UAE to support this claim. This current study has certainly found this to be the case within the entrepreneur sample. However, quantitative methodology should be employed with a larger sample to further investigate this aspect and produce findings that can be generalized.

The study has identified a gender imbalance within the entrepreneur sample. Furthermore, the study has also attributed the gender imbalance to key facets in the UAE culture, for example, the role of males in regard to financial responsibilities toward the family, negative perceptions of family commitment, and stigma of failure. Arguably these aspects lead to differences in motivation and perception of risk. This area represents an interesting area of research. Confirming and identifying these and additional factors that affect motivation and perception among males through empirical research would significantly improve support mechanisms designed to advance entrepreneurship within the UAE. The impact of social class on entrepreneurship lacks empirical data within the UAE. This study touches on the effects of social class on entrepreneurs. However, further research is required to assess and confirm the impact of social class on entrepreneurship within the UAE. Better understanding of this area can potentially help a large number of entrepreneurs, improve social mobility and enhance the support of entrepreneurship within the UAE and beyond. A regional study, using a qualitative approach, focusing on a two-tier sample of entrepreneurs, from different scales of the social class would provide the best means of understanding the experiences of entrepreneurs from diverse backgrounds.

Lastly, the impact of political role models clearly had an effect on entrepreneurs. The entrepreneurs sample consistently related their early personal ambition motivation to political role models, who were also a source of motivation throughout the entrepreneurial process. It would be interesting to explore this phenomenon on a wider scale with a larger sample, not only to be able to generalize but also compare with other parts of the world and political systems. This represents an important area of research, as it brings together different disciplines of economics, political science, and entrepreneurship. A comparative international study using a mixed method approach would be useful in exploring this area further.

Emirati Model of Entrepreneurship

This short section outlines how different themes interact and create the different stages within the entrepreneurial process, specifically in the context of Emirati nationals. The interrelated themes emerging from the interview data affected Emiratis at different stages and alluded to an EME. By understanding the experiences of participants, we can start to identify key elements that cause the entrepreneurial gap within the UAE. Based upon their experiences and a range of internal and external factors, Emirati entrepreneurs revealed ambition, intentions, action and success as the most important elements in their experiences (Fig. 9.1).

Emirati Model of Entrepreneurship: Critical Success Factors

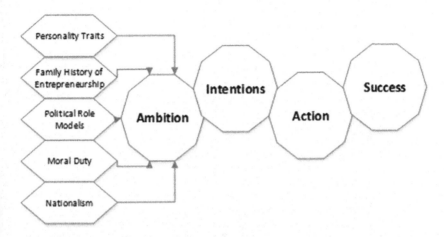

Fig. 9.1 Basic model outline

However, this oversimplifies a complicated set of processes and overlooks key elements of the individual context that provide insights into the origins of entrepreneurial motivation and factors that moderate behavior throughout different stages of the entrepreneurial process for nascent Emirati entrepreneurs. A combination of family, culture, political role models and, to a lesser extent, education seem to inspire Emiratis and develop crucial personality traits, such as the need for achievement and need for independence. This is the first stage and lays the foundation for personal ambition, which is deeply rooted in the desire to prove themselves, to improve their personal situation and that of others in the UAE. However, this ambition is largely undirected.

The combination of GSPs, family circumstance, education, and, to a lesser extent, culture highlight entrepreneurship as an appropriate vehicle to fulfill personal ambitions and thus develop entrepreneurial intentions. Therefore, the origins of entrepreneurial intentions, within the UAE context, stem from the individual context. The most important elements in the individual context are personality traits, the effect of political role models and family circumstances, specifically a history of entrepreneurship and the family's financial situation. These factors also determine the strength of entrepreneurial intentions.

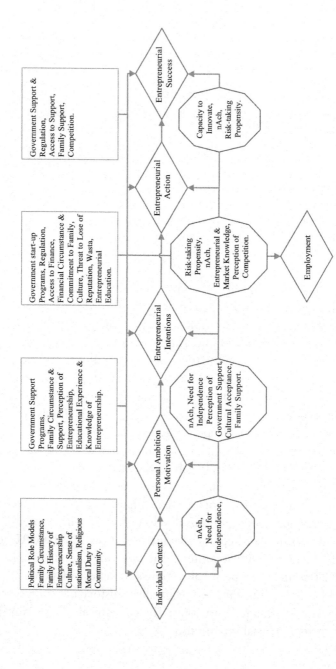

Fig. 9.2 Emirati Model of Entrepreneurship

As extensive empirical data suggests, intentions do not necessarily equate to action, which also applies in the UAE context (Bae et al. 2014; Bahrami 2014; Shane et al. 2003). Whether Emiratis acted on their entrepreneurial intentions or sought employment depended heavily on their perceived potential levels of success in any one of these behaviors. Key elements such as family, education, government regulation, and start-up programs played a vital role in moderating individual behavior. Perceived behavior control also moderated behavior and emerged as the essential component leading to entrepreneurial action. The entrepreneurial process does not stop at action, gathering the experiences of Emirati entrepreneurs also revealed what they considered to be important in achieving entrepreneurial success. This highlighted five key stages within the UAE entrepreneurial process for Emiratis, illustrated in the proposed EME (Fig. 9.2).

The model suggests a range of external factors at play that shape and influence personality traits and perceptions. Ultimately, the combination of these factors modifies the behavior of Emirati Nationals. This phenomenon is well researched (Berglund 2005; Carsrud and Brännback 2011; Liñan 2011; Reynolds et al. 1999). However, some elements within the external factors are unique to the UAE and, arguably, the wider Gulf region. For example, in comparison to studies in Europe, family plays a much stronger role in the UAE. The threat to the loss of reputation also seems to have a greater effect on Emiratis. The impact of political role models in inspiring young people has not been explored in great depth elsewhere and it would be interesting to see if political role models play a similar role in other parts of the world. It is clear they have a crucial role in inspiring young people to do better for themselves and for others.

The Entrepreneurial Gap

To conclude, the entrepreneurial gap within the UAE exists because of the inability of young Emiratis to translate their entrepreneurial intentions into action. However, there are a number of factors that develop entrepreneurial intentions and affect Emirati entrepreneurs after they have taken entrepreneurial action. Hence a number of conclusions can be drawn from findings that make important academic contributions to understanding the entrepreneurial process for nascent Emirati entrepreneurs within the UAE and beyond. On the surface, the answers may lie within the individual's personality traits and the low risk-taking propensity among Emirati graduates.

EME suggests that major opportunities to convert entrepreneurial intentions into action are rooted in providing access to finance, responsive GSPs, and financial regulation, along with effective entrepreneurial education. However, arguably, these factors are already available to most Emiratis, especially those interested in opening traditional businesses and despite these, the entrepreneurial gap remains. Indeed, to close the entrepreneurial gap within the UAE, a holistic approach is required which needs to consider additional factors such as an individual's personal circumstances, for example, their financial responsibility and commitment to family, their entrepreneurial and market knowledge, how they perceive competition, and threat to the loss of reputation. Addressing these key issues will also help pacify personality traits that deter individuals from taking entrepreneurial action such as low risk-taking propensity or fear of failure.

Lower propensity to take risks was a dividing factor between the entrepreneur and employee sample. This rationale is also supported by empirical data from around the world (Collins et al. 2004; Shane et al. 2003; Wagner and Ziltener 2008). However, this individual trait is a product of the sample's environment and results from a complex network of external factors that develop risk-taking propensity and influence individual behavior when faced with the choice of tasks with varying degrees of uncertainty. In this regard, the role of family and government came across as the most important influences on Emirati graduates.

A combination of an individual's position among siblings, the family's financial situation and the individual's commitment and financial responsibility toward the family dictated the level of acceptable risk when evaluating career options between employment and entrepreneurship. If an individual was responsible for providing for the family, which incidentally is normally a responsibility of the eldest child in the family and only required if the family is not financially secure, then the uncertainty posed by entrepreneurship is too much to bear. Emiratis are deeply affected by their family circumstances. If the family is not financially secure and an individual feels responsible to provide for the family financially, then they are unlikely to risk starting a business until their circumstances change. This is regardless of the strength of their entrepreneurial intentions. Therefore, unfavorable family financial circumstances are a key barrier for Emiratis trying to translate their intentions into action.

There is a direct link between the family's financial position and an individual's risk-taking propensity. However, this also highlights social class as an important factor in influencing entrepreneurship within the UAE. In a country stereotyped with excessive wealth, the impact of social class has not featured in empirical research. Variances in social class would also explain attitudes toward social standing or reputation. Along with family, culture, and specifically the threat to loss of reputation, came across as major barriers for Emirati graduates. Reputation only seemed to be a major factor for the male sample. The female sample was hindered by family approval but, although it was required, none of the participants highlighted difficulties in gaining family approval.

These variances highlight gender differences in the challenges faced by Emirati graduates. A combination of not letting the family down financially and in regard to social standing, led to a fear of failure in both male and female participants. Therefore, participants demonstrated they were more likely to choose tasks which they perceived to be safer and promised higher levels of success. This selection process was based on an individual's perceived behavior control or perceived likelihood of success in a given task.

It should also be noted that the differences in the average age between the entrepreneur and employee sample and the similarities between some employee and entrepreneur participants point to the likelihood of some employees becoming entrepreneurs in the future. Emp1F and Emp2M would certainly fall in this category. Thus, it can also be concluded that for Emiratis, the void between employment and entrepreneurship is not wholly static. Instead, at least for some, it is in a state of flux, where slight changes in personal circumstances can push Emiratis to make the leap from employment to entrepreneurship. This notion is supported by the fact that all but one of the entrepreneurs were employed at some point and only made the jump to entrepreneurship once their circumstances allowed.

Perceived behavior control was evaluated by gauging a range of factors that, in the participants' minds, influenced the likelihood of success in starting a business. Among these, access to finance and access to start-up support came across as the most important factors. None of the employees sample had access to finance and attributed this as the main barrier to starting the business. In contrast, all of the entrepreneurs had access to finance, which they saw as one of the most important steps in starting a business. The availability of finance gave participants confidence and motivated them to forge ahead. However, as many of the entrepreneurs revealed, access to finance was not a chance encounter; they had strong intentions of starting a business and accumulated the required finance over time. Entrepreneurs planned for a launch strategy that was in line with the finance available. Furthermore, as the incubator manager sample indicated, finance is readily available to Emiratis and does not represent a major barrier.

The importance of access to finance is supported by a plethora of empirical data (Gupta et al. 2012; Fayolle et al. 2014; Rocha et al. 2010). However, access to government support and its impact on entrepreneurs is less researched (Itani et al. 2011). Those who had access to government support were able to start their businesses successfully, highlighting start-up support programs as major contributors to entrepreneurship within the UAE context. The fact that the employee sample did not attempt to access start-up support demonstrates weak intentions rather than limitations of start-up programs. Furthermore, this also demonstrates that access to finance and start-up support are there for those who are suitably motivated. Therefore, although access to finance and start-up support programs are a major factor in explaining the entrepreneurial gap within the UAE, securing the required finance and start-up support depended upon the strength of an individual's entrepreneurial intentions.

The strength of entrepreneurial intentions related directly to the strength of individual ambition. Emirati graduates that had a strong history of entrepreneurship, whose family's financial position was sound and who were deeply inspired by political role models, had strong need for achievement and ambitions to improve themselves and their community.

These individuals were able to highlight opportunities and through educational and government input identified a career in entrepreneurship as the most viable option to fulfill their ambitions. Arguably, the strength of their conviction or ambition helped them overcome perceived risk and challenges such as access to finance and motivated them to seek and secure government start-up support to start their business.

Critical Success Factors

This section focuses on the main recommendations drawn from conclusions and other results of this study. These practical recommendations on critical success factors mainly focus on reducing the effects of barriers and creating better opportunities for nascent Emirati entrepreneurs to start business ventures rather than finding employment. There is also an emphasis on revamping support mechanisms that encourage and support Emiratis to develop and act on their entrepreneurial intentions. These recommendations are aimed at nascent Emirati entrepreneurs to better understand the challenges they face and how these may be overcome. However, primarily these recommendations are intended for key stakeholders supporting entrepreneurship and interested in advancing it in the UAE and beyond. Highlighting these critical success factors will enhance our understanding of nascent entrepreneurs. Before focusing on overarching recommendations, it is useful to address the support mechanisms that specifically focus on the needs of Emiratis who are at different stages of their entrepreneurial journey.

The last chapter highlighted the taxonomy of potential Emirati entrepreneurs with very specific support needs.

- Type A: Rough Diamonds
- Type B: Wondering Stars
- Type C: Free-Radicals
- Type D: Self-Starters
- Type E: Nascent Entrepreneurs

A critical success factor for advancing entrepreneurships in the UAE is supporting the development of individual Emiratis as discussed in the previous chapter. This section takes a slightly wider view and makes recommendations to support Emirati entrepreneurs as a whole.

Financial Safety Net for Emirati Entrepreneurs

The employee sample cited financial responsibility and commitment to family as one of the main reasons for not acting upon entrepreneurial intentions. This notion was also supported by one of the incubator managers, Inc01F. The incubator manager suggested a government funded program to create a financial net for new Emirati entrepreneurs. Therefore, those who have financial commitments toward family are able to meet these responsibilities by a temporary income provided through an extension of existing GSPs that focus on advancing entrepreneurship. Entrepreneurs gaining a stipendium income for starting a business venture seems far-fetched from a western perspective. This notion also conflicts with the theory of the entrepreneur because a guaranteed income essentially reduces the risk associated with starting a business, which diminishes the primary role of an entrepreneur as the risk bearer.

However, the UAE is recognized for providing one of the most generous social welfare systems in the region (Bradshaw et al. 2004). Furthermore, the advancement of entrepreneurship is one of its key priorities (Dubai SME 2011; Government of Abu Dhabi 2008; Sikdar and Vel 2011). This recommendation does not sit well with traditional concepts of entrepreneurship; however, we need bespoke localized and regional solutions to support entrepreneurs in an increasingly globalized world. A temporary financial safety net for new Emirati entrepreneurs is a practical proposition and provides an effective means of encouraging Emiratis to start new business ventures instead of finding employment. This initiative may require cooperation between different government agencies, such as the Ministry for Social Welfare and relevant departments of economic development in each Emirate. Furthermore, the entrepreneurs may also have to be means tested. These represent significant challenges and could lead to increased bureaucracy; nevertheless, it is an avenue worth exploring.

As the study has revealed, a slight change in circumstances makes the difference between whether Emiratis with entrepreneurial intentions actually start a business or find employment. To an extent, a financial safety net would also eliminate barriers created by social class and may bridge the gender gap identified in the study. For example, young Emiratis from moderate income families, especially males, who in the past had to find employment due to financial commitments to the family, would be able to act on their entrepreneurial intentions. This slight change in circumstances would also affect how young Emiratis perceive risk. A reduction in associated risk will have positive implications on attitudes and the way Emiratis evaluate entrepreneurial action. Thus, neutralizing some external factors would enable Emiratis to transcend external pressures, allowing them to take advantage of positive personality traits and act on their intentions.

Expansion of Government Support Programs

Although GSPs are playing an integral role in supporting Emirati entrepreneurs, they must widen their scope and enhance their capabilities. This will enable them to better support entrepreneurs engaged in non-traditional business activities. The entrepreneur sample acknowledged the benefit of GSPs, such as Dubai SME. These programs enabled entrepreneurs to start their businesses quicker and cheaper than non-nationals (a form of positive discrimination justified in a landscape where the national population represents just 13% of the total population). These programs also enabled entrepreneurs to gain access to new markets and helped further establish their businesses.

However, these benefits were limited to traditional businesses. Entrepreneurs engaged in non-traditional businesses were critical of support levels after the start-up stage. These entrepreneurs wanted to see an expansion of GSPs to an extent that they take an active role in identifying and closing sales opportunities, almost as if new businesses in non-traditional sectors were to be nationalized before being privatized. As with the first recommendation, this idea of handholding may seem alien and contrary to traditional concepts of entrepreneurship. However, as Ent01M highlighted, some entrepreneurs in the UAE are in direct competition with multinational firms that have been around for decades. These entrepreneurs are not just expected to compete in the market, but eventually to lead it. Therefore, they require support that goes beyond the start-up stage and helps them survive, establish, and grow their business.

This is not a new solution, as Inc02M indicated a number of incubators that have an equity stake in new businesses do actively engage to help them establish themselves. This process would also be instrumental in instilling experience and personal growth for young Emiratis who, in some cases, are venturing into the real world for the first time. The disadvantages of protectionism are well documented; however, with the advent of globalization, the regulatory role of competition in markets is obsolete (Boettke and Coyne 2003; Hayek 1968; Nee and Young 1991; Steele 2001). Large multinationals enjoy de-facto price monopolies across vast and diverse geographical regions that are almost impossible to regulate. Therefore, the government must go beyond traditional financial support mechanisms, such as subsidies, and play a proactive role in establishing nascent businesses after initiation. To an extent, this approach is being applied by a number of support programs in the UAE; however, as mentioned previously, they tend to focus on traditional businesses. This study recommends that programs such as Dubai SME or Khalifa fund expand their scope to cater to non-traditional businesses. Educational establishments have to play a greater role in supporting the taxonomy of potential and aspiring entrepreneurs.

Effective Promotion of Government Support Programs

As the study revealed, all participants, whether entrepreneurs or employees, knew of at least one GSPs. However, almost half of the participants, mostly from the employee sample, did not have appropriate knowledge of the types of services they could access. Furthermore, participants from both segments expressed negative perceptions of Wasta and the time associated with accessing government support (as mentioned in the previous section Wasta is an Arabic word referring to how connected you are or who you know). However, the study also revealed that participants who did not try and access government support, most likely did not do so because of their circumstances and weak entrepreneurial intentions, rather than a lack of information. Nevertheless, a crucial aspect creating successful GSPs is their effective promotion.

The fact that most participants knew about GSPs but did not know what they entailed, or how to access them, points to a change in communication strategy. Currently, a number of GSPs rely on sponsoring competitions as their main promotion strategy, especially for university students, which clearly works (Dubai SME 2011). However, it does not go far enough. This study recommends more information should be communicated on the types of services available and how these services can be accessed.

Integrating this information as an aspect of competitions would have added value. Apart from competitions and along with existing promotional tools, relevant GSPs could also offer dedicated in-house workshops and complementary tours of the organization to university students. This will not only attract more Emiratis to apply but also enable potential entrepreneurs to physically interact with staff and get a real feel of the services and support they can expect. As an added benefit, these practices may also quell some doubts about access to services without Wasta.

Educational Establishments and Public, Private Sector Collaboration

Participants from both sample segments stressed that their experiences with entrepreneurship education were most effective when it was delivered in collaboration with other public or private sector organizations. Participants who had not experienced this expressed a desire for entrepreneurship education to be delivered in this way. This reflects that all participants at least had an awareness that benefits of entrepreneurial education are enhanced when educational establishments deliver in collaboration with relevant public or private sector organizations. There is also extensive empirical data available in this area, especially in Western education systems, where experiential learning entails practical input from industry (Groenewegen and Steen 2007; Grossman 2008; Nelson 2007). However, the UAE and wider region still needs to catch up (Itani et al. 2011). As the MEEG model has outlined, education plays an integral part in the entrepreneurial process for Emirati graduates and affects multiple stages of the process. Therefore, the study recommends educational establishments develop relationships and collaborate effectively with a range of relevant public and private sector organizations to enhance entrepreneurial education.

As Ent02F highlighted, collaborations between educational institutions and public or private sector organizations to enhance entrepreneurial education were most beneficial when individual courses were linked to specific external partners that provided the best fit to gain the most relevant input. For Ent02F, this was one of the main experiences that highlighted entrepreneurship as a viable career option to satisfy her need for achievement. Similarly, Emp03F pointed out that a government funded entrepreneurial education program delivered through the university was key to developing her original ambition motivation. Thus, clearly education has a role to play within the UAE's entrepreneurial process. However, effective entrepreneurial education must be linked with practical input from experienced external entities. Furthermore, the benefits of entrepreneurial education must be extended to all disciplines and not just courses associated with business or economics.

The call for cross-curriculum integration of entrepreneurial education has gained momentum in recent years (Collinson 1999; Wilson 2008). However, in reality entrepreneurial education, in most educational establishments, is typically available within the school of business. Non-business students do have access through a number of entrepreneurial competitions and some universities offer entrepreneurship as an elective course. Some institutions offer entrepreneurship across the curriculum as a standalone course. For example, Higher Colleges of Technology students, whether studying engineering or graphic design, undertake a course in entrepreneurship. Hence, although there is a wide verity of techniques being employed to provide access to entrepreneurial education, its manifestation is limited and sporadic at best. Furthermore, one would argue that entrepreneurial education should go beyond a stand-alone course or the confines of competitions.

As the literature review has revealed, entrepreneurship provides the foundations for our modern civilization: it exists in every aspect of human life and therefore is relevant to every educational discipline. Hence, entrepreneurial education should be woven into every program, not as a separate course but integrated into programs students undertake, because ultimately every program provides students with options that either lead to employment or entrepreneurship. An effective entrepreneurial curriculum provides an effective solution to these issues (Collinson 1999). Lastly, most higher education institutions have a dedicated career center on campus. These centers need to be twinned with business incubators or innovation hubs so that graduating students not only have access to support in finding employment, but also have the same opportunities to start businesses.

Changes in Government Regulation

The UAE and the wider Middle East region have some of the most stringent bankruptcy laws in the world. Previous studies have called for a change in bankruptcy laws, as currently financial failure could land entrepreneurs in jail (Rocha et al. 2010; Gupta et al. 2012). Participants from both samples were clearly affected by this factor, which also had a knock-on effect on how Emiratis perceive risk associated with uncertainty and social stigma attached to financial failure. A combination of these factors significantly diminishes an individual's evaluation of entrepreneurial action. A relaxation in bankruptcy laws will significantly increase the number of Emirati owned nascent businesses as they ultimately reduce the risk associated with entrepreneurial action. Therefore, in line with previous studies, changes to current bankruptcy laws are strongly recommended. In fact, at the time of writing, news agencies were reporting imminent changes government regulation regarding bankruptcy laws.

And since then bankruptcy laws in particular have received significant reforms. Under the Federal Decree No 9, as of December 29, 2016, bankruptcy in the UAE was decriminalized. Although this law reform does not apply to private individuals and still requires commercial entities to meet several conditions, it is a significant step forward in increasing the UAE's international competitiveness and benchmarking the UAE's regulatory framework with advanced economies.

Changes to the bankruptcy laws allow companies, traders, and government funded companies to seek insolvency assistance without the criminal penalties, provided that the application has been made within 30 business days of the first default. There are four main routes companies can use. Insolvency with restructuring, where creditor approved debt restructuring, overseen by civil courts, is applied for over a period of five years. This period can be further extended to another three years, but, requires the same due process. Protective composition, which seems to be the most preferred option, encourages businesses to address imminent financial woes before they come to a head. Otherwise the same conditions as the insolvency with restructuring apply. Insolvency and liquidation, is the least preferred as it comes into place if the creditors do not agree with the protective composition or restructuring plan. The court itself can deem insolvency plan inappropriate and therefore call for trustees to oversee the liquidation process. In both cases the company and creditors have to meet a timeframe, set by the court, to make objections. Companies can also seek new financing to avoid bankruptcy, but this is only after protective composition or restructuring scheme have been agreed to and safeguards guaranteed for secured creditors. Ultimately these changes create a safer and more transparent environment for entrepreneurs when it comes to securing finance (KPMG International 2017; UAE Ministry of Finance 2016).

There are other nuances to bankruptcy laws but the scope of this book does not allow for further exploration. Suffice to say these changes have made it much easier to do business in the UAE: a factor signified in the 2017/18 World Bank Rankings for Ease of Doing Business which places the UAE 1st in the Middle East and North Africa region (MENA) and 21st globally (World Bank 2018). This is a significant improvement on its last ranking (2010) which placed it 3rd in the MENA region and 33rd globally (World Bank 2010). Yet it is still a long way from the top ten global ranking, the UAE political leadership has envisioned. Interestingly, when it comes to starting a business, the UAE is still ranked 3rd in the MENA region and only 51st globally (World Bank 2018). This indicates there are significant opportunities ahead to further improve the entrepreneurial ecosystem within the UAE. An important factor to consider here relates to Business licensing.

Participants in the entrepreneur sample were also critical of the level of bureaucracy associated with government services and support programs. The incubator manager sample also corroborated this notion and shared experiences where individuals had opted for a job specifically because of the time-lag in gaining government support. Although these cases are rare and mainly associated with non-traditional businesses, this study recommends relevant government departments should adopt strategies that reduce bureaucracy and improve flexibility, responsiveness and, ultimately, accessibility.

To an extent, some steps have been taken to improve accessibility. For example, the UAE government's E-Government program has brought almost all government services, including new business licenses, online. However, even though it is easier to apply, the time taken to gain relevant approvals has not improved. Similarly, even though there is a fast-track licensing service offered through GSPs, the service is limited to specific business types. This situation is further exacerbated when it comes to non-traditional businesses that are not pre-approved for licensing. As one of the incubator managers highlighted, these non-traditional businesses can take months to gain approval, by which time either the entrepreneur's circumstances have changed or the market opportunity is gone. Either way, this represents a significant disadvantage for entrepreneurship within the UAE. Reducing the time-lag, especially for non-traditional businesses needing new approvals, would significantly improve the prospects of entrepreneurship within the UAE.

Lastly, there is a need to recognize the potential pit falls of a target drive culture. The development of a long-term strategy has inevitably led to the formation of many key performance indicators (KPIs) across all industries in the UAE, public and private sector entities mandated with supporting entrepreneurship included. These performance indicators are crucial in mapping out the relative success of our efforts; however, we must also step with caution.

At times an insistent focus on these KPIs could be counterproductive. For example, at times the means of achieving a specific KPI might be in conflict with stakeholder needs. Support programs are expected to deliver a number of start-ups. And in a target driven environment, focused on the number of start-up businesses that are easier to launch, or that are ready, may be preferred. These tend to be traditional businesses that have precedence and fit into a prescribed type of business licenses. While there is of course a need to help support and launch these businesses, we also need to think about how we support the concepts that are not yet fully developed, or that break the mold completely. Ideas need the freedom to develop the way the innovator entrepreneur envisaged rather than being penned into an existing list of ideas because this is how we will find the next Emirati Steve Jobs.

References

Al Mazrouei, M., & Krotov, V. (2016). Gender barriers to e-commerce entrepreneurship: The case of the UAE. *Polish Journal of Management Studies, 14*(2). https://doi.org/10.17512/pjms.2016.14.2.01.

Bae, T., Qian, S., Miao, C., & Fiet, J. (2014). The relationship between entrepreneurship education and entrepreneurial intentions: A meta-analytic review. *Entrepreneurship Theory & Practice, 4*, 217–254.

Bahrami, S. (2014). Entrepreneurship intentions and perceptions in the UAE: A study of moderating effects of gender, culture and family. *International Journal of Small Business and Entrepreneurship Research, 2*(4), 37–50.

Berglund, H. (2005). *Toward a theory of entrepreneurial action: Exploring risk, opportunity and self in technology Entrepreneurship*. Göteborg: Chalmers Publication Library. ISBN: 91-7291-697-4.

Boettke, P., & Coyne, C. (2003). Entrepreneurship and development: Cause or consequence. In *Austrian economics and entrepreneurial studies* (pp. 67–87). Bingley: Emerald Insight.

Bradshaw, K., Tennant, L., & Lydiatt, S. (2004). Special education in the United Arab Emirates: Anxieties, attitudes and aspirations. *International Journal of Special Education, 19*(1), 49–55.

Carsrud, A., & Brännback, M. (2011). Entrepreneurial motivations: What do we still need to know?. *Journal of Small Business Management,* ProQuest, *49*(1), 9–26.

Collins, C. J., Hanges, P. J., & Locke, E. A. (2004). The relationship of achievement motivation to entrepreneurial behavior: A meta-analysis. *Human Performance, 17*(1), 95–117. Taylor & Francis

Collinson, E. (1999). The entrepreneurial curriculum: Equipping graduates for a career in the SME sector. *Journal of Research in Marketing and Entrepreneurship, 1*(1), 18–23.

Dubai SME. (2011). *The role of government in supporting entrepreneurship & SME development.* Dubai Department of Economic Development. Retrieved from http://www.oecd.org/mena/investment/47246782.pdf.

Erogul, M., & McCrohan, D. (2008). Preliminary investigation of Emirati women entrepreneurs in the UAE. *African Journal of Business Management, 2*(10), 177–185.

Fayolle, A., Liñán, F., & Moriano, J. (2014). Beyond entrepreneurial intentions values and motivations in entrepreneurship. *International Entrepreneurship Management Journal, 10*, 679–689. https://doi.org/10.1007/s11365-014-0306-7.

Gallant, M., & Pounder, J. (2008). The employment of female nationals in the United Arab Emirates (UAE). *Education, Business and Society: Contemporary Middle Eastern Issues, 1*(1), 26–33. Retrieved from https://doi.org/10.1108/17537980810861493

Gartner, W. (1988). Who is an entrepreneur? Is the wrong question. *American Journal of Small Business, 12*(4), 11–32.

Government of Abu Dhabi. (2008). *The Abu Dhabi Economic Vision 2030.* Retrieved from https://www.ecouncil.ae/PublicationsEn/economic-vision-2030-full-versionEn.pdf.

Grossman, S. (2008). The case of business improvement districts: Special district public-private cooperation in community revitalization. *Public Performance & Management Review, 32*(2), 290–308.

Groenewegen, J., & Steen, M. (2007). The evolutionary policy maker. *Journal of Economic Issues.* ProQuest Central, *41*(2), 351.

Gupta, V., Yayla, A., Sikdar, A., & Cha, M. (2012). Institutional environment for entrepreneurship: Evidence from the developmental states of South Korea and United Arab Emirates. *Journal of Developmental Entrepreneurship, 17*(3). https://doi.org/10.1142/S1084946712500136.

Haan, H. (2004). *Small enterprises: Women entrepreneurs in the UAE.* Centre for Labour Market Research & Information (CLMRI). Retrieved from http://

www.zu.ac.ae/infoasis/modules/mod8/business/documents/smallenterprisereport.pdf

Hayek, F. A. (1968). Competition as a discovery procedure. *QJAE, 5*(3).

Hossan, C., Parakandi, M., & Saber, H. (2013). Entrepreneurial knowledge, preferences and barriers of female business students in the Middle East. *Journal of Business and Policy Research, 8*(2), 83–99.

Itani, H., Sidani, S., & Baalbaki, I. (2011). United Arab Emirates female entrepreneurs: Motivations and frustrations. *Equality, Diversity and Inclusion: An International Journal, 30*(5), 409–424.

Jones, C. (2011). *Economic, social, and political attitudes in the UAE: A comparison of Emirati and non-Emirati youth in Ras al Khaimah.* Paper prepared for the Gulf Comparative Education Society (GCES) Symposium, United Arab Emirates.

Kirdar, S. (2010). United Arab Emirates, Chapter in Women's Rights in the Middle East and North Africa: Progress amid Resistance. Sanja Kelly and Julia Breslin. New York/Lanham: Freedom House, Rowman & Littlefield.

KMPG International. (2017). *KPMG Insights, UAE Bankruptcy Law.* Retrieved from https://home.kpmg.com/ae/en/home/insights/2016/12/uae-bankruptcy-law.html.

Liñan, F. (2011). Regional variations in entrepreneurial cognitions: Start-up intentions of university students in Spain. *Entrepreneurship & Regional Development, 23*(3–4), 187–215.

Nee, V., & Young, F. (1991). Peasant entrepreneurs in China's second economy: An institutional analysis. *Economic Development and Cultural Change, 39*(2), 293–310.

Nelson, J. (2007). *Building linkages for competitive and responsible entrepreneurship.* The United Nations Industrial Development Organization (UNIDO) and the Fellows of Harvard School. Puritan Press. https://www.unido.org/sites/default/files/2008-06/Building_Linkages_for_Competitive_and_Responsible_Entrepreneurship_0.pdf.

Oksana Tashakova/Dubai. Khaleej Times Filed on May 8, 2016 | Last updated on May 8, 2016 at 07.53 am UAE women rising in positions of power and influence. https://www.khaleejtimes.com/business/local/20160507/uae-women-rising-in-positions-of-power-and-influence

Patrinos, H., Osorio, F., & Guaqueta, J. (2009). *The role and impact of public-private partnerships in education.* Washington, DC: World Bank Publications. ISBN 0821379038.

Reynolds, P. D., Hay, M., & Camp, M. (1999). *Global entrepreneurship monitor* (Executive Report). Babson Park/London: Babson College, London Business School.

Rocha, R., Farazi, S., Khuori, R., & Pearce, D. (2010). *The status of bank lending to SMEs in the Middle East and North Africa Region: The results of a joint survey of the Union of Arab Banks and the World Bank*. Washington, DC/Bruit: The World Bank & The Union of Arab Banks.

Sarfaraz, L., Faghih, N., & Majd, A. (2014). The relationship between women entrepreneurship and gender equality. *Journal of Global Entrepreneurship Research, 4*, 6. https://doi.org/10.1186/2251-7316-2-6.

Shane, S., Lockea, E., & Collins, C. (2003). Entrepreneurial motivation. *Human Resource Management Review, 13*, 257–279. https://doi.org/10.1016/S1053-4822(03)00017-2. Elsevier Science Inc.

Sikdar, A., & Vel, P. (2011). Factors influencing entrepreneurial value creation in the UAE—An exploratory study. *International Journal of Business and Social Science, 2*(6), 77.

Sowmya, D., Majumdar, S., & Gallant, M. (2010). Relevance of education for potential entrepreneurs: An international investigation. *Journal of Small Business and Enterprise Development, 17*(4), 626–640.

Steele, G. R. (2001). *Keynes and Hayek, The money economy*. Abingdon: Routledge.

The Economic Review. (2013). Encouraging entrepreneurialism and economic growth. Abu Dhabi Council for Economic Development, 14.

UAE Ministry of Finance. (2016). *The final draft of the federal bankruptcy law*. Retrieved from https://www.mof.gov.ae/En/Media/News/Pages/06092016.aspx.

Wagner, K., & Ziltener, A. (2008). *The nascent entrepreneur at the crossroads: Entrepreneurial motives as determinants for different type of entrepreneurs*. Discussion Papers on Entrepreneurship and Innovation.

Wilson, K. (2008). Entrepreneurship education in Europe. *Entrepreneurship and Higher Education*. Chapter 5. Paris: OECD.

World Bank. (2010). *Doing business in the Arab world. World Bank and the International Finance Corporation*. Retrieved from http://www.doingbusiness.org/reports/-/media/WBG/DoingBusiness/Documents/Special-Reports/DB10-ArabWorld.pdf.

World Bank. (2018). *Doing business reforming to create jobs. World Bank and the International Finance Corporation*. Retrieved from http://www.doingbusiness.org/reports/-/media/WBG/DoingBusiness/Documents/Profiles/Regional/DB2018/MENA.pdf.

Young, K. (2016). *Women's labor force participation across the GCC*. Washington, DC: The Arab Gulf States Institute in Washington (AGSIW). 10, pp. 1–23.

Index

A
Acceleration, 211
Accessing support, 178
Access to finance, 100, 106, 135
Access to support, 100, 106, 135
Achievement, 42–46, 48, 60, 182
  motive, 107, 108, 192, 193, 204
Action, 217, 219, 221, 222,
  225–227, 235
Active entrepreneurs, 19
Adaptor, 19
Alertness, 19, 24, 32, 63
Alliances, 30
Allocative function, 32
Ambition, 108–110, 124, 175, 181,
  194–196, 199–202, 204–206,
  210, 220, 222, 223, 228, 234
American Psychological Association,
  89, 92
Antecedents, 40, 42, 44, 56
Anti-competitive, 174
Attitudes, 47
Austrian, 17–19, 22, 25–33, 40, 59

B
Bankruptcy, 179, 186, 187, 217,
  235, 236
Barriers, 43, 52, 105, 120, 125–127,
  130, 201
Baumol, W. J., 18–21, 23, 25, 31,
  32, 40, 57, 59, 62
Behavior, 23, 25, 30, 40, 42, 46, 47,
  49–52, 54, 60, 63, 64
  moderators, 192
Beliefs, 52, 54, 64
Bentham, Jeremy, 16
British Educational Research
  Association, 92
British Sociological Association, 91

Bureaucracy, 179
Business cycle, 28, 29
Business plans, 211

C

Cantillon, R., 14–16, 20, 22, 23, 57–59, 62
Capabilities, 174
Capacity building, 175
Capacity to innovate, 100, 106, 107, 119, 120, 199, 202, 205, 208
Capitalism, 27–29, 173
Capitalist, 15, 17, 20, 21
Cartels, 30
Casson, M., 13, 16, 17, 19, 20, 24, 25, 31, 39, 40, 57, 60, 62
Challenges, 75, 77–79, 84, 86, 93, 99, 105, 108, 135, 198, 204, 211, 215, 227, 229, 231
Characteristics, 17, 25, 40, 58, 62
Circumstance, 216, 221, 223
Civic duty, 193
Collaboration, 233
Collectivist culture, 193
Collectivist nationalism, 100, 106, 135
Commitment to family, 100, 106, 120
Communication, 178
Competencies, 120
Competition, 21, 25, 26, 29, 30, 100, 106, 118, 135, 201–204, 208, 226, 232
Competitive advantage, 1, 30, 174
Confidence, 109, 110, 119, 120, 128, 181, 182
Constructivism, 76

Conversational technology, 84, 91
Corporate governance, 212, 213
Creative destruction, 20
Creativity, 210
Credibility, 7, 8, 76–79, 81–84, 87–91, 93
Credulous listening, 84, 91
Criterion sampling, 79
Cross-curriculum integration, 234
Cultural factors, 43, 55
Culture, 74, 84, 100, 105, 106, 110, 124, 125, 135, 177, 178, 181, 191, 193–195, 199, 200, 205, 206

D

Darwinism, 19
Data analysis, 86–88
Decision-making, 18, 26, 32, 40
Deficiencies, 24, 25, 27, 31, 61
Demand, 14, 18, 19, 27, 28, 173, 174
Demographic Data, 101–106
Desirability, 48, 49, 51
Development, 1
Discontinuous, 21
Discovery process, 30
Disequilibrating, 21–23, 31
Drip feed, 31
Dubai SME, 175, 177, 178, 184, 230, 231, 233
Dynamic, 17, 31, 60

E

Economic functions, 15
Economic growth, 1, 28

Economic policy, 182
Economic progress, 20
Economic science, 13
Economic theory, 4, 17, 31, 53
Economy, 2
Education, 1, 3, 19, 24, 48, 51–57, 59, 60, 100, 101, 106, 111, 120, 127, 135, 136, 201, 202, 206, 213, 218, 220, 221, 223, 225, 226, 233–235
Educational institutions, 218, 234
E-Government, 237
Eighteenth century, 15, 16
Emirati entrepreneurs, 3, 5, 7, 191, 213, 215, 220, 222, 225, 229–231
Emirati Model of Entrepreneurship, 222
Employment, 75, 78, 79, 82, 83, 192, 194, 199–201, 206, 207
Entrepreneur, 5, 14–25, 30–32, 40, 44, 45, 48, 51, 57–63
Entrepreneurial ability, 24
Entrepreneurial action, 32, 40, 43, 45, 46, 49, 53, 55, 56, 61, 73, 110, 120, 181, 182, 217, 219, 220, 225, 226, 231, 235
Entrepreneurial activity, 74, 75, 78, 81, 82, 93
Entrepreneurial behavior, 23, 45, 46, 51, 60, 63, 107
Entrepreneurial education, 120, 218, 234
Entrepreneurial Event Model, 48–50
Entrepreneurial gap, 3, 6, 74, 99, 135, 215, 220, 222, 225, 226, 228

Entrepreneurial inspiration, 209
Entrepreneurial intentions, 2, 3, 6, 40, 44, 46–48, 50–53, 55, 56, 60, 61, 63, 73, 75, 77, 80, 83, 85, 99, 100, 105–107, 110, 111, 192, 197, 200–202, 204, 206, 207, 215, 217, 218, 220, 223, 225–231, 233
Entrepreneurial motivation, 40–42, 44, 61, 113
Entrepreneurial potential, 44
Entrepreneurial process, 3, 5, 74, 78, 100, 106, 128, 174, 176, 180, 181, 191, 199, 202, 204, 205, 213, 220, 222, 223, 225, 226, 234
Entrepreneurial State, 173
Entrepreneurial success, 207
Entrepreneurial traits, 41
Entrepreneurial venture, 15
Entrepreneurship, 1–7, 13–25, 31, 32, 39, 40, 43, 44, 46–50, 53, 55–63
Environment, 16, 19, 22, 32, 40, 42, 50, 52–54, 62
Environmental factors, 4, 22, 32, 39, 40, 43, 48, 51–56, 59, 61, 74, 75
Equilibrating, 21, 23, 31
Equilibrium, 21, 23, 24, 31
Expansion of Government Support Programs, 231–232
Expectations, 100, 106, 175, 184–186, 195–199, 208
External factors, 75, 219, 220, 222, 225, 226, 231
Extrinsic, 41

F

Family, 105, 109, 110, 112, 113, 120–131, 193–195, 199–208, 210, 216, 217, 219–221, 223, 225–228, 230, 231
  approval, 100, 106, 120, 124–126
  circumstances, 100, 106, 120, 121, 191, 192
  support, 100, 106, 120, 126–128
Fear of failure, 195, 226, 227
Feasibility, 48, 49, 51
Federal Law, 187
Finance, 15, 53, 54, 216, 226, 228, 229, 236
Financial, 174, 180, 187, 195, 201, 203, 205, 206
  failure, 217, 220, 235
  independence, 111, 112
  regulation, 220, 226
  responsibility, 192, 193, 207, 226, 230
  reward, 25
  Safety Net, 230–231
  security, 192
  support, 216, 232
Fiscal policy, 28
Foresighted bankers, 18
Fostering entrepreneurship, 4
Free market, 27, 59, 105, 198, 199
Free-Radicals, 210, 211

G

Gender imbalance, 217, 221
Generalizations, 76
Global Entrepreneurship Monitor, 1–2, 74

Government, 26–29, 31, 32, 53, 57, 59, 60, 63, 105
  regulations, 100, 106, 175, 179, 180, 186, 217, 225, 235
  support, 221, 228, 237
  support programs, 100, 195, 198, 199, 206, 208, 212
Guidance, 192, 210

H

Hayek, F. A., 24, 26–30, 59
Human action, 24, 26, 31, 41
Human experience, 76–78, 86

I

Idea generation, 210
Imperfect information, 14
Imperfections, 24, 27
Incentives, 17, 39, 41, 49
Income, 15, 216, 230, 231
Incubation, 3
Incubator, 99, 101, 110, 113, 117, 120, 124, 126, 128, 130, 136, 211, 218, 232, 235
  managers, 79, 80, 85, 87, 178, 183, 186, 196
Independence, 42–44
Individual context, 219, 220, 223
Inflation, 28
Informed consent, 92
Innovation, 15, 17–23, 27, 29, 31, 40, 58, 62, 63, 119, 120, 174, 180, 183
  hubs, 218, 235
Innovative, 17, 18, 21, 22, 30, 45

Index

Innovativeness, 58, 120
Innovator, 15, 16, 19, 62
Insolvency assistance, 236
Inspiration, 182, 183
Institutional, 32, 43, 53, 56, 57, 59
   environment, 176
Intelligence, 15
Intentionality, 76
Intentions, 73–75, 80, 85, 192, 197,
   200–202, 206, 207, 220–223,
   225, 227, 228, 231
Interest, 14–16, 28
Internal factors, 75
Interpreting findings, 86
Intervention, 25–28, 31, 59, 60,
   173, 210
Interviews, 6, 8, 73, 75, 77, 78,
   82–85, 87, 90, 93
Intrinsic, 41

K

Keynesian, 27, 32, 173
Khalifa Fund, 2, 175, 176, 178,
   232
Kirzner, I., 19, 26, 27, 31, 32, 40,
   57–59, 62
Knight, F., 19–23, 57, 59

L

Leader, 17, 57, 62
Leadership, 18, 40, 62, 63
Legal Issues, 91–93
License/licensing, 176, 179, 187,
   211, 212
Limitations, 8, 177–179
Liquidation, 236
Locus of control, 45, 48, 60, 115

M

Managerial function, 20
Market, 13, 15, 17, 20, 24, 30, 40,
   59, 62, 174, 180, 184, 185
   economy, 14, 16, 26, 27, 29, 32
   forces, 173
   knowledge, 100, 106, 135, 201,
      203, 204, 207
   place, 211
   process, 18, 25, 26, 28, 32
   research, 211
Marshall, Alfred, 19, 20, 22–24, 39,
   58, 59
Masdar City, 175
Mentorship, 212, 213
Microtheory, 32
Ministry of Finance, 236
Mises, L., 19, 26, 28–31, 40, 57, 59,
   62
Mohammad Bin Rashid
   Establishment, 2
Monetary, 28
Monopolies, 27, 29, 30
Moral duty, 205
Motivational factors, 4
Motivations, 4, 25, 39–46, 49, 60,
   75, 175, 181–183, 194, 196,
   200, 203–206, 217, 220–223,
   234
Multinationals, 29

N

Nascent, 2, 3, 45, 55, 174, 191, 208
   Entrepreneurs, 212
Nationalism, 115, 205
Need for achievement, 100,
   106–113, 192, 196, 199, 200,
   203, 205–208

Need for independence, 100, 106–108, 111–113, 122, 192, 199, 206
Neoclassical, 19, 24, 25
Nineteenth century, 14, 16, 17
Nodes, 86, 87
NVivo10, 9, 86–91

O

Oligopolies, 174
Ontological position, 76
Operational Definitions, 61–64
Opportunities, 2–4, 6, 7, 14, 24, 27, 29, 32, 45, 52, 53, 56, 59, 63, 64, 99, 135, 174, 176–178, 182, 184, 186, 187

P

Partnership, 184, 185
Passive entrepreneurs, 19
Perceived behavior control, 100, 105, 106, 115, 120, 135, 183, 191, 206, 219, 227
Perceptions, 41, 42, 47, 48, 50, 52, 61, 194, 197, 200, 201, 204, 206, 207
  of entrepreneurship, 100, 106, 135
Perfect information, 18
Perfect markets, 18, 24
Personal characteristics, 100, 105, 106
Personality traits, 105, 107, 120, 192, 199, 200, 204, 205, 207, 208, 219, 220, 223, 225, 226, 231

Personal traits, 50, 191
Phenomenological, 74, 77, 78, 82, 93, 99, 104
Political economy, 13, 14
Political leadership, 175, 182
Political role models, 100, 106, 195, 196, 198, 199, 205, 220, 222, 223, 225, 228
Population, 2, 3, 5, 73, 76
Post-commercialization, 208
Price, 14, 18, 26, 28, 29
  monopolies, 232
Principles of Economics, 18, 25
Privacy, 84, 92
Process matrix, 26
Profit, 14–20, 26, 40, 62
Promotion of Government Support Programs, 232–233
Propensity to act, 48
Protective composition, 236
Punishment, 25

Q

Qualitative, 6–9, 73, 74, 76–79, 82, 83, 86, 88, 90, 93, 99, 104
  phenomenological approach, 5
Quantitative, 73, 76–78, 86

R

Reasoned Action Approach, 47
Reckless speculators, 18
Recognition, 44, 59, 107, 115
Regulation, 195, 196, 198, 199, 207, 208
Regulatory framework, 180, 187
Reliability, 76

Religion, 54, 100, 106, 110, 135, 193
Rent controls, 173
Reputation, 100, 106, 109, 114, 116, 117, 135, 193–195, 200, 203, 217, 219, 225–227
Research question, 75
Responsibility, 27, 44, 59, 107, 111, 114–116, 122, 123
Restructuring, 236
Risk, 14, 15, 17–21, 23, 45, 52, 57–59, 62, 100, 106, 107, 113–116, 120, 124, 126, 129, 179, 182, 183, 192, 194–196, 199, 200, 202, 203, 205, 207, 216, 217, 219–221, 226, 227, 229–231, 235
Risk-taking propensity, 100, 106, 107, 114, 120, 192, 199, 200, 202, 205, 207
Role of government, 99, 100, 105, 106
Rough Diamonds, 209, 210

S

Sampling strategies, 73
Say, Jean-Baptiste, 16
Schumpeter, J., 19–23, 25, 27, 30–32, 40, 57–59, 62
Self-determination, 111
Self-efficacy, 47–50, 52, 53, 75
Self-Starters, 211, 212
Self-sufficiency, 112
Sense of responsibility, 192
Smith, Adam, 15, 18, 29
Social, 13, 16, 22, 25, 27, 43, 47, 48, 51–56, 60, 63

class, 215
sciences, 4
Social Learning Theory, 47, 51
Society, 13, 17, 27, 55, 58
Socio-cognitive, 46
Start a business, 192, 201, 203, 207, 211, 216, 220, 221, 231
Starting a business, 192–194, 196, 200, 201, 203, 204, 206, 209
Start-up, 1, 2, 6–8, 75, 105, 117, 174, 195–199, 201, 202, 207, 208, 217, 225, 228, 229, 231, 238
Subjective norms, 47
Subsidies, 173
Success, 222, 225, 227–230, 238
Supply, 14, 27, 28, 30
Support, 27, 43, 45, 50, 51, 53, 56, 57, 59, 60, 63
  mechanism, 4, 216, 217
  organization, 211, 212
  programs, 175, 177, 178, 181

T

Taxonomy, 208
Themes, 106–107
Theory of Achievement, 42
Theory of entrepreneurship, 4, 13, 15–17, 20, 22, 23, 39, 41, 57, 58, 61
Theory of Planned Behavior, 40, 47–48
Theory of X-efficiency, 24–25, 49
Time, 100, 106, 108, 109, 111, 114–119, 122, 123, 126, 127, 129, 130, 135, 203
Tradition, 100, 106, 135

Training, 48, 54–57, 175
Transactions, 26
Transcription, 87
Transparency, 8, 9, 86, 88, 90, 91
Triangulate/triangulating, 99, 191
Triangulation, 81
Twentieth century, 16, 19, 22

U

Uncertainty, 14, 15, 17, 18, 20–23, 25, 40, 45, 52, 57–59, 62, 114–116, 119, 120, 199, 200, 216, 217, 219, 226, 235
Unemployment, 28
Unfortunate legacy, 17
United Arab Emirates, 1, 2

Unregulated markets, 29
Utility, 75–77, 79, 81, 82, 84, 88–91, 93

V

Validity, 76

W

Wasta, 219, 233
Wondering Stars, 210

Z

Zaid, Shaikh, 121, 122